When we look hard into God's Word, we always learn something new about Jesus. Thanks, Philip, for pointing the way in your new book.

Joni Eareckson Tada
President, JAF Ministries

In the more than twenty years I've known Philip Yancey, he's shown a deep and persistent hunger for the truth in Jesus. I would rather read his words on Jesus than almost any other contemporary's, for I know that he speaks from deep learning and deep passion.

Tim Stafford

This is the best book about Jesus I have ever read, probably the best book about Jesus in the whole century. Yancey gently took away my blinders and blazed the trail through my own doubting fears, pious know-it-all, and critical balderdash until I saw the Savior anew and thought I heard him ask me, "Now whom do you say that I am?" and I understood the question as I never had before.

Lewis B. Smedes
Senior Professor
Fuller Seminary

In this, *The Jesus I Never Knew,* Philip Yancey is both more personal and more focused on Jesus than perhaps he has ever been before. He remembers the experiences of his childhood church with honest sight and astonishing insight—and then he holds himself and his reader to a true biblical and historical investigation of who this Jesus was (and is) after all. Jesus becomes, under his faithful eye, human and divine and powerfully present, in the text of Scripture and in our lives. It is this progression—from a view of our Lord too narrow for the full promises of the Bible to a presence both broad and blessed—which is the genuine gift of Yancey's book. I am grateful for the gift.

Walter Wangerin Jr.

Philip Yancey can always be counted on not only to tell the truth, but to pursue it with passion. In *The Jesus I Never Knew,* he continues the hunt.

Virginia Stem Owens
Kansas Newman College

Philip Yancey takes the reader with him on his very personal journey to Jesus. In *The Jesus I Never Knew*, I became convinced that the Jesus I met—in some ways for the first time—has known me all along. This book is destined to become a favorite—to recommend to those still seeking Jesus and to pass along to those who've met him, but long to know him more.

Elisa Morgan
President, MOPS International

In *The Jesus I Never Knew*, Yancey both educates and inspires the reader to take a closer look at the biblical Jesus and his motivations. In doing so, he helps us gain new perspective on what it truly means to be a follower of Christ. Even those who think they know Jesus well will find new information and meaning in this remarkable book.

Dale Hanson Bourke

In his unique, challenging, and careful way, Philip Yancey breaks through stale stereotypes to give us a powerful antidote to the "Prozac Jesus" and other inadequate images, to reveal the complex reality and impact of Jesus of Nazareth on all of life. A fresh and helpful book.

Roberta Hestenes
President, Eastern College

Yancey's flair for honest, vivid, well-informed down-to-earthness gives piercing power to these broodings on the gospel facts about Jesus Christ. In a day when novel ideas about Jesus are all the rage, Yancey's pages offer major help for seeing the Savior as he really was.

James I. Packer
Regent College
Sangwoo Youtong Chee Professor of Theology

There is no writer in the evangelical world that I admire and appreciate more.

Billy Graham

Philip Yancey

THE JESUS I NEVER KNEW

SPECIAL LIMITED EDITION

Featuring an excerpt from
The Bible Jesus Read

Philip Yancey

ZondervanPublishingHouse
Grand Rapids, Michigan

A Division of HarperCollinsPublishers

The Jesus I Never Knew—Special Limited Edition
Copyright © 1995 by Philip Yancey
Excerpt from *The Bible Jesus Read* Copyright © 1999 by Philip D. Yancey

Requests for information should be addressed to:

📕 ZondervanPublishingHouse
Grand Rapids, Michigan 49530

   ISBN: 0-310-23055-1

This edition printed on acid-free paper and meets the American National Standards Institute Z39.48 standard.

All Scripture quotations, unless otherwise indicated, are taken from the *Holy Bible: New International Version*®. NIV®. Copyright © 1973, 1978, 1984 by International Bible Society. Used by permission of Zondervan Publishing House. All rights reserved.

"Seven Stanzas at Easter," from *Telephone Poles and Other Poems* by John Updike. Copyright © 1961 by John Updike. Reprinted by permission of Alfred A. Knopf,Inc.

Interior design by Sue Koppenol
Cover illustration: "The Lord's Image" by Heinrich Hoffman, courtesy of Superstock

Printed in the United States of America

99 00 01 02 03 04 05 06 / ❖ DC/ 10 9 8 7 6 5 4 3 2 1

Contents

Thanks...

To the class I taught, and was taught by, at LaSalle Street Church in Chicago.

To Tim Stafford, Bud Ogle, and Walter Wangerin Jr., whose perceptive comments caused me to rewrite this book several more times than I would have on my own.

To Verlyn Verbrugge, for his careful technical editing on matters of biblical accuracy.

To my editor John Sloan, who patiently endured, and helped improve, all those drafts.

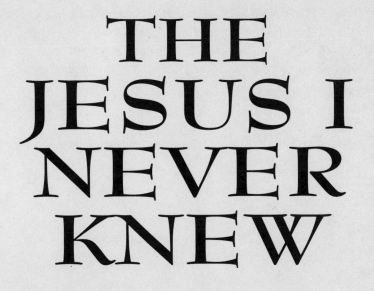

THE
JESUS I
NEVER
KNEW

Part One

Who He Was

1
The Jesus I Thought I Knew

Suppose we hear an unknown man spoken of by many men.
Suppose we were puzzled to hear that some men said he was too tall
and some too short; some objected to his fatness, some lamented his
leanness; some thought him too dark, and some too fair. One
explanation . . . would be that he might be an odd shape. But there
is another explanation. He might be the right shape. . . . Perhaps
(in short) this extraordinary thing is really the ordinary thing; at
least the normal thing, the centre.

G. K. Chesterton

1
The Jesus
I Thought I Knew

I first got acquainted with Jesus when I was a child, singing "Jesus Loves Me" in Sunday school, addressing bedtime prayers to "Dear Lord Jesus," watching Bible Club teachers move cutout figures across a flannelgraph board. I associated Jesus with Kool-Aid and sugar cookies and gold stars for good attendance.

I remember especially one image from Sunday school, an oil painting that hung on the concrete block wall. Jesus had long, flowing hair, unlike that of any man I knew. His face was thin and handsome, his skin waxen and milky white. He wore a robe of scarlet, and the artist had taken pains to show the play of light on its folds. In his arms, Jesus cradled a small sleeping lamb. I imagined myself as that lamb, blessed beyond all telling.

Recently, I read a book that the elderly Charles Dickens had written to sum up the life of Jesus for his children. In it, the portrait emerges of a sweet Victorian nanny who pats the heads of boys and girls and offers such advice as, "Now, children, you must be nice to your mummy and daddy." With a start I recalled the Sunday school image of Jesus that I grew up with: someone kind and reassuring, with no sharp edges at all—a Mister Rogers before the age of children's television. As a child I felt comforted by such a person.

Later, while attending a Bible college, I encountered a different image. A painting popular in those days depicted Jesus, hands outstretched, suspended in a Dalí-like pose over the United Nations building in New York City. Here was the cosmic Christ, the One in whom all things inhere, the still point of the turning world. This world figure had come a long way from the lamb-toting shepherd of my childhood.

Still, students spoke of the cosmic Jesus with a shocking intimacy. The faculty urged us to develop a "personal relationship with Jesus Christ," and in chapel services we hymned our love for him in most familiar terms. One song told about walking beside him in a garden with dew still on the roses. Students testifying about their faith casually dropped in phrases like "The Lord told me. . . ." My own faith hung in a kind of skeptical suspension during my time there. I was wary, confused, questioning.

Looking in retrospect on my years at Bible college, I see that, despite all the devotional intimacies, Jesus grew remote from me there. He became an object of scrutiny. I memorized the list of thirty-four specific miracles in the Gospels but missed the impact of just one miracle. I learned the Beatitudes yet never faced the fact that none of us—I above all—could make sense of those mysterious sayings, let alone live by them.

A little later, the decade of the 1960s (which actually reached me, along with most of the church, in the early 1970s) called everything into question. Jesus freaks—the very term would have been an oxymoron in the tranquil 1950s—suddenly appeared on the scene, as if deposited there by extraterrestrials. No longer were Jesus' followers well-scrubbed representatives of the middle class; some were unkempt, disheveled radicals. Liberation theologians began enshrining Jesus on posters in a troika along with Fidel Castro and Che Guevara.

It dawned on me that virtually all portrayals of Jesus, including the Good Shepherd of my Sunday school and the United Nations Jesus of my Bible college, showed him wearing a mustache and beard, both of which were strictly banned from the Bible college. Questions now loomed that had never occurred to me in childhood. For example, How would telling people to be nice to one another get a man crucified? What government would execute Mister Rogers or Captain Kangaroo? Thomas Paine said that no religion could be truly divine which has in it any doctrine that offends the sensibilities of a little child. Would the cross qualify?

In 1971 I first saw the movie *The Gospel According to St. Matthew*, directed by Italian filmmaker Pier Paolo Pasolini. Its release had scandalized not only the religious establishment, who barely recognized the Jesus on-screen, but also the film community, who knew Pasolini as an outspoken homosexual and Marxist. Pasolini wryly dedicated the film to Pope John XXIII, the man indirectly responsible for its creation. Trapped in an enormous traffic jam during a papal visit to Florence, Pasolini had checked into a hotel room where, bored, he picked up a copy of the New Testament from the bedside table and read through Matthew. What he discovered in those pages so startled him that he determined to make a film using no text but the actual words from Matthew's gospel.

Pasolini's film captures well the reappraisal of Jesus that took place in the 1960s. Shot in southern Italy on a tight budget, it evokes in chalky whites and dusty grays something of the Palestinian surroundings Jesus lived in. The Pharisees wear towering headpieces, and Herod's soldiers faintly resemble Fascist *squadristi*. The disciples act like bumbling raw recruits, but Jesus himself, with a steady gaze and a piercing intensity, seems fearless. The parables and other sayings, he fires in clipped phrases over his shoulder as he dashes from place to place.

The impact of Pasolini's film can only be understood by one who passed through adolescence during that tumultuous period. Back then it had the power to hush scoffing crowds at art theaters. Student radicals realized they were not the first to proclaim a message that was jarringly antimaterialistic, antihypocritical, pro-peace, and pro-love.

For me, the film helped to force a disturbing revaluation of my image of Jesus. In physical appearance, Jesus favored those who would have been kicked out of Bible college and rejected by most churches. Among his contemporaries he somehow gained a reputation as "a wine-bibber and a glutton." Those in authority, whether religious or political, regarded him as a troublemaker, a disturber of the peace. He spoke and acted like a revolutionary, scorning fame, family, property, and other traditional measures of success. I could not dodge the fact that the words in Pasolini's film were taken entirely from Matthew's gospel, yet their message clearly did not fit my prior conception of Jesus.

About this same time a Young Life worker named Bill Milliken, who had founded a commune in an inner-city neighborhood, wrote *So Long, Sweet Jesus.* The title of that book gave words to the change at work inside me. In those days I was employed as the editor of *Campus Life* magazine, an official publication of Youth For Christ. *Who was this Christ, after all?* I wondered. As I wrote, and edited the writing of others, a tiny dybbuk of doubt hovered just to my side. *Do you really believe that? Or are you merely dispensing the party line, what you're paid to believe? Have you joined the safe, conservative establishment—modern versions of the groups who felt so threatened by Jesus?*

As often as not I avoided writing directly about Jesus.

When I switched on my computer this morning, Microsoft Windows flashed the date, implicitly acknowledging that, whatever you may believe about it, the birth of Jesus was so important that it split history into two parts. Everything that has ever happened on this planet falls into a category of before Christ or after Christ.

Richard Nixon got carried away with excitement in 1969 when Apollo astronauts first landed on the moon. "It's the greatest day since Creation!" crowed the president, until Billy Graham solemnly reminded him of Christmas and Easter. By any measure of history Graham was right. This Galilean, who in his lifetime spoke to fewer people than would fill just one of the many stadia Graham has filled, changed the world more than any other person. He introduced a new force field into history, and now holds the allegiance of a third of all people on earth.

Today, people even use Jesus' name to curse by. How strange it would sound if, when a businessman missed a golf putt, he yelled, "Thomas Jefferson!" or if a plumber screamed "Mahatma Gandhi!" when his pipe wrench mashed a finger. We cannot get away from this man Jesus.

"More than 1900 years later," said H. G. Wells, "a historian like myself, who doesn't even call himself a Christian, finds the picture centering irresistibly around the life and character of this most significant man. . . . The historian's test of an individual's greatness is 'What did he leave to grow?' Did he start men to thinking along fresh lines with a vigor that persisted after him? By this test Jesus stands first." You can gauge the size of a ship that has passed out of sight by the huge wake it leaves behind.

And yet I am not writing a book about Jesus because he is a great man who changed history. I am not tempted to write about Julius Caesar or the Chinese emperor who built the Great Wall. I am drawn to Jesus, irresistibly, because he positioned himself as the dividing point of life—my life. "I tell you, whoever acknowledges me before men, the Son of Man will also acknowledge him before the angels of God," he said. According to Jesus, what I think about him and how I respond will determine my destiny for all eternity.

Sometimes I accept Jesus' audacious claim without question. Sometimes, I confess, I wonder what difference it should make to my life that a man lived two thousand years ago in a place called Galilee. Can I resolve this inner tension between doubter and lover?

I tend to write as a means of confronting my own doubts. My book titles—*Where Is God When It Hurts*, *Disappointment with God*—betray me. I return again and again to the same questions, as if fingering an old wound that never quite heals. Does God care about the misery down here? Do we really matter to God?

Once, for a two-week period, I was snowbound in a mountain cabin in Colorado. Blizzards closed all roads and, somewhat like Pasolini, I had nothing to do but read the Bible. I went through it slowly, page by page. In the Old Testament I found myself identifying with those who boldly stood up to God: Moses, Job, Jeremiah, Habakkuk, the psalmists. As I read, I felt I was watching a play with human characters who acted out their lives of small triumph and large tragedy onstage, while periodically calling to an unseen Stage Manager, "You don't know what it's like out here!" Job was most brazen, flinging to God this accusation: "Do you have eyes of flesh? Do you see as a mortal sees?"

Every so often I could hear the echo of a booming voice from far offstage, behind the curtain. "Yeah, and you don't know what it's like back here either!" it said, to Moses, to the prophets, most loudly to Job. When I got to the Gospels, however, the accusing voices stilled. God, if I may use such language, "found out" what life is like in the confines of planet earth. Jesus got acquainted with grief in person, in a brief, troubled life not far from the dusty plains where Job had travailed. Of the many reasons for Incarnation, surely one was to answer Job's accusation: Do you have eyes of flesh? For a time, God did.

If only I could hear the voice from the whirlwind and, like Job, hold a conversation with God himself! I sometimes think. And perhaps that is why I now choose to write about Jesus. God is not mute: the Word spoke, not out of a whirlwind, but out of the human larynx of a Palestinian Jew. In Jesus, God lay down on the dissection table, as it were, stretched out in cruciform posture for the scrutiny of all skeptics who have ever lived. Including me.

> *The vision of Christ that thou dost see*
> *Is my vision's greatest enemy:*
> *Thine has a great hook nose like thine,*
> *Mine has a snub nose like to mine....*
> *Both read the Bible day and night,*
> *But thou read'st black where I read white.*
> WILLIAM BLAKE

As I think about Jesus, an analogy from Karl Barth comes to mind. A man stands by a window gazing into the street. Outside, people are shading their eyes with their hands and looking up into the sky. Because of the overhang of the building though, the man cannot see what it is they are pointing toward. We who live two thousand years after Jesus have a viewpoint not unlike the man standing by the window. We hear the shouts of exclamation. We study the gestures and words in the Gospels and the many books they have spawned. Yet no amount of neck-craning will allow us a glimpse of Jesus in the flesh.

For this reason, as William Blake's poem expresses so well, sometimes those of us who look for Jesus cannot see past our own noses. The Lakota tribe, for example, refers to Jesus as "the buffalo calf of God." The Cuban government distributes a painting of Jesus with a carbine slung over his shoulder. During the wars of religion with France, the English used to shout, "The pope is French but Jesus Christ is English!"

Modern scholarship further muddies the picture. If you peruse the academic books available at a seminary bookstore you may encounter Jesus as a political revolutionary, as a magician who married Mary Magdalene, as a Galilean charismatic, a rabbi, a peasant Jewish Cynic, a Pharisee, an anti-Pharisee Essene, an eschatological prophet, a "hippie in a world of Augustan yuppies," and as the hallucinogenic leader of a sacred mushroom cult. Serious scholars write these works, with little sign of embarrassment.*

Athletes come up with creative portrayals of Jesus that elude modern scholarship. Norm Evans, former Miami Dolphins lineman, wrote in his book *On God's Squad*, "I guarantee you Christ would be the toughest guy who ever played this game. . . . If he were alive today I would picture a six-foot-six-inch 260-pound defensive tackle who would always make the big plays and would be hard to keep out of the backfield for offensive linemen like myself." Fritz Peterson, former New York Yankee, more easily fancies Jesus in a baseball uniform: "I firmly believe that if Jesus Christ was sliding into second base, he would knock the second baseman into left field to break up the double play. Christ might not throw a spitball, but he would play hard within the rules."

In the midst of such confusion, how do we answer the simple question, "Who was Jesus?" Secular history gives few clues. In a delicious irony, the figure who has changed history more than any other

*The U.S. public tends to ignore such trendy portrayals. A recent Gallup survey revealed that 84 percent of Americans believe Jesus Christ was God or the Son of God. Overwhelmingly Americans believe that Jesus was sinless, brave, and emotionally stable. By lesser margins they regard him as easy to understand (!), physically strong and attractive, practical, warm, and accepting.

managed to escape the attention of most scholars and historians of his own time. Even the four men who wrote the Gospels omitted much that would interest modern readers, skipping over nine-tenths of his life. Since none devotes a word to physical description, we know nothing about Jesus' shape or stature or eye color. Details of his family life are so scant that scholars still debate whether or not he had brothers and sisters. The facts of biography considered essential to modern readers simply did not concern the gospel writers.

Before beginning this book I spent several months in three seminary libraries—one Catholic, one liberal Protestant, one conservative evangelical—reading about Jesus. It was daunting in the extreme to walk in the first day and see not just shelves but entire walls devoted to books about Jesus. A scholar at the University of Chicago estimates that more has been written about Jesus in the last twenty years than in the previous nineteen centuries. I felt almost as if the hyperbolic comment at the end of John's gospel had come true: "Jesus did many other things as well. If every one of them were written down, I suppose that even the whole world would not have room for the books that would be written."

The agglomeration of scholarship began to have a numbing effect on me. I read scores of accounts of the etymology of Jesus' name, discussions of what languages he spoke, debates about how long he lived at Nazareth or Capernaum or Bethlehem. Any true-to-life image receded into a fuzzy, indistinct blur. I had a hunch that Jesus himself would be appalled by many of the portrayals I was reading.

At the same time, with great consistency I found that whenever I returned to the Gospels themselves the fog seemed to lift. J. B. Phillips wrote, after translating and paraphrasing the Gospels, "I have read, in Greek and Latin, scores of myths, but I did not find the slightest flavour of myth here. . . . No man could have set down such artless and vulnerable accounts as these unless some real Event lay behind them."

Some religious books have about them the sour smell of propaganda—but not the Gospels. Mark records what may be the most important event in all history, an event that theologians strive to interpret with words like "propitiation, atonement, sacrifice," in one sentence: "With a loud cry, Jesus breathed his last." Odd, unpredictable scenes show up, such as Jesus' family and neighbors trying to put him away under suspicion of insanity. Why include such scenes if you are writing hagiography? Jesus' most devoted followers usually come off as scratching their heads in wonderment—*Who is this guy?*—more baffled than conspiratorial.

Jesus himself, when challenged, did not offer airtight proofs of his identity. He dropped clues here and there, to be sure, but he also said, after appealing to the evidence, "Blessed is he who takes no offense at me." Reading the accounts, it is hard to find anyone who does not at some point or another take offense. To a remarkable degree the Gospels throw the decision back to the reader. They operate more like a "whodunit" (or as Alister McGrath has pointed out, a "whowashe") detective story than like a connect-the-dots drawing. I found fresh energy in this quality of the Gospels.

It occurs to me that all the contorted theories about Jesus that have been spontaneously generating since the day of his death merely confirm the awesome risk God took when he stretched himself out on the dissection table—a risk he seemed to welcome. Examine me. Test me. You decide.

The Italian movie *La Dolce Vita* opens with a shot of a helicopter ferrying a giant statue of Jesus to Rome. Arms outstretched, Jesus hangs in a sling, and as the helicopter passes over the landscape, people begin to recognize him. "Hey, it's Jesus!" shouts one old farmer, hopping off his tractor to race across the field. Nearer Rome, bikini-clad girls sunbathing around a swimming pool wave a friendly greeting, and the helicopter pilot swoops in for a closer look. Silent, with an almost doleful expression on his face, the concrete Jesus hovers incongruously above the modern world.

My search for Jesus took off in a new direction when the filmmaker Mel White loaned me a collection of fifteen movies on the life of Jesus. They ranged from *King of Kings*, the 1927 silent classic by Cecil B. DeMille, to musicals such as *Godspell* and *Cotton Patch Gospel* to the strikingly modern French-Canadian treatment *Jesus of Montreal*.

I reviewed these films carefully, outlining them scene by scene. Then, for the next two years, I taught a class on the life of Jesus, using the movies as a springboard for our discussion.

The class worked like this. As we came to a major event in Jesus' life, I would scout through the various films and from them select seven or eight treatments that seemed notable. As class began, I would show the two- to four-minute clips from each film, beginning with the comical and stiff renditions and working toward profound or evocative treatments. We found that the process of viewing the same event through the eyes of seven or eight filmmakers helped to strip away the patina of predictability that had built up over years of Sunday school and Bible reading. Obviously, some of the film interpretations had to be wrong—they blatantly contradicted each other—but which ones? What really happened? After reacting to the film clips we turned to the gospel accounts, and the discussion took off.

This class met at LaSalle Street Church, a lively congregation in downtown Chicago, which included Ph.D.'s from Northwestern as well as homeless men who used the hour in a warm room as a chance to catch up on sleep. Thanks largely to the class, I gradually underwent a transformation in how I viewed Jesus. Walter Kasper has said, "Extreme notions ... see God dressed as a Father Christmas, or slipping into human nature like someone putting on dungarees in order to repair the world after a breakdown. The biblical and church doctrine that Jesus was a complete man with a human intellect and human freedom, does not seem to prevail in the average Christian head." It did not prevail in my head, I admit, until I taught the class at LaSalle Street Church and sought to encounter the historical person Jesus.

Essentially, the films helped restore Jesus' humanity for me. The creeds repeated in churches tell about Christ's eternal preexistence and glorious afterlife, but largely ignore his earthly career. The Gospels themselves were written years after Jesus' death, from the far side of Easter, reporting on events as distant from the authors as the Korean War is from us today. The films helped me get further back, closer to a sense of Jesus' life as seen by his contemporaries. What would it have been like to hang on the edges of the crowd? How would I have responded to this man? Would I have invited him over for dinner, like

Zacchaeus? Turned away in sadness, like the rich young ruler? Betrayed him, like Judas and Peter?

Jesus, I found, bore little resemblance to the Mister Rogers figure I had met in Sunday school, and was remarkably unlike the person I had studied in Bible college. For one thing, he was far less tame. In my prior image, I realized, Jesus' personality matched that of a *Star Trek* Vulcan: he remained calm, cool, and collected as he strode like a robot among excitable human beings on spaceship earth. That is not what I found portrayed in the Gospels and in the better films. Other people affected Jesus deeply: obstinacy frustrated him, self-righteousness infuriated him, simple faith thrilled him. Indeed, he seemed more emotional and spontaneous than the average person, not less. More passionate, not less.

The more I studied Jesus, the more difficult it became to pigeonhole him. He said little about the Roman occupation, the main topic of conversation among his countrymen, and yet he took up a whip to drive petty profiteers from the Jewish temple. He urged obedience to the Mosaic law while acquiring the reputation as a lawbreaker. He could be stabbed by sympathy for a stranger, yet turn on his best friend with the flinty rebuke, "Get behind me, Satan!" He had uncompromising views on rich men and loose women, yet both types enjoyed his company.

One day miracles seemed to flow out of Jesus; the next day his power was blocked by people's lack of faith. One day he talked in detail of the Second Coming; another, he knew neither the day nor hour. He fled from arrest at one point and marched inexorably toward it at another. He spoke eloquently about peacemaking, then told his disciples to procure swords. His extravagant claims about himself kept him at the center of controversy, but when he did something truly miraculous he tended to hush it up. As Walter Wink has said, if Jesus had never lived, we would not have been able to invent him.

Two words one could never think of applying to the Jesus of the Gospels: boring and predictable. How is it, then, that the church has tamed such a character—has, in Dorothy Sayers' words, "very efficiently pared the claws of the Lion of Judah, certified Him as a fitting household pet for pale curates and pious old ladies"?

Pulitzer prize-winning historian Barbara Tuchman insists on one rule in writing history: no "flash-forwards." When she was writing about the Battle of the Bulge in World War II, for example, she resisted the temptation to include "Of course we all know how this turned out" asides. In point of fact, the Allied troops involved in the Battle of the Bulge did *not* know how the battle would turn out. From the look of things, they could well be driven right back to the beaches of Normandy where they had come from. A historian who wants to retain any semblance of tension and drama in events as they unfold dare not flash-forward to another, all-seeing point of view. Do so, and all tension melts away. Rather, a good historian re-creates for the reader the conditions of the history being described, conveying a sense that "you were there."

That, I concluded, is the problem with most of our writing and thinking about Jesus. We read the Gospels through the flash-forward lenses of church councils like Nicea and Chalcedon, through the church's studied attempts to make sense of him.

Jesus was a human being, a Jew in Galilee with a name and a family, a person who was in a way just like everyone else. Yet in another way he was something different than anyone who had ever lived on earth before. It took the church five centuries of active debate to agree on some sort of epistemological balance between "just like everyone else" and "something different." For those of us raised in the church, or even raised in a nominally Christian culture, the balance inevitably tilts toward "something different." As Pascal said, "The Church has had as much difficulty in showing that Jesus Christ was man, against those who denied it, as in showing that he was God; and the probabilities were equally great."

Let me make it clear that I affirm the creeds. But in this book I hope to go back beyond those formulations. I hope, as far as is possible, to look at Jesus' life "from below," as a spectator, one of the many who followed him around. If I were a Japanese filmmaker, given $50 million and no script but the Gospels' text, what kind of film would I make? I hope, in Luther's words, to "draw Christ as deep as possible into the flesh."

In the process, sometimes I have felt like a tourist walking around a great monument, awed and overwhelmed. I circle the monument of Jesus inspecting its constituent parts—the birth stories, the teachings, the miracles, the enemies and followers—in order to reflect on and try to comprehend the man who has changed history.

Other times I have felt like an art restorer stretched out on the scaffolding of the Sistine Chapel, swabbing away the grime of history with a moistened Q-tip. If I scrub hard enough, will I find the original beneath all those layers?

In this book I attempt to tell the story of Jesus, not my own story. Inevitably, though, a search for Jesus turns out to be one's own search. No one who meets Jesus ever stays the same. I have found that the doubts that afflict me from many sources—from science, from comparative religion, from an innate defect of skepticism, from aversion to the church—take on a new light when I bring those doubts to the man named Jesus. To say more at this stage, in this first chapter, would cause me to break Barbara Tuchman's cherished principle.

2

Birth:
The Visited Planet

> The God of power, as he did ride
> In his majestick robes of glorie
> Resolv'd to light; and so one day
> He did descend, undressing all the way.
>
> *George Herbert*

2
Birth:
The Visited Planet

Sorting through the stack of cards that arrived at our house last Christmas, I note that all kinds of symbols have edged their way into the celebration. Overwhelmingly, the landscape scenes render New England towns buried in snow, usually with the added touch of a horse-drawn sleigh. On other cards, animals frolic: not only reindeer, but also chipmunks, raccoons, cardinals, and cute gray mice. One card shows an African lion reclining with a foreleg draped affectionately around a lamb.

Angels have made a huge comeback in recent years, and Hallmark and American Greetings now feature them prominently, though as demure, cuddly-looking creatures, not the type who would ever need to announce "Fear not!" The explicitly religious cards (a distinct minority) focus on the holy family, and you can tell at a glance these folks are different. They seem unruffled and serene. Bright gold halos, like crowns from another world, hover just above their heads.

Inside, the cards stress sunny words like love, goodwill, cheer, happiness, and warmth. It is a fine thing, I suppose, that we honor a sacred holiday with such homey sentiments. And yet when I turn to the gospel accounts of the first Christmas, I hear a very different tone and sense mainly disruption at work.

I recall watching an episode of the TV show *Thirtysomething* in which Hope, a Christian, argues with her Jewish husband, Michael, about the holidays. "Why do you even bother with Hanukkah?" she asks. "Do you really believe a handful of Jews held off a huge army by using a bunch of lamps that miraculously wouldn't run out of oil?"

Michael exploded. "Oh, and Christmas makes more sense? Do you really believe an angel appeared to some teenage girl who then got pregnant without ever having had sex and traveled on horseback to Bethlehem where she spent the night in a barn and had a baby who turned out to be the Savior of the world?"

Frankly, Michael's incredulity seems close to what I read in the Gospels. Mary and Joseph must face the shame and derision of family and neighbors, who react, well, much like Michael ("Do you really believe an angel appeared …").

Even those who accept the supernatural version of events concede that big trouble will follow: an old uncle prays for "salvation from our enemies and from the hand of all who hate us"; Simeon darkly warns the virgin that "a sword will pierce your own soul too"; Mary's hymn of thanksgiving mentions rulers overthrown and proud men scattered.

In contrast to what the cards would have us believe, Christmas did not sentimentally simplify life on planet earth. Perhaps this is what I sense when Christmas rolls around and I turn from the cheeriness of the cards to the starkness of the Gospels.

Christmas art depicts Jesus' family as icons stamped in gold foil, with a calm Mary receiving the tidings of the Annunciation as a kind of benediction. But that is not at all how Luke tells the story. Mary was "greatly troubled" and "afraid" at the angel's appearance, and when the angel pronounced the sublime words about the Son of the Most High whose kingdom will never end, Mary had something far more mundane on her mind: *But I'm a virgin!*

Once, a young unmarried lawyer named Cynthia bravely stood before my church in Chicago and told of a sin we already knew about: we had seen her hyperactive son running up and down the aisles every

Sunday. Cynthia had taken the lonely road of bearing an illegitimate child and caring for him after his father decided to skip town. Cynthia's sin was no worse than many others, and yet, as she told us, it had such conspicuous consequences. She could not hide the result of that single act of passion, sticking out as it did from her abdomen for months until a child emerged to change every hour of every day of the rest of her life. No wonder the Jewish teenager Mary felt greatly troubled: she faced the same prospects even without the act of passion.

In the modern United States, where each year a million teenage girls get pregnant out of wedlock, Mary's predicament has undoubtedly lost some of its force, but in a closely knit Jewish community in the first century, the news an angel brought could not have been entirely welcome. The law regarded a betrothed woman who became pregnant as an adulteress, subject to death by stoning.

Matthew tells of Joseph magnanimously agreeing to divorce Mary in private rather than press charges, until an angel shows up to correct his perception of betrayal. Luke tells of a tremulous Mary hurrying off to the one person who could possibly understand what she was going through: her relative Elizabeth, who miraculously got pregnant in old age after another angelic annunciation. Elizabeth believes Mary and shares her joy, and yet the scene poignantly highlights the contrast between the two women: the whole countryside is talking about Elizabeth's healed womb even as Mary must hide the shame of her own miracle.

In a few months, the birth of John the Baptist took place amid great fanfare, complete with midwives, doting relatives, and the traditional village chorus celebrating the birth of a Jewish male. Six months later, Jesus was born far from home, with no midwife, extended family, or village chorus present. A male head of household would have sufficed for the Roman census; did Joseph drag his pregnant wife along to Bethlehem in order to spare her the ignominy of childbirth in her home village?

C. S. Lewis has written about God's plan, "The whole thing narrows and narrows, until at last it comes down to a little point, small as the point of a spear—a Jewish girl at her prayers." Today as I read the accounts of Jesus' birth I tremble to think of the fate of the world resting on the responses of two rural teenagers. How many times did Mary review the angel's words as she felt the Son of God kicking against the walls of her uterus? How many times did Joseph second-guess his own encounter with an angel—*just a dream?*—as he endured the hot shame of living among villagers who could plainly see the changing shape of his fiancée?

We know nothing of Jesus' grandparents. What must they have felt? Did they respond like so many parents of unmarried teenagers today, with an outburst of moral fury and then a period of sullen silence until at last the bright-eyed newborn arrives to melt the ice and arrange a fragile family truce? Or did they, like many inner-city grandparents today, graciously offer to take the child under their own roof?

Nine months of awkward explanations, the lingering scent of scandal—it seems that God arranged the most humiliating circumstances possible for his entrance, as if to avoid any charge of favoritism. I am impressed that when the Son of God became a human being he played by the rules, harsh rules: small towns do not treat kindly young boys who grow up with questionable paternity.

Malcolm Muggeridge observed that in our day, with family-planning clinics offering convenient ways to correct "mistakes" that might disgrace a family name, "It is, in point of fact, extremely improbable, under existing conditions, that Jesus would have been permitted to be born at all. Mary's pregnancy, in poor circumstances, and with the father unknown, would have been an obvious case for an abortion; and her talk of having conceived as a result of the intervention of the Holy Ghost would have pointed to the need for psychiatric treatment, and made the case for terminating her pregnancy even stronger. Thus our generation, needing a Savior more, perhaps, than any that has ever existed, would be too humane to allow one to be born."

The virgin Mary, though, whose parenthood was unplanned, had a different response. She heard the angel out, pondered the repercussions, and replied, "I am the Lord's servant. May it be to me as you have said." Often a work of God comes with two edges, great joy and great pain, and in that matter-of-fact response Mary embraced both. She was the first person to accept Jesus on his own terms, regardless of the personal cost.

* * *

When the Jesuit missionary Matteo Ricci went to China in the sixteenth century, he brought along samples of religious art to illustrate the Christian story for people who had never heard it. The Chinese readily adopted portraits of the Virgin Mary holding her child, but when he produced paintings of the crucifixion and tried to explain that the God-child had grown up only to be executed, the audience reacted with revulsion and horror. They much preferred the Virgin and insisted on worshiping her rather than the crucified God.

As I thumb once more through my stack of Christmas cards, I realize that we in Christian countries do much the same thing. We observe a mellow, domesticated holiday purged of any hint of scandal. Above all, we purge from it any reminder of how the story that began at Bethlehem turned out at Calvary.

In the birth stories of Luke and Matthew, only one person seems to grasp the mysterious nature of what God has set in motion: the old man Simeon, who recognized the baby as the Messiah, instinctively understood that conflict would surely follow. "This child is destined to cause the falling and rising of many in Israel, and to be a sign that will be spoken against . . ." he said, and then made the prediction that a sword would pierce Mary's own soul. Somehow Simeon sensed that though on the surface little had changed—the autocrat Herod still ruled, Roman troops were still stringing up patriots, Jerusalem still overflowed with beggars—underneath, everything had changed. A new force had arrived to undermine the world's powers.

At first, Jesus hardly seemed a threat to those powers. He was born under Caesar Augustus, at a time when hope wafted through the Roman Empire. More than any other ruler, Augustus raised the expectations of what a leader could accomplish and what a society could achieve. It was Augustus, in fact, who first borrowed the Greek word for "Gospel" or "Good News" and applied it as a label for the new world order represented by his reign. The empire declared him a god and established rites of worship. His enlightened and stable regime, many believed, would last forever, a final solution to the problem of government.

Meanwhile, in an obscure corner of Augustus's empire the birth of a baby named Jesus was overlooked by the chroniclers of the day. We know about him mainly through four books written years after his death, at a time when less than one-half of one percent of the Roman world had ever heard of him. Jesus' biographers would also borrow the word *gospel*, proclaiming a different kind of new world order altogether. They would mention Augustus only once, a passing reference to set the date of a census that ensured Jesus would be born in Bethlehem.

The earliest events in Jesus' life, though, give a menacing preview of the unlikely struggle now under way. Herod the Great, King of the Jews, enforced Roman rule at the local level, and in an irony of history we know Herod's name mainly because of the massacre of the innocents. I have never seen a Christmas card depicting that state-sponsored act of terror, but it too was a part of Christ's coming. Although secular history does not refer to the atrocity, no one acquainted with the life of Herod doubts him capable. He killed two brothers-in-law, his own wife Mariamne, and two of his own sons. Five days before his death he ordered the arrest of many citizens and decreed that they be executed on the day of his death, in order to guarantee a proper atmosphere of mourning in the country. For such a despot, a minor extermination procedure in Bethlehem posed no problem.

Scarcely a day passed, in fact, without an execution under Herod's regime. The political climate at the time of Jesus' birth resembled that of Russia in the 1930s under Stalin. Citizens could not gather in public meetings. Spies were everywhere. In Herod's mind, the command to slaughter Bethlehem's infants was probably an act of utmost rationality, a rearguard action to preserve the stability of his kingdom against a rumored invasion from another.

In *For the Time Being*, W. H. Auden projects what might have been going on inside Herod's mind as he mused about ordering the massacre:

> Today has been one of those perfect winter days, cold, brilliant, and utterly still, when the bark of a shepherd's dog carries for miles, and the great wild mountains come up quite close to the city walls, and the mind feels intensely awake, and this evening as I stand at this window high up in the citadel there is

nothing in the whole magnificent panorama of plain and mountains to indicate that the Empire is threatened by a danger more dreadful than any invasion of Tartar on racing camels or conspiracy of the Praetorian Guard. . . .

O dear, Why couldn't this wretched infant be born somewhere else?

And so Jesus the Christ entered the world amid strife and terror, and spent his infancy hidden in Egypt as a refugee. Matthew notes that local politics even determined where Jesus would grow up. When Herod the Great died, an angel reported to Joseph it was safe for him to return to Israel, but not to the region where Herod's son Archelaus had taken command. Joseph moved his family instead to Nazareth in the north, where they lived under the domain of another of Herod's sons, Antipas, the one Jesus would call "that fox," and also the one who would have John the Baptist beheaded.

A few years later the Romans took over direct command of the southern province that encompassed Jerusalem, and the cruelest and most notorious of these governors was a man named Pontius Pilate. Well-connected, Pilate had married the granddaughter of Augustus Caesar. According to Luke, Herod Antipas and the Roman governor Pilate regarded each other as enemies until the day fate brought them together to determine the destiny of Jesus. On that day they collaborated, hoping to succeed where Herod the Great had failed: by disposing of the strange pretender and thus preserving the kingdom.

From beginning to end, the conflict between Rome and Jesus appeared to be entirely one-sided. The execution of Jesus would put an apparent end to any threat, or so it was assumed at the time. Tyranny would win again. It occurred to no one that his stubborn followers just might outlast the Roman empire.

The facts of Christmas, rhymed in carols, recited by children in church plays, illustrated on cards, have become so familiar that it is easy to miss the message behind the facts. After reading the birth stories once more, I ask myself, *If Jesus came to reveal God to us, then what do I learn about God from that first Christmas?*

The word associations that come to mind as I ponder that question take me by surprise. Humble, approachable, underdog, courageous—these hardly seem appropriate words to apply to deity.

Humble. Before Jesus, almost no pagan author had used "humble" as a compliment. Yet the events of Christmas point inescapably to what seems like an oxymoron: a humble God. The God who came to earth came not in a raging whirlwind nor in a devouring fire. Unimaginably, the Maker of all things shrank down, down, down, so small as to become an ovum, a single fertilized egg barely visible to the naked eye, an egg that would divide and redivide until a fetus took shape, enlarging cell by cell inside a nervous teenager. "Immensity cloistered in thy dear womb," marveled the poet John Donne. He "made himself nothing ... he humbled himself," said the apostle Paul more prosaically.

I remember sitting one Christmas season in a beautiful auditorium in London listening to Handel's *Messiah*, with a full chorus singing about the day when "the glory of the Lord shall be revealed." I had spent the morning in museums viewing remnants of England's glory—the crown jewels, a solid gold ruler's mace, the Lord Mayor's gilded carriage—and it occurred to me that just such images of wealth and power must have filled the minds of Isaiah's contemporaries who first heard that promise. When the Jews read Isaiah's words, no doubt they thought back with sharp nostalgia to the glory days of Solomon, when "the king made silver as common in Jerusalem as stones."

The Messiah who showed up, however, wore a different kind of glory, the glory of humility. "'God is great,' the cry of the Moslems, is a truth which needed no supernatural being to teach men," writes Father Neville Figgis. "That *God is little*, that is the truth which Jesus taught man." The God who roared, who could order armies and empires about like pawns on a chessboard, this God emerged in Palestine as a baby who could not speak or eat solid food or control his bladder, who depended on a teenager for shelter, food, and love.

In London, looking toward the auditorium's royal box where the queen and her family sat, I caught glimpses of the more typical way rulers stride through the world: with bodyguards, and a trumpet fanfare, and a flourish of bright clothes and flashing jewelry. Queen Elizabeth II had recently visited the United States, and reporters delighted in spelling out the logistics involved: her four thousand pounds of luggage included two outfits for every occasion, a mourning outfit in case someone died, forty pints of plasma, and white kid leather toilet seat covers. She brought along her own hairdresser, two valets, and a host of other attendants. A brief visit of royalty to a foreign country can easily cost twenty million dollars.

In meek contrast, God's visit to earth took place in an animal shelter with no attendants present and nowhere to lay the newborn king but a feed trough. Indeed, the event that divided history, and even our calendars, into two parts may have had more animal than human witnesses. A mule could have stepped on him. "How silently, how silently, the wondrous gift is given."

For just an instant the sky grew luminous with angels, yet who saw that spectacle? Illiterate hirelings who watched the flocks of others, "nobodies" who failed to leave their names. Shepherds had such a randy reputation that proper Jews lumped them together with the "godless," restricting them to the outer courtyards of the temple. Fittingly, it was they whom God selected to help celebrate the birth of one who would be known as the friend of sinners.

In Auden's poem the wise men proclaim, "O here and now our endless journey stops." The shepherds say, "O here and now our endless journey starts." The search for worldly wisdom has ended; true life has just begun.

Approachable. Those of us raised in a tradition of informal or private prayer may not appreciate the change Jesus wrought in how human beings approach deity. Hindus offer sacrifices at the temple. Kneeling Muslims bow down so low that their foreheads touch the ground. In most religious traditions, in fact, *fear* is the primary emotion when one approaches God.

Certainly the Jews associated fear with worship. The burning bush of Moses, the hot coals of Isaiah, the extraterrestrial visions of Ezekiel—a person "blessed" with a direct encounter with God expected to come away scorched or glowing or maybe half-crippled like Jacob. These were the fortunate ones: Jewish children also learned stories of the sacred mountain in the desert that proved fatal to everyone who touched it. Mishandle the ark of the covenant, and you died. Enter the Most Holy Place, and you'd never come out alive.

Among people who walled off a separate sanctum for God in the temple and shrank from pronouncing or spelling out the name, God made a surprise appearance as a baby in a manger. What can be less scary than a newborn with his limbs wrapped tight against his body? In Jesus, God found a way of relating to human beings that did not involve fear.

In truth, fear had never worked very well. The Old Testament includes far more low points than high ones. A new approach was needed, a New Covenant, to use the words of the Bible, one that would not emphasize the vast gulf between God and humanity but instead would span it.

A friend of mine named Kathy was using a "Can you guess?" game to help her six-year-old learn the different animals. His turn: "I'm thinking of a mammal. He's big and he does magic." Kathy thought for a while and then gave up. "I don't know." "It's Jesus!" said her son in triumph. The answer seemed irreverent at the time, Kathy told me, but later as she thought about it she realized her son had hit upon an unsettling insight into the depths of incarnation: Jesus as a mammal!

I learned about incarnation when I kept a salt-water aquarium. Management of a marine aquarium, I discovered, is no easy task. I had to run a portable chemical laboratory to monitor the nitrate levels and the ammonia content. I pumped in vitamins and antibiotics and sulfa drugs and enough enzymes to make a rock grow. I filtered the water through glass fibers and charcoal, and exposed it to ultraviolet light. You would think, in view of all the energy expended on their behalf, that my fish would at least be grateful. Not so. Every time my shadow loomed above the tank they dove for cover into the nearest shell. They showed me one "emotion" only: fear. Although I opened the lid and dropped in food on a regular schedule, three times a day, they responded to each visit as a sure sign of my designs to torture them. I could not convince them of my true concern.

To my fish I was deity. I was too large for them, my actions too incomprehensible. My acts of mercy they saw as cruelty; my attempts at healing they viewed as destruction. To change their perceptions, I began to see, would require a form of incarnation. I would have to become a fish and "speak" to them in a language they could understand.

A human being becoming a fish is nothing compared to God becoming a baby. And yet according to the Gospels that is what happened at Bethlehem. The God who created matter took shape within it, as an artist might become a spot on a painting or a playwright a character within his own play. God wrote a story, only using real characters, on the pages of real history. The Word became flesh.

Underdog. I wince even as I write the word, especially in connection with Jesus. It's a crude word, probably derived from dogfighting and applied over time to predictable losers and victims of injustice. Yet as I read the birth stories about Jesus I cannot help but conclude that though the world may be tilted toward the rich and powerful, God is tilted toward the underdog. "He has brought down rulers from their thrones but has lifted up the humble. He has filled the hungry with good things but has sent the rich away empty," said Mary in her Magnificat hymn.

Laszlo Tokes, the Romanian pastor whose mistreatment outraged the country and prompted rebellion against the Communist ruler Ceausescu, tells of trying to prepare a Christmas sermon for the tiny mountain church to which he had been exiled. The state police were rounding up dissidents, and violence was breaking out across the country. Afraid for his life, Tokes bolted his doors, sat down, and read again the stories in Luke and Matthew. Unlike most pastors who would preach that Christmas, he chose as his text the verses describing Herod's massacre of the innocents. It was the single passage that spoke most directly to his parishioners. Oppression, fear, and violence, the daily plight of the underdog, they well understood.

The next day, Christmas, news broke that Ceausescu had been arrested. Church bells rang, and joy broke out all over Romania. Another King Herod had fallen. Tokes recalls, "All the events of the Christmas story now had a new, brilliant dimension for us, a dimension of history rooted in the reality of our lives. . . . For those of us who lived through them, the days of Christmas 1989 represented a rich, resonant embroidery of the Christmas story, a time when the providence of God and the foolishness of human wickedness seemed as easy to comprehend as the sun and the moon over the timeless Transylvanian hills." For the first time in four decades, Romania celebrated Christmas as a public holiday.

Perhaps the best way to perceive the "underdog" nature of the incarnation is to transpose it into terms we can relate to today. An unwed mother, homeless, was forced to look for shelter while traveling to meet the heavy taxation demands of a colonial government. She lived in a land recovering from violent civil wars and still in turmoil— a situation much like that in modern Bosnia, Rwanda, or Somalia. Like half of all mothers who deliver today, she gave birth in Asia, in its far western corner, the part of the world that would prove least receptive to the son she bore. That son became a refugee in Africa, the continent where most refugees can still be found.

I wonder what Mary thought about her militant Magnificat hymn during her harrowing years in Egypt. For a Jew, Egypt evoked bright memories of a powerful God who had flattened a pharaoh's army and brought liberation; now Mary fled there, desperate, a stranger in a strange land hiding from her own government. Could her baby, hunted, helpless, on the run, possibly fulfill the lavish hopes of his people?

Even the family's mother-tongue summoned up memories of their underdog status: Jesus spoke Aramaic, a trade language closely related to Arabic, a stinging reminder of the Jews' subjection to foreign empires.

Some foreign astrologers (probably from the region that is now Iraq) had dropped by to visit Jesus, but these men were considered "unclean" by Jews of the day. Naturally, like all dignitaries they had checked first with the ruling king in Jerusalem, who knew nothing about a baby in Bethlehem. After they saw the child and realized who he was, these visitors engaged in an act of civil disobedience: they deceived Herod and went home another way, to protect the child. They had chosen Jesus' side, against the powerful.

Growing up, Jesus' sensibilities were affected most deeply by the poor, the powerless, the oppressed—in short, the underdogs. Today theologians debate the aptness of the phrase "God's preferential option for the poor" as a way of describing God's concern for the underdog. Since God arranged the circumstances in which to be born on planet earth—without power or wealth, without rights, without justice—his preferential options speak for themselves.

Courageous. In 1993 I read a news report about a "Messiah sighting" in the Crown Heights section of Brooklyn, New York. Twenty thousand Lubavitcher Hasidic Jews live in Crown Heights, and in 1993 many of them believed the Messiah was dwelling among them in the person of Rabbi Menachem Mendel Schneerson.

Word of the Rabbi's public appearance spread like a flash fire through the streets of Crown Heights, and Lubavitchers in their black coats and curly sideburns were soon dashing down the sidewalks toward the synagogue where the Rabbi customarily prayed. Those lucky enough to be connected to a network of beepers got a head start, sprinting toward the synagogue the instant they felt a slight vibration. They jammed by the hundreds into a main hall, elbowing each other and even climbing the pillars to create more room. The hall filled with an air of anticipation and frenzy normally found at a championship sporting event, not a religious service.

The Rabbi was ninety-one years old. He had suffered a stroke the year before and had not been able to speak since. When the curtain finally pulled back, those who had crowded into the synagogue saw a frail old man in a long beard who could do little but wave, tilt his head, and move his eyebrows. No one in the audience seemed to mind, though. "Long live our master, our teacher, and our rabbi, King, Messiah, forever and ever!" they sang in unison, over and over, building in volume until the Rabbi made a small, delphic gesture with his hand, and the curtain closed. They departed slowly, savoring the moment, in a state of ecstasy.*

When I first read the news account I nearly laughed out loud. Who are these people trying to kid—a nonagenarian mute Messiah in Brooklyn? And then it struck me: I was reacting to Rabbi Schneer-

---

*Rabbi Schneerson died in June 1994. Now many Lubavitchers are anticipating his bodily resurrection.

son exactly as people in the first century had reacted to Jesus. A Messiah from Galilee? A carpenter's kid, no less?

The scorn I felt as I read about the Rabbi and his fanatical followers gave me a clue to the responses Jesus faced throughout his life. His neighbors asked, "Isn't his mother's name Mary, and aren't his brothers James, Joseph, Simon, and Judas? Where did this man get this wisdom and these miraculous powers?" Other countrymen scoffed, "Nazareth! Can anything good come from there?" His own family tried to put him away, believing he was out of his mind. The religious experts sought to kill him. As for the whipsaw commoners, one moment they judged him "demon-possessed and raving mad," the next they forcibly tried to crown him king.

It took courage, I believe, for God to lay aside power and glory and to take a place among human beings who would greet him with the same mixture of haughtiness and skepticism that I felt when I first heard about Rabbi Schneerson of Brooklyn. It took courage to risk descent to a planet known for its clumsy violence, among a race known for rejecting its prophets. What more foolhardy thing could God have done?

The first night in Bethlehem required courage as well. How did God the Father feel that night, helpless as any human father, watching his Son emerge smeared with blood to face a harsh, cold world? Lines from two different Christmas carols play in my mind. One, "The little Lord Jesus, no crying he makes," seems to me a sanitized version of what took place in Bethlehem. I imagine Jesus cried like any other baby the night he entered the world, a world that would give him much reason to cry as an adult. The second, a line from "O Little Town of Bethlehem," seems as profoundly true today as it did two thousand years ago: "The hopes and fears of all the world do rest on thee tonight."

"Alone of all creeds, Christianity has added courage to the virtues of the Creator," said G. K. Chesterton. The need for such courage began with Jesus' first night on earth and did not end until his last.

There is one more view of Christmas I have never seen on a Christmas card, probably because no artist, not even William Blake, could do it justice. Revelation 12 pulls back the curtain to give us a glimpse of Christmas as it must have looked from somewhere far beyond Andromeda: Christmas from the angels' viewpoint.

The account differs radically from the birth stories in the Gospels. Revelation does not mention shepherds and an infanticidal king; rather, it pictures a dragon leading a ferocious struggle in heaven. A woman clothed with the sun and wearing a crown of twelve stars cries out in pain as she is about to give birth. Suddenly the enormous red dragon enters the picture, his tail sweeping a third of the stars out of the sky and flinging them to the earth. He crouches hungrily before the woman, anxious to devour her child the moment it is born. At the last second the infant is snatched away to safety, the woman flees into the desert, and all-out cosmic war begins.

Revelation is a strange book by any measure, and readers must understand its style to make sense of this extraordinary spectacle. In daily life two parallel histories occur simultaneously, one on earth and one in heaven. Revelation, however, views them together, allowing a quick look behind the scenes. On earth a baby was born, a king got wind of it, a chase ensued. In heaven the Great Invasion had begun, a daring raid by the ruler of the forces of good into the universe's seat of evil.

John Milton expressed this point of view majestically in *Paradise Lost* and *Paradise Regained*, poems which make heaven and hell the central focus and earth a mere battleground for their clashes. The modern author J. B. Phillips also attempted such a point of view, on a much less epic scale, and last Christmas I turned to Phillips's fantasy to try to escape my earthbound viewpoint.

In Phillips's version, a senior angel is showing a very young angel around the splendors of the universe. They view whirling galaxies and blazing suns, and then flit across the infinite distances of space until at last they enter one particular galaxy of 500 billion stars.

> As the two of them drew near to the star which we call our sun and to its circling planets, the senior angel pointed to a small and rather insignificant sphere turning very slowly on its axis. It looked as dull as a dirty tennis-ball to the little angel, whose mind was filled with the size and glory of what he had seen.

"I want you to watch that one particularly," said the senior angel, pointing with his finger.

"Well, it looks very small and rather dirty to me," said the little angel. "What's special about that one?"

When I read Phillips's fantasy, I thought of the pictures beamed back to earth from the Apollo astronauts, who described our planet as "whole and round and beautiful and small," a blue-green-and-tan globe suspended in space. Jim Lovell, reflecting on the scene later, said, "It was just another body, really, about four times bigger than the moon. But it held all the hope and all the life and all the things that the crew of Apollo 8 knew and loved. It was the most beautiful thing there was to see in all the heavens." That was the viewpoint of a human being.

To the little angel, though, earth did not seem so impressive. He listened in stunned disbelief as the senior angel told him that this planet, small and insignificant and not overly clean, was the renowned Visited Planet.

"Do you mean that our great and glorious Prince ... went down in Person to this fifth-rate little ball? Why should He do a thing like that?" ...

The little angel's face wrinkled in disgust. "Do you mean to tell me," he said, "that He stooped so low as to become one of those creeping, crawling creatures of that floating ball?"

"I do, and I don't think He would like you to call them 'creeping, crawling creatures' in that tone of voice. For, strange as it may seem to us, He loves them. He went down to visit them to lift them up to become like Him."

The little angel looked blank. Such a thought was almost beyond his comprehension.

It is almost beyond my comprehension too, and yet I accept that this notion is the key to understanding Christmas and is, in fact, the touchstone of my faith. As a Christian I believe that we live in parallel worlds. One world consists of hills and lakes and barns and politicians and shepherds watching their flocks by night. The other consists of angels and sinister forces and somewhere out there places called heaven and hell. One night in the cold, in the dark, among the wrinkled hills of Bethlehem, those two worlds came together at a dramatic point of intersection. God, who knows no before or after, entered time and space. God, who knows no boundaries took on the shocking confines of a baby's skin, the ominous restraints of mortality.

"He is the image of the invisible God, the firstborn over all creation," an apostle would later write; "He is before all things, and in him all things hold together." But the few eyewitnesses on Christmas night saw none of that. They saw an infant struggling to work never-before-used lungs.

Could it be true, this Bethlehem story of a Creator descending to be born on one small planet? If so, it is a story like no other. Never again need we wonder whether what happens on this dirty little tennis ball of a planet matters to the rest of the universe. Little wonder a choir of angels broke out in spontaneous song, disturbing not only a few shepherds but the entire universe.

3
Background: Jewish Roots and Soil

This again is a great contradiction: though he was a Jew, his followers
were not Jews.

Voltaire

3
Background: Jewish Roots and Soil

As a boy growing up in a WASP community in Atlanta, Georgia, I did not know a single Jew. I pictured Jews as foreigners with thick accents and strange hats who lived in Brooklyn or some such faraway place where they all studied to become psychiatrists and musicians. I knew the Jews had something to do with World War II, but I had heard little about the Holocaust. Certainly these people had no relation to my Jesus.

Not until my early twenties did I befriend a Jewish photographer who disabused me of many notions about his race. One night when we stayed up late talking, he described what it was like to lose twenty-seven members of his family to the Holocaust. Later, he acquainted me with Elie Wiesel, Chaim Potok, Martin Buber, and other Jewish writers, and after these encounters I began reading the New Testament through new eyes. How could I have missed it! Jesus' true-blue Jewishness leaps out from Matthew's very first sentence, which introduces him as "the son of David, son of Abraham."

In church we affirmed Jesus as "the only-begotten Son of God, begotten of his Father before all worlds ... Very God of Very God." Those creedal statements, though, are light-years removed from the Gospels' account of Jesus growing up in a Jewish family in the agricultural town of Nazareth. I later learned that not even converted

Jews—who might have rooted Jesus more solidly in Jewish soil—were invited to the Council of Chalcedon that composed the creed. We Gentiles face the constant danger of letting Jesus' Jewishness, and even his humanity, slip away.

In historical fact, we are the ones who have co-opted *their* Jesus. As I got to know Jesus, the realization sank in that he probably did not spend his life among Jews in the first century merely to save Americans in the twentieth. Alone of all people in history, he had the privilege of choosing where and when to be born, and he chose a pious Jewish family living in a backwater protectorate of a pagan empire. I can no more understand Jesus apart from his Jewishness than I can understand Gandhi apart from his Indianness. I need to go back, way back, and picture Jesus as a first-century Jew with a phylactery on his wrist and Palestinian dust on his sandals.

Martin Buber said, "We Jews know [Jesus] in a way—in the impulses and emotions of his essential Jewishness—that remains inaccessible to the Gentiles subject to him." He is right, of course. To know Jesus' story I must, in the same way I get to know anyone else's story, learn something of his culture, family, and background.

Following this principle, Matthew opens his gospel not as I might be tempted to begin, with a teaser on "How this book will change your life," but rather with a dry list of names, the genealogy of Jesus. Matthew chose a representative sampling from forty-two generations of Jews in order to establish Jesus' royal bloodline. Much like the shabby descendants of deposed European royalty, the peasant family of Joseph and Mary could trace their lineage back to some impressive ancestors, including Israel's greatest king, David, and its original founder, Abraham.*

---

*Matthew's list of names also lets some skeletons out of the closet. Consider the women mentioned (a rarity in Jewish genealogies). At least three of the four were foreigners, which may have been Matthew's way of hinting that Jesus held out universal promise. The Jewish Messiah had gentile blood!

Tamar, a childless widow, had to dress like a prostitute and seduce her father-in-law in order to produce her contribution to Jesus' line. Rahab did not merely pre-

Jesus grew up during a time of resurgent "Jewish pride." In a backlash against the pressure to embrace Greek culture, families had recently begun adopting names that harked back to the times of the patriarchs and the Exodus from Egypt (not unlike ethnic Americans who choose African or Hispanic names for their children). Thus Mary was named for Miriam, the sister of Moses, and Joseph was named after one of the twelve sons of Jacob, as were Jesus' four brothers.

Jesus' own name comes from the word *Joshua*—"he shall save"— a common name in those days. (As major-league baseball rosters reveal, the name Jesus remains popular among Latin Americans.) Its very ordinariness, not unlike "Bob" or "Joe" today, must have grated on Jewish ears in the first century as they listened to Jesus' words. Jews did not pronounce the Honorable Name of GOD, save for the high priest one day a year, and even today Orthodox Jews carefully spell out G_D. For people raised in such a tradition, the idea that an ordinary person with a name like Jesus could be the Son of God and Savior of the world seemed utterly scandalous. Jesus was a man, for goodness' sake, Mary's boy.

Signs of Jesus' Jewishness surface throughout the Gospels. He was circumcised as a baby. Significantly, the one scene included from Jesus' childhood shows his family attending an obligatory festival in Jerusalem, several days' journey from their home. As an adult Jesus worshiped in the synagogue and temple, followed Jewish customs, and spoke in terms his fellow Jews would understand. Even his controversies with other Jews, such as the Pharisees, underscored the fact that they expected him to share their values and act more like them.

As the German theologian Jürgen Moltmann has pointed out, if Jesus had lived during the Third Reich, very likely he would have been branded like other Jews and shipped to the gas chambers. A pogrom of his own time, Herod's massacre of infants, was specifically targeted against Jesus.

---

tend, but actually made her living as a prostitute. And "Uriah's wife," or Bathsheba, was the object of David's lust, which led to the most famous royal scandal of the Old Testament. These shady ancestors show that Jesus entered human history in the raw, a willing descendant of its shame. In contrast, Herod the Great, reigning king at Jesus' birth, had his genealogical records destroyed out of vanity because he wanted no one to compare his background with others'.

A rabbi friend mentioned to me that Christians perceive Jesus' cry from the cross, "My God, my God why have you forsaken me?" as a profound moment of struggle between Father and Son; Jews, however, hear those words as the death cry of yet another Jewish victim. Jesus was not the first and certainly not the last Jew to cry out words from the Psalms at a time of torture.

Yet a strange reversal occurred within a few generations of Jesus' life. With rare exceptions, Jews stopped following him and the church became thoroughly Gentile. What happened? It seems clear to me that Jesus failed to meet the expectations of Messiah the Jews were awaiting.

It would be impossible to exaggerate the import of the word *Messiah* among faithful Jews. The Dead Sea Scrolls discovered in 1947 confirm that the Qumram community imminently expected a Messiah-like figure, setting aside an empty seat for him each day at the sacred meal. Audacious as it may be to dream that a tiny province wedged in among great powers would produce a worldwide ruler, nonetheless Jews believed just that. They staked their future on a king who would lead their nation back to glory.

During Jesus' lifetime, revolt was in the air. Pseudo-messiahs periodically emerged to lead rebellions, only to be crushed in ruthless crackdowns. To take just one example, a prophet known as "the Egyptian" attracted multitudes into the wilderness where he proclaimed that at his command the walls of Jerusalem would fall; the Roman governor sent a detachment of soldiers after them and killed four thousand of the rebels.

When another report spread that the long-awaited prophet had turned up in the desert, crowds flocked to see the wild man dressed in camel skin. "I am not the Christ [Messiah]," insisted John the Baptist, who then proceeded to raise hopes even higher by speaking in exalted terms of one who would soon appear. John's question of Jesus, "Are you the one who was to come, or shall we expect someone else?" was in a real sense the question of the age, whispered everywhere.

Every Hebrew prophet had taught that someday God would install his kingdom on earth, and that is why rumors about the "Son of David" so inflamed Jewish hopes. God would prove in person that he had not forsaken them. He would, as Isaiah had cried, "rend the heavens and come down, that the mountains would tremble before you! . . . come down to cause the nations to quake before you."

But let us be honest. When the one John pointed to arrived on the scene, neither the mountains trembled nor the nations quaked. Jesus did not come close to satisfying the lavish hopes of the Jews. The opposite happened: within a generation Roman soldiers razed Jerusalem to the ground. The young Christian church accepted the destruction of the temple as a sign of the end of the covenant between God and Israel, and after the first century very few Jews converted to Christianity. Christians appropriated Jewish Scriptures, renaming them "Old Testament," and put an end to most Jewish customs.

Rejected by the church, blamed for Jesus' death, some Jews began a counter-campaign against the Christians. They spread a rumor that Jesus was the illegitimate offspring of Mary's liaison with a Roman soldier, and wrote a cruel parody of the Gospels. Jesus was hanged on the eve of Passover, said one report, because "he hath practiced sorcery and beguiled and led astray Israel." The man whose birth angels celebrated with a proclamation of peace on earth became the great divide of human history.

A few years ago I met with ten Christians, ten Jews, and ten Muslims in New Orleans. The psychiatrist and author M. Scott Peck had invited us there to see if we could overcome our differences enough to produce some sort of community. Each faith held a worship service—Muslims on Friday, Jews on Saturday, Christians on Sunday—which the others were invited to observe. The services had striking similarities and reminded us how much the three faiths have in common. Perhaps the intensity of feeling among the three traditions stems from a common heritage: family disputes are always the stubbornest, and civil wars the bloodiest.

I learned a new word in New Orleans: *supersessionism*. The Jews resented the notion that Christian faith had superseded Judaism. "I feel like a curiosity of history, as if my religion should be put in a nursing home," said one. "It grates on me to hear the term 'Old Testament God' or even 'Old' Testament, for that matter." Christians had also taken over the word Messiah, or at least its Greek equivalent, "Christ." One rabbi told of growing up in the only Jewish household in a small Virginia town. Each year the Christians asked his father, a respected member of the community (and, as a Jew, impartial in judgment), to rank the displays of Christmas lights and decide which houses deserved prizes. As a young boy, this rabbi drove with his father past every house in town, staring with longing and incomprehension at the bright displays of *Christ*-mas lights: literally, "Messiah lights."

I had not realized that Muslims look on both faiths with a supersessionist attitude. As they see it, just as Christianity grew out of and incorporated parts of Judaism, Islam grew out of and incorporated parts of both religions. Abraham was a prophet, Jesus was a prophet, but Muhammad was The Prophet. The Old Testament has a place, as does the New Testament, but the Qur'an is "the final revelation." Hearing my own faith talked about in such paternalistic terms gave me insight into how Jews have felt for two millennia.

I also realized, after listening to three faiths articulate their differences, how deep is the divide that Jesus introduced. The Muslim worship service consisted mostly of reverential prayers to the Almighty. The Jewish service incorporated readings from Psalms and the Torah and some warmhearted singing. Any of those elements can be found in a Christian service. What divided us from the others was the celebration of the Lord's Supper. "This is my body, broken for you," our leader read, before distributing the bread—Christ's body, the divergence point.

When Muslims conquered Asia Minor they converted many Christian churches into mosques, carving this stern inscription for the admonition of any remaining Christians: "God did not beget and is not begotten." The same phrase could be painted on synagogue walls. The great divide of history traces back to Bethlehem and Jerusalem. Was Jesus really Messiah, the Son of God? As the Jews in New

Orleans explained, a Messiah who dies at the age of thirty-three, a nation that goes downhill after its Savior's death, a world that grows more fractured, not less—these facts do not seem to add up for the members of Jesus' own race.

Nevertheless, despite two thousand years of the great divide, despite all that has taken place in this century of violent anti-Semitism, interest in Jesus is resurging among the Jews. In 1925, when the Hebrew scholar Joseph Klausner decided to write a book about Jesus, he could find only three full-length treatments of Jesus' life by contemporary Jewish scholars. Now there are hundreds, including some of the most illuminating studies available. Modern Israeli schoolchildren learn that Jesus was a great teacher, perhaps the greatest Jewish teacher, who was subsequently "co-opted" by the Gentiles.

Is it possible to read the Gospels without blinders on? Jews read with suspicion, preparing to be scandalized. Christians read through the refracted lenses of church history. Both groups, I believe, would do well to pause and reflect on Matthew's first words, "A record of the genealogy of Jesus Christ, son of David, son of Abraham." The son of David speaks of Jesus' messianic line, which Jews should not ignore; "a title which he would not deny to save his life cannot have been without significance for him," notes C. H. Dodd. The son of Abraham speaks of Jesus' Jewish line, which we Christians dare not ignore either. Jaroslav Pelikan writes,

> Would there have been such anti-Semitism, would there have been so many pogroms, would there have been an Auschwitz, if every Christian church and every Christian home had focused its devotion and icons of Mary not only as Mother of God and Queen of Heaven but as the Jewish maiden and the new Miriam, and on icons of Christ not only as a Pantocrator but as *Rabbi Jeshua bar-Joseph*, Rabbi Jesus of Nazareth?

Growing up, I did not know a single Jew. I do now. I know something of their culture. The close ties that keep sacred holidays alive even for families who no longer believe in their meaning. The passionate arguments that at first intimidated me but soon attracted me as a style of personal engagement. The respect, even reverence, for legalism amid a society that mainly values autonomy. The tradition of scholarship that has helped sustain a culture despite others' relentless attempts to obliterate it. The ability to link arms and dance and sing and laugh even when the world offers scant reason for celebration.

This was the culture Jesus grew up in, a Jewish culture. Yes, he changed it, but always from his starting point as a Jew. Now when I find myself wondering what Jesus was like as a teenager, I think of Jewish boys I know in Chicago. And when the thought jars me, I remember that in his own day Jesus got the opposite reaction. A Jewish teenager, surely—but the Son of God?

Not only did Jesus choose a race, he also chose a time and place in which to be born. History became, in Bonhoeffer's phrase, "the womb of the birth of God." Why that particular history? I sometimes wonder why Jesus did not come in modern times, when he could have taken advantage of mass communications. Or back in Isaiah's day, when expectations for the Messiah also ran high and Israel was still an independent nation. What about the first century made it the right time to ease God into the world?

Every age has its prevailing mood: the sunny confidence of the nineteenth century, the violent chaos of the twentieth. In the era of Jesus' birth, at the height of the Roman Empire, hope and optimism held sway. As in the Soviet Union before its breakup or the British Empire in Queen Victoria's day, Rome kept peace at the point of a sword, but by and large even the conquered peoples cooperated. Except in Palestine, that is.

Anticipation soared for "a new order of the ages" at the time of Jesus' birth. The Roman poet Virgil coined that phrase, sounding like an Old Testament prophet as he declared that "a new human race is descending from the heights of heaven," a change that would come about due to "the birth of a child, with whom the iron age of humanity will end and the golden age begin." Virgil wrote these messianic words not about Jesus, however, but about Caesar Augustus, the "present deity," the "restorer of the world," who had managed to reunite the empire after the civil war sparked by Julius Caesar's assassination.

To loyal Roman subjects Augustus offered peace, security, and entertainment: in two words, bread and circuses. The Pax Romana assured that citizens had protection from outside enemies and enjoyed the benefits of Roman justice and civil government. Meanwhile, a Greek soul filled the Roman body politic. People throughout the empire dressed like the Greeks, built their buildings in the Greek style, played Greek sports, and spoke the Greek language. Except in Palestine.

Palestine, the one lump the anaconda could not digest, exasperated Rome to no end. Contrary to Roman tolerance for many gods, the Jews held tenaciously to the notion of one God, their God, who had revealed to them a distinct culture as the Chosen People. William Barclay describes what happened when these two societies collided. "It is the simple historical fact that in the thirty years from 67 to 37 B.C. before the emergence of Herod the Great, no fewer than one hundred and fifty thousand men perished in Palestine in revolutionary uprisings. There was no more explosive and inflammable country in the world than Palestine."

Jews resisted Hellenization (imposed Greek culture) as fiercely as they fought the Roman legions. Rabbis kept this aversion alive by reminding Jews of the attempts by a Seleucid madman named Antiochus to Hellenize the Jews more than a century before. Antiochus had compelled young boys to undergo reverse circumcision operations so they could appear nude in Greek athletic contests. He flogged an aged priest to death for refusing to eat pig's flesh, and butchered a mother and her seven children for not bowing down to an image. In a heinous act that became known as the "abomination of desolation," he invaded the Most Holy Place of the temple, sacrificed an unclean pig on the altar in honor of the Greek god Zeus, and smeared the sanctuary with its blood.

Antiochus's campaign failed miserably, driving Jews to an open revolt led by the Maccabeans. (Jews still celebrate Hanukkah in memory of this victory.) For nearly a century, in fact, the Maccabeans held off foreign invaders, until the Roman juggernaut rolled into Palestine. It took thirty years for Roman armies to quash all signs of rebellion; then they installed the local strongman Herod as their puppet "King of the Jews." As Herod watched the Romans killing women and children in their houses, markets, and even in the temple, he asked a general, "Would the Romans deprive the city of all its inhabitants and possessions and leave me a king of the wilderness?" Almost. By the time Herod ascended the throne, not only Jerusalem but the entire country lay in ruins.

Herod the Great still reigned when Jesus was born. Comparatively, Palestine stayed quiet under his iron thumb, for the long wars had drained both the spirit and resources of the Jews. An earthquake in 31 B.C. killed 30,000 people and much livestock, leading to more destitution. The Jews called such tragedies "pangs of the Messiah" and pled with God for a deliverer.

It is difficult to find a modern parallel, now that the Soviet empire has collapsed, to the brittle situation the Jews faced under Roman rule. Tibet under China perhaps? The blacks in South Africa before they gained freedom from minority rule? The most provocative suggestion comes from visitors to modern Israel, who cannot help noticing the similar plights of Galilean Jews in Jesus' day and Palestinians in modern times. Both served the economic interests of their richer neighbors. Both lived in small hamlets, or refugee camps, in the midst of a more modern and alien culture. Both were subject to curfews, crackdowns, and discrimination.

As Malcolm Muggeridge observed in the 1970s, "The role of the Roman legionnaires had been taken over by the Israeli army. Now it was the Arabs who were in the position of a subject people; entitled, like the Jews in Jesus' lifetime, to attend their mosques and practise their religion, but otherwise treated like second-class citizens."

Both groups, modern Palestinians and Galilean Jews, also share a susceptibility to hotheads who would call them to armed revolt. Think of the modern Middle East with all its violence, intrigues, and squabbling parties. Into such an incendiary environment, Jesus was born.

The journey from Judea to Galilee in springtime is a journey from brown to green, from an arid, rocky terrain to some of the lushest fields in the Mediterranean basin. Fruits and vegetables grow in abundance, fishermen work the Sea of Galilee, and beyond rolling hills to the west lies the shimmering blue of the Mediterranean itself. Jesus' hometown of Nazareth, so obscure that it does not make the list of sixty-three Galilean towns mentioned in the Talmud, sits on a hillside 1,300 feet above sea level. The view from a ridge allows a sweeping panorama all the way from Mt. Carmel by the ocean to the snowy peak of Mt. Hermon to the north.

With fertile land, beautiful vistas, and moderate climate, Galilee had its attractions, and clearly Jesus enjoyed his childhood there. The wildflowers and weeds growing among the crops, the laborious method of separating wheat and chaff, the fig trees and grapevines dotting the hillsides, the fields white unto harvest—all these would show up later in his parables and sayings. Just as telling, some obvious features of Galilee did not show up. A mere three miles north, in easy view of Nazareth, sat the gleaming city of Sepphoris, just then in the process of being rebuilt. Jesus' neighbors—perhaps his own father—were employed in building trades there.

For most of Jesus' life, construction crews worked on this beautiful Greco-Roman metropolis, which featured colonnaded streets, a forum, a palace, a bath and gymnasium, and luxurious villas, all constructed in white limestone and colored marble. In an imposing theater that seated four thousand, Greek actors, or *hypocrites*, entertained the multinational crowds. (Jesus would later borrow the word to describe one who played a false role in public.) During Jesus' lifetime Sepphoris served as Galilee's capital, second in importance only to Jerusalem in all of Palestine. Not once, however, do the Gospels record that Jesus visited or even mentioned the city. Nor did he visit Tiberias, Herod's winter resort town situated nearby on the shore of Lake Galilee. He gave centers of wealth and political power a wide berth.

Although Herod the Great managed to make Galilee the most prosperous province in Palestine, only a few reaped the benefits. Landless peasants mainly served the interests of wealthy landlords (another fact that would surface in Jesus' parables). An illness or back-to-back seasons of bad weather would bring disaster to most families. We know that Jesus was raised in poverty: his family could not afford a lamb for the sacrifice at the temple and offered instead a pair of doves or two young pigeons.

Galilee had a reputation as a breeding ground for revolutionaries. In 4 B.C., around the time of Jesus' birth, a rebel broke into the arsenal in Sepphoris and looted it to arm his followers. Roman troops recaptured and burned the town—which explains why it had to be rebuilt—crucifying two thousand Jews who had participated in the uprising. Ten years later another rebel, named Judas, incited a revolt, urging his countrymen to pay no taxes to the pagan Roman emperor. He helped found the Zealot party which would harass Rome for the next six decades. Two of Judas's sons would be crucified after Jesus' death, and his last son would ultimately capture the stronghold of Masada from the Romans, vowing to defend it until every last Jew had died. In the end, 960 Jewish men, women, and children took their own lives rather than fall captive to the Romans. Galileans were freedom-lovers to the core.

For all its prosperity and political activism, Galilee got little respect from the rest of the country. It was the farthest province from Jerusalem and the most backward culturally. Rabbinic literature of the time portrays Galileans as bumpkins, fodder for ethnic jokes. Galileans who learned Hebrew pronounced it so crudely that they were not called on to read the Torah in other synagogues. Speaking the common language of Aramaic in a slipshod way was a telltale sign of Galilean roots (as Simon Peter would one day find out, betrayed in a courtyard by his rural accent). The Aramaic words preserved in the Gospels show that Jesus, too, spoke in that northern dialect, no doubt encouraging skepticism about him. "How can the Christ come from Galilee?" "Nazareth! Can anything good come from there?"

Other Jews regarded Galilee as lax about spiritual matters as well. One Pharisee, after eighteen fruitless years there, lamented, "Galilee, Galilee, you hate the Torah!" Nicodemus, who stuck up for Jesus, was silenced by the rebuke, "Are you from Galilee, too? Look into it, and you will find that a prophet does not come out of Galilee." Jesus' own brothers encouraged him, "You ought to leave here and go to Judea." From the perspective of the religious power base in Jerusalem, Galilee seemed a most unlikely place for the Messiah to arise.

As I read the Gospels, I try to project myself back into those times. How would I have responded to oppression? Would I strive to be a model citizen and keep out of trouble, to live and let live? Would I be tempted by fiery insurrectionists like the Zealots? Would I fight back in more devious ways, by avoiding taxes perhaps? Or would I throw my energies into a religious movement and shun political controversies? What kind of Jew would I have made in the first century?

Eight million Jews lived in the Roman Empire then, just over a quarter of them in Palestine itself,* and sometimes they stretched Roman forbearance to the breaking point. Romans branded Jews "atheists" for their refusal to honor Greek and Roman gods, and regarded them as social misfits because of their peculiar customs: Jews refused to eat the "unclean" food of their neighbors, eschewed all business on Friday evenings and Saturdays, and disdained civic office. Nevertheless, Rome had granted Judaism legal status.

In many ways the plight of Jewish leaders resembled that of the Russian churches under Stalin. They could cooperate, which meant submitting to government interference, or they could go their own way, which meant harsh persecution. Herod the Great fit the Stalin pattern well, keeping the religious community in a state of suspicion and terror through his network of spies. "His High Priests he changed as he might change his clothes," complained one Jewish writer.

In response, the Jews splintered into parties that followed different paths of collaboration or separatism. These were the parties who would follow Jesus around, listening to him, testing him, taking his measure.

The Essenes were the most separate of all. Pacifistic, they did not actively resist Herod or the Romans, but rather withdrew into monkish communities in the caves of a barren desert. Convinced that the Roman invasion had come as a punishment for their failure to keep the Law, they devoted themselves to purity. The Essenes took ritual baths every day, maintained a strict diet, did not defecate on the Sabbath, wore no jewelry, took no oaths, and held all material goods in common. They hoped their faithfulness would encourage the advent of the Messiah.

---

*Due largely to the Holocaust, the number of Jews is approximately the same nineteen centuries later, and the same proportion lives in Palestine.

Zealots, representing a different strategy of separatism, advocated armed revolt to throw out impure foreigners. One branch of the Zealots specialized in acts of political terrorism against the Romans while another operated as a kind of "morals police" to keep fellow Jews in line. In an early version of ethnic cleansing, the Zealots declared that anyone who married into another race should be lynched. During Jesus' years of ministry, observers surely would have noted that his group of disciples included Simon the Zealot. On the other hand, Jesus' social contacts with Gentiles and foreigners, not to mention parables like the Good Samaritan, would have driven the jingoistic Zealots to fury.

At the other extreme, collaborationists tried to work within the system. The Romans had granted limited authority to a Jewish council called the Sanhedrin, and in return for their privileges the Sanhedrin cooperated with Romans in scouting out any sign of insurrection. It was in their best interests to prevent uprisings and the harsh reprisals they would surely bring.

The Jewish historian Josephus tells of a mentally ill peasant who would cry out "Woe to Jerusalem!" in the midst of popular festivals, agitating the crowds. The Sanhedrin tried punishing him, to no avail, so they turned him over to the Roman governor for a proper flogging. He was flayed to the bone and peace was restored. In the same vein, the Sanhedrin sent representatives to examine John the Baptist and Jesus. Did they represent a true threat to the peace? If so, should they be turned in to the Romans? Caiphas, the high priest, perfectly captured the collaborationist point of view: "It is better for you that one man die for the people than that the whole nation perish."

Sadducees were the most blatant collaborationists. They had first Hellenized under the Greeks, and then cooperated in turn with Maccabeans, Romans, and now Herod. Humanistic in theology, the Sadducees did not believe in an afterlife or divine intervention on this earth. What happens, happens, and since there is no future system of reward and punishment, a person might as well enjoy the limited time on earth. From the palatial homes and silver and gold kitchen utensils that archaeologists have uncovered, it appears that Sadducees enjoyed life very well indeed. Of all parties in Palestine, the mandarin Sadducees had the most to lose from any threat to the status quo.

Pharisees, the popular party of the middle class, often found themselves on the fence, vacillating between separatism and collaboration. They held to high standards of purity, particularly on such matters as Sabbath observance, ritual cleanliness, and the exact time of feast days. They treated nonobservant Jews "as Gentiles," shutting them out of local councils, boycotting their businesses, and ostracizing them from meals and social affairs. Yet the Pharisees had already suffered their share of persecution: in one instance eight hundred Pharisees were crucified on a single day. Although they believed passionately in the Messiah, Pharisees hesitated to follow too quickly after any impostor or miracle worker who might bring disaster on the nation.

The Pharisees picked their battles carefully, putting their lives on the line only when necessary. Once, Pontius Pilate spurned a prior agreement with the Jews that Roman troops would not enter Jerusalem carrying standards that bore an image ("icon") of the emperor. The Pharisees regarded this act as idolatry. In protest a crowd of Jews, mostly Pharisees, stood outside Pilate's palace for five days and nights in a kind of sit-down strike, weeping and begging him to change. Pilate ordered them to the hippodrome, where soldiers lay in ambush, and threatened to put to death any who did not cease their begging. As one, they fell on their faces, bared their necks, and announced they were prepared to die rather than have their laws broken. Pilate backed down.

As I consider each one of these groups, I conclude that most likely I would have ended up in the party of Pharisees. I would have admired their pragmatic approach to the ruling government, balanced by their willingness to stand up for principle. Orderly people, the Pharisees produced good citizens.* Radicals like the Essenes and

---

*Scholars have debated why the Gospels record so much conflict between Jesus and the Pharisees, when actually he had more in common with them than with the Sadducees, Essenes, or Zealots. One explanation is that the Gospels were written several decades after Jesus' death. By then Jerusalem had been destroyed and the other parties had virtually disappeared. Understandably, the gospel writers focused on the sole surviving threat to Christians, the Pharisees.

Zealots would have made me nervous; the Sadducees I would have scorned as opportunists. Thus as a sympathizer of the Pharisees, I would have stood on the edge of Jesus' audience, watching him deal with the burning issues of the day.

Would Jesus have won me over? Much as I wish, I cannot easily answer that question. At one time or another, Jesus managed to confound and alienate each of the major groups in Palestine. He held out a third way, neither separation nor collaboration, radically changing the emphasis from the kingdom of Herod or Caesar to the kingdom of God.

Looking back now, it may seem difficult to sort out the nuances that divided one party from another, or to understand why controversy flared over minor aspects of Jesus' teaching. For all their differences, though, Essenes, Zealots, Pharisees, and even Sadducees shared one goal: to preserve what was distinctively Jewish, no matter what. To that goal, Jesus represented a threat, and I'm sure I would have perceived that threat.

The Jews were, in effect, erecting a fence around their culture in hopes of saving their tiny nation of high ideals from the pagans around them. Could God liberate them from Rome as he had once liberated them from Egypt? One tradition promised that if all Israel repented for an entire day, or if Israel kept two Sabbaths perfectly, then redemption by the Messiah would soon follow. Something of a spiritual revival was under way, spurred by a splendid new temple. Constructed on a huge platform that dominated the entire city of Jerusalem, the temple had become the focal point of national pride and hope for the future.

It was against this background that I, like other Jews, would have judged Jesus' statements about legalism, about Sabbath-keeping, and about the temple. How could I reconcile my respect for family values with a comment like, "If anyone comes to me and does not hate his father and mother, his wife and children, his brothers and sisters . . . he cannot be my disciple"? What could Jesus possibly mean? Similarly, to official Sanhedrin ears, a reported comment like "I am able to destroy the temple of God and rebuild it in three days" was no idle boast but a form of blasphemy and even treason, striking against the very thing that held Jews together. Jesus' offer to forgive a person's sin seemed to them as bizarrely inappropriate as a private individual today offering to issue someone a passport or a building permit. Who did he think he was, preempting the entire temple system?

As it turned out, Jewish fears about cultural suicide proved entirely justified. Not Jesus, but other charismatic figures would lead revolts that finally, in A.D. 70, provoked Rome to destroy the temple and level Jerusalem. The city would later be rebuilt as a Roman colony, with a temple to the god Jupiter occupying the site of the demolished Jewish temple. Jews were forbidden to enter the city on pain of death. Rome set in motion an exile that would not end until our own generation, and it changed the face of Judaism forever.

4

Temptation: Showdown in the Desert

Love consents to all and commands only those who consent. Love is abdication. God is abdication.

Simone Weil

4
Temptation: Showdown in the Desert

The Gospels assert that Jesus, the Jew who grew up in rural Galilee, was none other than God's own Son, dispatched from heaven to lead the fight against evil. With that mission in view, certain questions about Jesus' priorities immediately come to mind. At the top of the list, natural disasters: If Jesus had the power to cure illness and raise the dead, why not tackle a few macro-problems like earthquakes and hurricanes, or perhaps the whole sinister swarm of mutating viruses that plague the earth?

Philosophers and theologians blame many of the rest of earth's ills on the consequences of human freedom, which raises a whole new set of questions. Do we in fact enjoy too much freedom? We have the freedom to harm and kill each other, to fight global wars, to despoil our planet. We are even free to defy God, to live without restraints as though the other world did not exist. At the least, Jesus could have devised some irrefutable proof to silence all skeptics, tilting the odds decisively in God's favor. As it is, God seems easy to ignore or deny.

Jesus' first "official" act as an adult, when he went into the wilderness to meet the accuser face-to-face, gave him the occasion to address these problems. Satan himself tempted the Son of God to change the rules and achieve his goals by a dazzling, shortcut method. More than

Jesus' character was at stake on the sandy plains of Palestine; human history hung in the balance.

When John Milton wrote a sequel to his epic *Paradise Lost*, he made the Temptation, not the crucifixion, the hinge event in Jesus' effort to regain the world. In a garden, a man and woman had fallen for Satan's promise of a way to rise above their assigned state. Millennia later, another representative—the Second Adam, in Paul's phrase—faced a similar test, though curiously inverted. *Can you be like God?* the serpent had asked in Eden; *Can you be truly human?* asked the tempter in the desert.

As I read the Temptation story it occurs to me that, in the absence of eyewitnesses, all details must have come from Jesus himself. For some reason, Jesus felt obliged to disclose to his disciples this moment of struggle and personal weakness. I presume the Temptation was a genuine conflict, not a role Jesus acted out with a prearranged outcome. The same tempter who had found a fatal spot of vulnerability in Adam and Eve aimed his thrust against Jesus with deadly accuracy.

Luke sets the stage with a tone of understated drama. "Jesus, full of the Holy Spirit, returned from the Jordan and was led by the Spirit in the desert, where for forty days he was tempted by the devil. He ate nothing during those days, and at the end of them he was hungry." Like single combat warriors, two giants of the cosmos converged on a scene of desolation. One, just beginning his mission in enemy territory, arrived in a badly weakened state. The other, confident and on home turf, seized the initiative.

I puzzle over certain details of the Temptation. Satan asked Jesus to turn a stone into bread, offered him all the kingdoms of the world, and urged him to jump from a high place in order to test God's promise of physical safety. Where is the evil in these requests? The three temptations seem like Jesus' prerogatives, the very qualities to be expected in a Messiah. Would not Jesus go on to multiply bread for five thousand, a far more impressive display? He would also conquer death and rise again to become King of Kings. The three temptations do not seem evil in themselves—and yet clearly something pivotal happened in the desert.

The British poet Gerard Manley Hopkins presents the Temptation as something of a get-acquainted session between Jesus and Satan. In the dark about the Incarnation, Satan did not know for certain whether Jesus was an ordinary man or a theophany or perhaps an angel with limited powers like himself. He challenged Jesus to perform miracles as a means of scouting his adversary's powers. Martin Luther goes further, speculating that throughout his life Jesus "conducted himself so humbly and associated with sinful men and women, and as a consequence was not held in great esteem," on account of which "the devil overlooked him and did not recognize him. For the devil is farsighted; he looks only for what is big and high and attaches himself to that; he does not look at that which is low down and beneath himself."

In the gospel accounts, the single combat warriors treat each other with a kind of wary respect, like two boxers circling one another in the ring. For Jesus, the greatest strain was probably a willingness to put up with the Temptation in the first place. Why not simply destroy the tempter, saving human history from his evil plague? Jesus demurred.

For his part, Satan offered to trade away his dominion over the world in exchange for the satisfaction of prevailing over the Son of God. Although Satan posed the tests, in the end it was he who flunked them. In two tests he merely asked Jesus to prove himself; by the third he was demanding worship, something God would never accede to.

The Temptation unmasked Satan, while God remained masked. *If you are God,* said Satan, *then dazzle me. Act like God should act.* Jesus replied, *Only God makes those decisions, therefore I do nothing at your command.*

In Wim Wender's elegant films about angels (*Wings of Desire*; *Faraway, So Close*), celestial beings discuss together in childlike wonder what it must be like to drink coffee and digest food, to experience warmth and pain, to sense a skeleton moving as you walk, to feel the touch of another human being, to say "Ah!" and "Oh!" because not everything is known in advance, to live by minutes and hours and thus to encounter *now* instead of just forever. At the age of thirty or so, when Jesus first squared off with Satan in the desert, he had realized all those "advantages" of being human. He lived comfortably inside his suit of skin.

As I look back on the three temptations, I see that Satan proposed an enticing improvement. He tempted Jesus toward the good parts of being human without the bad: to savor the taste of bread without being subject to the fixed rules of hunger and of agriculture, to confront risk with no real danger, to enjoy fame and power without the prospect of painful rejection—in short, to wear a crown but not a cross. (The temptation that Jesus resisted, many of us, his followers, still long for.)

Apocryphal gospels, judged spurious by the church, suggest what it might have looked like had Jesus succumbed to Satan's temptations. These fantastic accounts show the child Jesus making clay sparrows that he could bring to life with a puff of breath, and dropping dried fish into water to see them miraculously start swimming. He turned his playmates into goats to teach them a lesson, and made people go blind or deaf just for the thrill of healing them. The apocryphal gospels are the second-century counterparts to modern comic books about Superboy and Batgirl. Their value lies mainly in the contrast they form with the actual Gospels, which reveal a Messiah who did not use miraculous powers to benefit himself. Beginning with the Temptation, Jesus showed a reluctance to bend the rules on earth.

Malcolm Muggeridge, while filming a documentary in Israel, found himself musing on the Temptation:

> Curiously enough, just at the right moment to begin filming, when the shadows were long enough and the light not too weak, I happened to notice near by a whole expanse of stones, all identical, and looking uncommonly like loaves well baked and brown. How easy for Jesus to have turned these stone loaves into edible ones, as, later, he would turn water into wine at a wedding feast! And, after all, why not? The Roman authorities distributed free bread to promote Caesar's kingdom, and Jesus could do the same to promote his. . . .

Jesus had but to give a nod of agreement and he could have constructed Christendom, not on four shaky Gospels and a defeated man nailed on a Cross, but on a basis of sound socio-economic planning and principles.... Every utopia could have been brought to pass, every hope have been realized and every dream been made to come true. What a benefactor, then, Jesus would have been. Acclaimed, equally, in the London School of Economics and the Harvard Business School; a statue in Parliament Square, and an even bigger one on Capitol Hill and in the Red Square.... Instead, he turned the offer down on the ground that only God should be worshipped.

As Muggeridge sees it, the Temptation revolved around the question uppermost in the minds of Jesus' countrymen: What should the Messiah look like? A People's Messiah who could turn stones into bread to feed the multitudes? A Torah Messiah, standing tall at the lofty pinnacle of the temple? A King Messiah, ruling over not just Israel but all the kingdoms of earth? In short, Satan was offering Jesus the chance to be the thundering Messiah we think we want. Certainly, I recognize in Muggeridge's description the Messiah I think I want.

We want anything but a Suffering Messiah—and so did Jesus, at one level. Satan hit closest to home with his suggestion that Jesus throw himself from a high place to test God's care. That temptation would surface again. Once, in a flash of anger Jesus gave Peter a strong rebuke. "Out of my sight, Satan!" he said. "You do not have in mind the things of God, but the things of men." Peter had recoiled at Jesus' prediction of suffering and death—"Never, Lord! This shall never happen to you!"—and that instinctively protective reaction had hit a nerve. In Peter's words, Jesus heard again the allure of Satan tempting him toward an easier way.

Nailed to the cross, Jesus would hear the last temptation repeated as a taunt. A criminal scoffed, "Aren't you the Christ? Save yourself and us." Spectators took up the cry: "Let him come down from the cross, and we will believe in him.... Let God rescue him now if he wants him." But there was no rescue, no miracle, no easy, painless path. For Jesus to save others, quite simply, he could not save himself. That fact, he must have known as he faced Satan in the desert.

* * *

My own temptations tend to involve common vices such as lust and greed. As I reflect on Jesus' temptations, though, I realize they centered on his reason for coming to earth, his "style" of working. Satan was, in effect, dangling before Jesus a speeded-up way of accomplishing his mission. He could win over the crowds by creating food on demand and then take control of the kingdoms of the world, all the while protecting himself from danger. "Why move thy feet so slow to what is best?" Satan jeered in Milton's version.

I first found this insight in the writings of Dostoevsky, who made the Temptation scene the centerpiece of his great novel *The Brothers Karamazov*. The agnostic brother Ivan Karamazov writes a poem called "The Grand Inquisitor" set in sixteenth-century Seville at the height of the Inquisition. In the poem, a disguised Jesus visits the city at a time when heretics are daily being burned at the stake. The Grand Inquisitor, a cardinal, "an old man, almost ninety, tall and erect, with a withered face and sunken eyes," recognizes Jesus and has him thrown into prison. There, the two visit in a scene intentionally reminiscent of the Temptation in the desert.

The Inquisitor has an accusation to make: by turning down the three temptations, Jesus forfeited the three greatest powers at his disposal, "miracle, mystery, and authority." He should have followed Satan's advice and performed the miracles on demand in order to increase his fame among the people. He should have welcomed the offer of authority and power. Did Jesus not realize that people want more than anything else to worship what is established beyond dispute? "Instead of taking possession of men's freedom, you increased it, and burdened the spiritual kingdom of mankind with its sufferings forever. You desired man's free love, that he should follow you freely, enticed and taken captive by you."

By resisting Satan's temptations to override human freedom, the Inquisitor maintains, Jesus made himself far too easy to reject. He surrendered his greatest advantage: the power to compel belief. Fortunately, continues the sly Inquisitor, the church recognized the error and corrected it, and has been relying on miracle, mystery, and authority ever since. For this reason, the Inquisitor must execute Jesus one more time, lest he hinder the church's work.

The scene from *Karamazov* has added poignancy because at the time of its composition, communist revolutionaries were organizing themselves in Russia. As Dostoevsky noted, they too would borrow techniques from the church. They promised to turn stones into bread and to guarantee safety and security for all citizens in exchange for one simple thing: their freedom. Communism would become the new church in Russia, one likewise founded on miracle, mystery, and authority.

More than a century after Dostoevsky wrote this chilling dialogue about power and freedom, I had the opportunity to visit his homeland and observe in person the results of seven decades of Communist rule. I went in November of 1991, when the Soviet empire was crumbling, Mikhail Gorbachev was giving way to Boris Yeltsin, and the entire nation was trying to rediscover itself. The iron grasp of power had loosened, and people were now reveling in the freedom to say whatever they wished.

I remember vividly a meeting with the editors of *Pravda*, formerly the official mouthpiece of the Communist Party. *Pravda* as much as any institution had slavishly served the Communist "church." Now, though, *Pravda*'s circulation was falling dramatically (from eleven million to 700,000) in concert with communism's fall from grace. The editors of *Pravda* seemed earnest, sincere, searching—and shaken to the core. So shaken that they were now asking advice from emissaries of a religion their founder had scorned as "the opiate of the people."

The editors remarked wistfully that Christianity and communism have many of the same ideals: equality, sharing, justice, and racial harmony. Yet they had to admit the Marxist pursuit of that vision had produced the worst nightmares the world has ever seen. Why?

"We don't know how to motivate people to show compassion," said the editor-in-chief. "We tried raising money for the children of Chernobyl, but the average Russian citizen would rather spend his money on drink. How do you reform and motivate people? How do you get them to be good?"

Seventy-four years of communism had proved beyond all doubt that goodness could not be legislated from the Kremlin and enforced at the point of a gun. In a heavy irony, attempts to compel morality tend to produce defiant subjects and tyrannical rulers who lose their moral core. I came away from Russia with the strong sense that we Christians would do well to relearn the basic lesson of the Temptation. Goodness cannot be imposed externally, from the top down; it must grow internally, from the bottom up.

The Temptation in the desert reveals a profound difference between God's power and Satan's power. Satan has the power to coerce, to dazzle, to force obedience, to destroy. Humans have learned much from that power, and governments draw deeply from its reservoir. With a bullwhip or a billy club or an AK–47, human beings can force other human beings to do just about anything they want. Satan's power is external and coercive.

God's power, in contrast, is internal and noncoercive. "You would not enslave man by a miracle, and craved faith given freely, not based on miracle," said the Inquisitor to Jesus in Dostoevsky's novel. Such power may seem at times like weakness. In its commitment to transform gently from the inside out and in its relentless dependence on human choice, God's power may resemble a kind of abdication. As every parent and every lover knows, love can be rendered powerless if the beloved chooses to spurn it.

"God is not a Nazi," said Thomas Merton. Indeed God is not. The Master of the universe would become its victim, powerless before a squad of soldiers in a garden. God made himself weak for one purpose: to let human beings choose freely for themselves what to do with him.*

Søren Kierkegaard wrote about God's light touch: "Omnipotence which can lay its hand so heavily upon the world can also make its touch so light that the creature receives independence." Sometimes, I concede, I wish that God used a heavier touch. My faith suffers from too much freedom, too many temptations to disbelieve. At times I

_____

*In Dorothy Sayers' play *The Man Born to Be King*, King Herod tells the Magi, "You cannot rule men by love. When you find your king, tell him so. Only three things will govern a people—fear and greed and the promise of security." King Herod understood the management principles Satan operates by, the same ones Jesus declined in the wilderness.

want God to overwhelm me, to overcome my doubts with certainty, to give final proofs of his existence and his concern.

I want God to take a more active role in human affairs as well. If God had merely reached down and flicked Saddam Hussein off the throne, how many lives would have been saved in the Gulf War? If God had done the same with Hitler, how many Jews would have been spared? Why must God "sit on his hands"?

I want God to take a more active role in my personal history too. I want quick and spectacular answers to my prayers, healing for my diseases, protection and safety for my loved ones. I want a God without ambiguity, One to whom I can point for the sake of my doubting friends.

When I think these thoughts, I recognize in myself a thin, hollow echo of the challenge that Satan hurled at Jesus two thousand years ago. God resists those temptations now as Jesus resisted them on earth, settling instead for a slower, gentler way. In George MacDonald's words,

> Instead of crushing the power of evil by divine force; instead of compelling justice and destroying the wicked; instead of making peace on earth by the rule of a perfect prince; instead of gathering the children of Jerusalem under His wings whether they would or not, and saving them from the horrors that anguished His prophetic soul—He let evil work its will while it lived; He contented Himself with the slow unencouraging ways of help essential; making men good; casting out, not merely controlling Satan. . . .
>
> To love righteousness is to make it grow, not to avenge it. . . . He resisted every impulse to work more rapidly for a lower good.

"O Jerusalem, Jerusalem," Jesus cried, in the scene MacDonald alludes to, "how often I have longed to gather your children together, as a hen gathers her chicks under her wings, but you were not willing." The disciples had proposed that Jesus call down fire on unrepentant cities; in contrast, Jesus uttered a cry of helplessness, an astonishing "if only" from the lips of the Son of God. He would not force himself on those who were not willing.

The more I get to know Jesus, the more impressed I am by what Ivan Karamazov called "the miracle of restraint." The miracles Satan suggested, the signs and wonders the Pharisees demanded, the final proofs I yearn for—these would offer no serious obstacle to an omnipotent God. More amazing is his *refusal* to perform and to overwhelm. God's terrible insistence on human freedom is so absolute that he granted us the power to live as though he did not exist, to spit in his face, to crucify him. All this Jesus must have known as he faced down the tempter in the desert, focusing his mighty power on the energy of restraint.

I believe God insists on such restraint because no pyrotechnic displays of omnipotence will achieve the response he desires. Although power can force obedience, only love can summon a response of love, which is the one thing God wants from us and the reason he created us. "I, when I am lifted up from the earth, will draw all men to myself," Jesus said. In case we miss the point John adds, "He said this to show the kind of death he was going to die." God's nature is self-giving; he bases his appeal on sacrificial love.

I remember one afternoon in Chicago sitting in an outdoor restaurant listening to a broken man relate the story of his prodigal son. Jake, the son, could not keep a job. He wasted all his money on drugs and alcohol. He rarely called home, and brought little joy and much grief to both parents. Jake's father described to me his feeling of helplessness in words not unlike those Jesus used about Jerusalem. "If only I could bring him back, and shelter him and try to show how much I love him," he said. He paused to gain control of his voice, then added, "The strange thing is, even though he rejects me, Jake's love means more to me than that of my other three, responsible children. Odd, isn't it? That's how love is."

I sense in that final four-word sentence more insight into the mystery of God's restraint than I have found in any book of theodicy. Why does God content himself with the slow, unencouraging way of making righteousness grow rather than avenging it? *That's how love is.* Love has its own power, the only power ultimately capable of conquering the human heart.

* * *

Though rebuffed in all three temptations, Satan may well have departed from the confrontation wearing a smirk. Jesus' steadfast refusal to play by Satan's rules meant that Satan himself could continue playing by those rules. He still had the kingdoms of the world at his disposal, after all, and now he had learned a lesson about God's restraint. Restraint by God creates opportunity for those opposed to God.

Other skirmishes would come, of course. Jesus would forcibly cast out demons, but the Spirit he replaced them with was far less possessive and depended always on the will of the one possessed. Occasions for mischief abounded: Jesus admitted as much in his analogy of the kingdom of God growing up in the midst of evil, like wheat among the weeds.

From Satan's perspective, the Temptation offered a new lease on life. The kids from *Lord of the Flies* could roam the island awhile longer, apparently free of adult authority. Furthermore, God could be blamed for what went wrong. If God insisted on sitting on his hands while devilment like the Crusades and the Holocaust went on, why not blame the Parent, not the kids?

It occurs to me that by turning down the temptations in the desert, Jesus put God's own reputation at risk. God has promised to restore earth to perfection one day, but what about the meantime? The swamp of human history, the brutality even of church history, the apocalypse to come—are all these worth the divine restraint? To put it bluntly, is human freedom worth the cost?

No one who lives in the midst of the restoration process, not at its end, can answer that question fairly. All I can do is recall that Jesus, a single combat warrior facing Evil head-on with the power to destroy it, chose a different way. For him, preserving the free will of a notoriously flawed species seemed worth the cost. The choice could not have been easy, for it involved his own pain as well as his followers'.

As I survey the rest of Jesus' life, I see that the pattern of restraint established in the desert persisted throughout his life. I never sense Jesus twisting a person's arm. Rather, he stated the consequences of a choice, then threw the decision back to the other party. He answered a wealthy man's question with uncompromising words and then let him walk away. Mark pointedly adds this comment: "Jesus looked at him and loved him." Jesus had a realistic view of how the world would respond to him: "Because of the increase of wickedness, the love of most will grow cold."

We sometimes use the term "savior complex" to describe an unhealthy syndrome of obsession over curing others' problems. The true Savior, however, seemed remarkably free of such a complex. He had no compulsion to convert the entire world in his lifetime or to cure people who were not ready to be cured. In Milton's words, Jesus "held it more humane, more heavenly first / By winning words to conquer willing hearts, / And make persuasion do the work of fear."

In short, Jesus showed an incredible respect for human freedom. When Satan asked for the chance to test Peter and sift him as wheat, even then Jesus did not refuse the request. His response: "I have prayed for you, Simon, that your faith may not fail." When the crowds turned away and many disciples deserted him, Jesus said to the Twelve, almost plaintively, "You do not want to leave too, do you?" As his life moved toward doom in Jerusalem, he exposed Judas but did not try to prevent his evil deed—that, too, a consequence of restraint.

"Take up your *cross* and follow me," Jesus said, in the least manipulative invitation that has ever been given.

This quality of restraint in Jesus—one could almost call it a divine shyness—took me by surprise. I realized, as I absorbed the story of Jesus in the Gospels, that I had expected from him the same qualities I had met in the southern fundamentalist church of my childhood. There, I often felt the victim of emotional pressures. Doctrine was dished out in a "Believe and don't ask questions!" style. Wielding the power of miracle, mystery, and authority, the church left no place for doubt. I also learned manipulative techniques for "soul-winning," some of which involved misrepresenting myself to the person I was talking to. Yet now I am unable to find any of these qualities in the life of Jesus.

If I read church history correctly, many other followers of Jesus have yielded to the very temptations he resisted. Dostoevsky shrewdly replayed the Temptation scene in the torture cell of the Grand Inquisitor. How could a church founded by the One who withstood the Temptation carry out an Inquisition of forced belief that lasted half a millennium? Meanwhile, in a milder Protestant version in the city of Geneva, officials were making attendance at church compulsory and refusal to take the Eucharist a crime. Heretics there, too, were burned at the stake.

To its shame, Christian history reveals unrelieved attempts to improve on the way of Christ. Sometimes the church joins hands with a government that offers a shortcut path to power. "The worship of success is generally *the* form of idol worship which the devil cultivates most assiduously," wrote Helmut Thielicke about the German church's early infatuation with Adolf Hitler. "We could observe in the first years after 1933 the almost suggestive compulsion that emanates from great successes and how, under the influence of these successes, men, even Christians, stopped asking in whose name and at what price...."

Sometimes the church grows its own mini-Hitlers, men with names like Jim Jones and David Koresh, who understand all too well the power represented in miracle, mystery, and authority. And sometimes the church simply borrows the tools of manipulation perfected by politicians, salesmen, and advertising copywriters.

I am quick to diagnose these flaws. Yet when I turn from church history and examine myself, I find that I too am vulnerable to the Temptation. I lack the willpower to resist shortcut solutions to human needs. I lack the patience to allow God to work in a slow, "gentlemanly" way. I want to seize control myself, to compel others to help accomplish the causes I believe in. I am willing to trade away certain freedoms for the guarantee of safety and protection. I am willing to trade away even more for the chance to realize my ambitions.

When I feel those temptations rising within me, I return to the story of Jesus and Satan in the desert. Jesus' resistance against Satan's temptations preserved for me the very freedom I exercise when I face my own temptations. I pray for the same trust and patience that Jesus showed. And I rejoice that, as Hebrews said, "We do not have a high priest who is unable to sympathize with our weaknesses, but we have one who has been tempted in every way, just as we are—yet without sin. . . . Because he himself suffered when he was tempted, he is able to help those who are being tempted."

5
Profile: What Would I Have Noticed?

Everything in Christ astonishes me. His spirit overawes me, and his will confounds me. Between him and whoever else in the world, there is no possible term of comparison. He is truly a being by himself. . . . I search in vain in history to find the similar to Jesus Christ, or anything which can approach the gospel. Neither history, nor humanity, nor the ages, nor nature, offer me anything with which I am able to compare it or to explain it. Here everything is extraordinary.

Napoleon

5
Profile: What Would I Have Noticed?

The Apostles' Creed hustles through Jesus' life in one paragraph, beginning with his birth and skipping immediately to his death, descent into hell, and ascent into heaven. Wait a minute—isn't something missing? What happened in the interval between his being born of the Virgin Mary and his suffering under Pontius Pilate? Somehow everything Jesus said and did in thirty-three years on earth gets swept aside in the rush to interpret his life. How did he spend his time here?

Memories from Sunday school actually detract from my efforts to picture Jesus' everyday life, for he was rendered in lifeless flannel-board scenes. There he is teaching. That's him holding a lamb. Now he's talking with a Samaritan woman and, look, another conversation with a man named Nicodemus. The closest thing to action came when the disciples in their miniature sailboats bobbed across the blue flannelboard sea. I remember one scene of Jesus standing in the temple with a whip in his hand, but it matched nothing else I had learned about him. I certainly never saw him at a party. I may have learned facts about Jesus' life in Sunday school, but as a person he remained remote and two-dimensional.

Movies about Jesus helped bring him to life for me. Some of them, such as *Jesus of Nazareth* by Zeffirelli, take great pains to recreate settings faithful to the gospel accounts. Unlike the placid flannelgraph

scenes, the movies show Jesus in action, surrounded by unruly spectators who jostle each other for a better view and press their demands
on him.

As I watch these movies, and then return to the Gospels, I try to
place myself in my familiar role as a journalist, or at least the first-century equivalent. I stand on the margins, listening and taking notes, intent
to capture something of Jesus in my reports, while at the same time aware
he is having an effect on me personally. What do I see? What impresses
me? Disturbs me? How can I convey him to my readers?

I cannot begin where I normally begin in reporting on a person,
by describing what my subject looked like. No one knows. The first
semi-realistic portraits of Jesus did not come until the fifth century,
and these were pure speculation; until then the Greeks had portrayed
him as a young, beardless figure resembling the god Apollo.

In 1514 someone forged a document under the name of Publius
Lentulus, the Roman governor who succeeded Pontius Pilate, which
contained this description of Jesus:

> He is a tall man, well shaped and of an amiable and reverend
> aspect; his hair is of a color that can hardly be matched, falling into
> graceful curls ... parted on the crown of his head, running as a
> stream to the front after the fashion of the Nazarites; his forehead
> high, large and imposing; his cheeks without spot or wrinkle, beau-
> tiful with a lovely red; his nose and mouth formed with exquisite
> symmetry; his beard, and of a color suitable to his hair, reaching
> below his chin and parted in the middle like a fork; his eyes bright
> blue, clear and serene....

I recognize that Jesus from the oil paintings hanging on the
concrete-block walls of my childhood church. The forger gave himself away, however, with his next sentence: "No man has seen him
laugh." Was he reading the same Gospels that I read, documents that
say not a word about Jesus' physical appearance yet depict him per-
forming his first miracle at a wedding, giving playful nicknames to his
disciples, and somehow gaining a reputation as a "gluttonous man and

a wine-bibber"? When the pious criticized his disciples for their laxity in spiritual disciplines, Jesus replied, "How can the guests of the bridegroom fast while he is with them?" Of all the images he could have chosen for himself, Jesus settled on that of the groom whose radiance cheers up the entire wedding party.

I once showed to a class several dozen art slides portraying Jesus in a variety of forms—African, Korean, Chinese—and then asked the class to describe what they thought Jesus looked like. Virtually everyone suggested he was tall (unlikely for a first-century Jew), most said handsome, and no one said overweight. I showed a BBC film on the life of Christ that featured a pudgy actor in the title role, and some in the class found it offensive. We prefer a tall, handsome, and, above all, slender Jesus.

One tradition dating back to the second century suggested Jesus was a hunchback. In the Middle Ages, Christians widely believed that Jesus had suffered from leprosy. Most Christians today would find such notions repulsive and perhaps heretical. Was he not a perfect specimen of humanity? Yet in all the Bible I can find only one physical description of sorts, a prophecy written hundreds of years before Christ's birth. Here is Isaiah's portrayal, in the midst of a passage that the New Testament applies to the life of Jesus:

> Just as there were many who were appalled at him—his appearance was so disfigured beyond that of any man and his form marred beyond human likeness. . . . He had no beauty or majesty to attract us to him, nothing in his appearance that we should desire him. He was despised and rejected by men, a man of sorrows, and familiar with suffering. Like one from whom men hide their faces he was despised, and we esteemed him not.

Because of the Gospels' silence, we cannot answer with certainty the basic question of what Jesus looked like. That is a good thing, I believe. Our glamorized representations of Jesus say more about us than about him. He had no supernatural glow about him: John the Baptist admitted he never would have recognized Jesus apart from special revelation. According to Isaiah, we cannot point to his beauty or majesty or anything else in his appearance to explain his attraction. The key lies elsewhere.

* * *

I move beyond physical appearance to consider what Jesus was like as a person. How would he have scored on a personality profile test?

The personality that emerges from the Gospels differs radically from the image of Jesus I grew up with, an image I now recognize in some of the older Hollywood films about Jesus. In those films, Jesus recites his lines evenly and without emotion. He strides through life as the one calm character among a cast of flustered extras. Nothing rattles him. He dispenses wisdom in flat, measured tones. He is, in short, the Prozac Jesus.

In contrast, the Gospels present a man who has such charisma that people will sit three days straight, without food, just to hear his riveting words. He seems excitable, impulsively "moved with compassion" or "filled with pity." The Gospels reveal a range of Jesus' emotional responses: sudden sympathy for a person with leprosy, exuberance over his disciples' successes, a blast of anger at coldhearted legalists, grief over an unreceptive city, and then those awful cries of anguish in Gethsemane and on the cross. He had nearly inexhaustible patience with individuals but no patience at all with institutions and injustice.

I once attended a men's movement retreat designed to help men "get in touch with their emotions" and break out of restrictive stereotypes of masculinity. As I sat in a small group, listening to other men tell of their struggles to express themselves and to experience true intimacy, I realized that Jesus lived out an ideal for masculine fulfillment that nineteen centuries later still eludes most men. Three times, at least, he cried in front of his disciples. He did not hide his fears or hesitate to ask for help: "My soul is overwhelmed with sorrow to the point of death," he told them in Gethsemane; "Stay here and keep watch with me." How many strong leaders today would make themselves so vulnerable?

Unlike most men I know, Jesus also loved to praise other people. When he worked a miracle, he often deflected credit back on the recipient: "Your faith has healed you." He called Nathanael "a true Israelite, in whom there is nothing false." Of John the Baptist, he said there was none greater born of women. Volatile Peter he renamed "the Rock." When a cringing woman offered him an extravagant act of devotion, Jesus defended her against critics and said the story of her generosity would be told forever.

The Gospels show that Jesus quickly established intimacy with the people he met. Whether talking with a woman at a well, a religious leader in a garden, or a fisherman by a lake, he cut instantly to the heart of the matter, and after a few brief lines of conversation these people revealed to Jesus their innermost secrets. People of his day tended to keep rabbis and "holy men" at a respectful distance, but Jesus drew out something else, a hunger so deep that people crowded around him just to touch his clothes.

Novelist Mary Gordon mentions Jesus' sensitivity to women and children as one of the main qualities that attracted her: "Surely, He is the only affectionate hero in literature. Who can imagine an affectionate Odysseus, Aeneas?" To Jesus' aside to the daughters of Jerusalem, "Alas for women with child in those days," Gordon responds, "I knew I wanted children; I felt those words were for me. Now I think: how many men would take into consideration the hardships of pregnancy and nursing?"

Jesus did not mechanically follow a list of "Things I Gotta Do Today," and I doubt he would have appreciated our modern emphasis on punctuality and precise scheduling. He attended wedding feasts that lasted for days. He let himself get distracted by any "nobody" he came across, whether a hemorrhaging woman who shyly touched his robe or a blind beggar who made a nuisance of himself. Two of his most impressive miracles (the raising of Lazarus and of Jairus's daughter) took place because he arrived too late to heal the sick person.

Jesus was "the man for others," in Bonhoeffer's fine phrase. He kept himself free—free for the other person. He would accept almost anybody's invitation to dinner, and as a result no public figure had a more diverse list of friends, ranging from rich people, Roman centurions, and Pharisees to tax collectors, prostitutes, and leprosy victims. People *liked* being with Jesus; where he was, joy was.

And yet, for all these qualities that point toward what psychologists like to call self-actualization, Jesus broke the mold. As C. S.

Lewis puts it, "He was not at all like the psychologist's picture of the integrated, balanced, adjusted, happily married, employed, popular citizen. You can't really be very well 'adjusted' to your world if it says you 'have a devil' and ends by nailing you up naked to a stake of wood."

Like most of Jesus' contemporaries, no doubt I would have balked at the odd combination of extravagant claims coming from an ordinary-looking Jewish man. He claimed to be the Son of God, and yet he ate and drank like other men, and even got tired and lonely. What kind of creature was he?

In some ways Jesus seemed to feel "at home" here, and in other ways he felt unequivocally "not at home." I think of the single scene preserved from his adolescence, when he disappeared in Jerusalem and got scolded by his mother. The cryptic record of her Jewish-mother response, "Son, why have you treated us like this?" probably does not do justice to the scene—his parents had, after all, been searching for three days. Jesus replied, "Why were you searching for me? Didn't you know I had to be in my Father's house?" Already a cleft, a conflict of loyalties, was dividing Jesus and his family.

Living on a planet of free will and rebellion, Jesus often must have felt "not at home." At such times he went aside and prayed, as if to breathe pure air from a life-support system that would give him the strength to continue living on a polluted planet. Yet he did not always get formulaic answers to his prayers. Luke reports that he prayed all night before choosing the twelve disciples—even so, the group included a traitor. In Gethsemane he prayed at first that the cup of suffering be taken from him, but of course it was not. That scene in the garden shows a man desperately "not at home," yet resisting all temptations toward supernatural rescue.

For me, one scene in the Gospels brings together the "at home" and "not at home" nature of Jesus. A storm blew up on the Sea of Galilee, nearly capsizing the boat in which Jesus lay sleeping. He stood up and yelled into the wind and spray, "Quiet! Be still!" The disciples shrank back in terror. What kind of person could shout to the weather as if correcting an unruly child?

The display of power in the midst of a storm helped convince the disciples that Jesus was unlike any other man. Yet it also hints at the depths of Incarnation. "God is vulnerable," said the philosopher Jacques Maritain. Jesus had, after all, fallen asleep from sheer fatigue. Moreover, the Son of God was, but for this one instance of miracle, one of its victims: the creator of rain clouds was rained on, the maker of stars got hot and sweaty under the Palestine sun. Jesus subjected himself to natural laws even when, at some level, they went against his desires ("If it is possible, may this cup be taken from me"). He would live, and die, by the rules of earth.

* * *

He comes as yet unknown into a hamlet of Lower Galilee. He is watched by the cold, hard eyes of peasants living long enough at subsistence level to know exactly where the line is drawn between poverty and destitution. He looks like a beggar, yet his eyes lack the proper cringe, his voice the proper whine, his walk the proper shuffle. He speaks about the rule of God, and they listen as much from curiosity as anything else. They know all about rule and power, about kingdom and empire, but they know it in terms of tax and debt, malnutrition and sickness, agrarian oppression and demonic possession. What, they really want to know, can this kingdom of God do for a lame child, a blind parent, a demented soul screaming its tortured isolation among the graves that mark the edges of the village? (John Dominic Crossan)

Jesus' neighbors soon found out what he could do for them. He made the lame child walk and the blind parent see, and exorcised demons from the demented soul among the graves. When Jesus inaugurated his ministry of healing and teaching, his neighbors scratched their heads and asked, flabbergasted, "Isn't he Mary's boy, Joseph the carpenter's son? Where did he get such wisdom and such miraculous power?"

Initially, for perhaps a year, Jesus met with great success. So many people flocked to him that he sometimes had to flee to a boat offshore. Without doubt it was the physical healings that first put him on the map. The Jews, who believed the Devil caused illness and thus holy men could be channels for God's intervention, had a long history of miracle workers. (One named Honi lived just before Jesus' time and is mentioned by the historian Josephus.) Jesus apparently knew of some rivals, for he subdued his disciples' impulse to condemn them.

About a third of the Gospels' stories about Jesus involve physical healings, and by journalistic instinct I probably would have investigated these stories, searching out medical records and interviewing the families of those who claimed a miracle. The healings were diverse and fit no real pattern. At least one person Jesus healed long-distance; some were instant and some gradual; many required the healed person to follow specific instructions.

I would have noticed in Jesus a curious ambivalence about miracles. On the one hand, Jesus healed in spontaneous response to human need: he saw a suffering person before him, felt compassion, and healed the person. Not once did he turn down a direct request for help. On the other hand, Jesus certainly did not advertise his powers. He condemned the "wicked and adulterous generation" who clamored for signs and, just as he had in the desert, resisted all temptation toward spectacle. Mark records seven separate occasions when Jesus instructed a person he had healed, "Tell no one!" In regions where people had no faith, he did no miracles.

Probably I would have speculated about what a man with such powers might have accomplished in Rome, Athens, or Alexandria. Jesus' brothers proposed that at the least he should concentrate his work in Jerusalem, Israel's capital. Jesus himself, though, preferred to keep out of the spotlight. Distrusting crowds and public opinion, he spent most of his time in towns of small size and little importance.

Despite his ambivalence, Jesus did not hesitate to use the miracles as proof of who he was: "Believe me when I say that I am in the Father and the Father is in me; or at least believe on the evidence of the miracles themselves," he told his disciples. And when his cousin John the Baptist, languishing in a jail cell, entertained doubts about whether Jesus was indeed the Messiah, Jesus gave John's disciples this message (as paraphrased by Frederick Buechner):

> You go tell John what you've seen around here. Tell him there are people who have sold their seeing-eye dogs and taken up bird-watching. Tell him there are people who've traded in aluminum walkers for hiking boots. Tell him the down-and-out have turned into the up-and-coming and a lot of dead-beats are living it up for the first time in their lives.

* * *

If I had sought a one-word label to describe Jesus to his contemporaries, I would have chosen the word *rabbi*, or teacher. In the United States now I know of no parallels to Jesus' life. Surely his style had little in common with that of modern mass evangelists, with their tents and stadia, their advance teams and billboards and direct-mail campaigns, their electronically enhanced presentations. His little band of followers, possessing no permanent base of operations, wandered from town to town without much discernible strategy.

"Foxes have holes and birds of the air have nests, but the Son of Man has no place to lay his head," Jesus said. Were they living in modern times, with the crackdown on homelessness, Jesus and his disciples would likely be harassed by police and forced to move on. Ancient times, though, knew many such teachers (there was actually a school of philosophers called the Peripatetics based on this common style of wisdom-sharing on the run).

In India I had the chance to observe in person something like the life Jesus led. There, Christian evangelists follow in the path of itinerant Hindu and Buddhist "holy men." Some hang around train stations, introducing themselves to waiting travelers and asking if they want to know more about God. Some walk from town to town, accompanied by their disciples. Others invite disciples to meet with them in *ashrams*, where together they worship and study the Scriptures.

The group Jesus led functioned with no headquarters or other property and apparently no officers except a treasurer (Judas). Financially, it seems, they barely scraped by. In order to scrounge up money for taxes, Jesus sent Peter fishing. He borrowed a coin to make a point about Caesar and had to borrow a donkey the one time he opted against traveling on foot. As his disciples walked through fields they pulled off the heads of standing grain to eat the raw kernels, taking advantage of Mosaic laws that made allowances for the poor. When Jesus met with influential people like Nicodemus or the rich young ruler it never seemed to occur to him that a person with money and influence could be of potential use.

How did Jesus support himself? In the Middle East of that day, teachers lived off the gifts of appreciative listeners. Luke points out that certain women who had been healed by Jesus—including the wife of Herod's finance minister!—helped provide for him. Touchingly, some of these women made the long and dangerous journey from Galilee to Jerusalem at the time of the Passover Feast, and stayed by Jesus at the cross after his closest disciples had deserted him.

By any account, Jesus was a master teacher. Followers were drawn by the magnetic power of his words which, in poet John Berryman's description, were "short, precise, terrible, and full of refreshment." Jesus gave his most enduring lessons on the spot, in spontaneous response to questions. A woman had seven successive husbands: Whose wife will she be in the life to come? Is it lawful to pay taxes to pagan authorities? What must I do to inherit eternal life? Who is the greatest in the kingdom of heaven? How can a man be born when he is old?

Jaroslav Pelikan tells of an old rabbi asked by his pupil, "Why is it that you rabbis so often put your teaching in the form of a question?" The rabbi shot back, "So what's wrong with a question?" Very often Jesus too deflected the question back in Socratic style, pressing the seeker toward a crisis point. His answers cut to the heart of the question and to the hearts of his listeners. I doubt I would have left any encounter with Jesus feeling smug or self-satisfied.

I would have marveled at Jesus' parables, a form that became his trademark. Writers ever since have admired his skill in communicating profound truth through such everyday stories. A scolding woman wears down the patience of a judge. A king plunges into an ill-planned war. A group of children quarrel in the street. A man is mugged and left for dead by robbers. A single woman who loses a penny acts as if she has lost everything. There are no fanciful creatures and sinuous plots in Jesus' parables; he simply describes the life around him.

The parables served Jesus' purposes perfectly. Everyone likes a good story, and Jesus' knack for storytelling held the interest of a mostly illiterate society of farmers and fishermen. Since stories are easier to remember than concepts or outlines, the parables also helped preserve his message: years later, as people reflected on what Jesus had taught, his parables came to mind in vivid detail. It is one thing to talk in abstract terms about the infinite, boundless love of God. It is quite another to tell of a man who lays down his life for friends, or of a heartsick father who scans the horizon every night for some sign of a wayward son.

Jesus came to earth "full of grace and truth," says the gospel of John, and that phrase makes a good summary of his message. First, grace: in contrast to those who tried to complicate the faith and petrify it with legalism, Jesus preached a simple message of God's love. For no reason—certainly not because we deserve it—God has decided to extend to us love that comes free of charge, no strings attached, "on the house."

In a rabbinic story of the time, the owner of a farm went into town to hire temporary workers for the harvest. The day wore on, and as late as the eleventh hour he recruited one last batch of workers, who had a mere hour remaining to prove their worth. In the familiar version of the story, the latecomers made up for lost time by working so hard that the foreman decided to reward them with a whole day's pay. Jesus' version, though, says nothing about the diligence of the workers. He accents instead the generosity of the employer—God—who lavishes his grace on veterans and newcomers alike. No one gets cheated and everyone gets rewarded, far beyond what they deserve.

Despite this emphasis on grace, no one could accuse Jesus of watering down the holiness of God. I would likely have stumbled over the truth that Jesus proclaimed, a truth more uncompromising by far than that taught by the strictest rabbis of his day. Contemporary teachers strove to "not impose a restriction upon the community unless the majority of the community will be able to stand it." Jesus had no such reticence. He broadened murder to include anger, adultery to include lust, theft to include coveting. "Be perfect, therefore, as your heavenly Father is perfect," he said, setting down an ethical standard that no one could reach.

As Elton Trueblood has observed, all the major symbols that Jesus used had a severe, even offensive quality: the yoke of burden, the cup of suffering, the towel of servanthood, and finally the cross of execution. "Count the cost," Jesus said, giving fair warning to any who dared follow him.

A modern rabbi named Jacob Neusner, the world's preeminent scholar on Judaism of the early Christian era, devoted one of his five hundred books (*A Rabbi Talks with Jesus*) to the question of how he would have responded to Jesus. Neusner has great respect for Jesus and for Christianity, and he admits that such teaching as the Sermon on the Mount leaves him "impressed—and moved." It would have quickened enough interest, he says, that he likely would have joined the crowd who followed Jesus from place to place, feasting on his wisdom.

Ultimately, though, Neusner concludes he would have parted company with the rabbi from Nazareth. "Jesus takes an important step—in the wrong direction," he says, by moving the emphasis from "us" as a Jewish community to an "I." Neusner could not go along with the shift from the Torah to Jesus himself as the central authority. "At issue is the figure of Jesus, not the teachings at all. . . . In the end the master, Jesus, makes a demand that only God makes." Respectfully, Neusner turns away, unable to make that leap of faith.

Neusner is right that Jesus' content hardly fit the pattern of other rabbis, not to mention wandering masters such as Confucius or Socrates. He was not so much seeking truth as pointing to it, by pointing to himself. In Matthew's words, "he taught as one who had authority, and not as their teachers of the law." The scribes endeavored to offer no personal opinions, rather basing their remarks on the Scriptures and approved commentaries. Jesus had many personal opinions, and used Scripture as the commentary. "You have heard that it was said . . . but I tell you . . ." went his commanding refrain. *He* was the source, and as he spoke he made no distinction between his own words and God's. His listeners understood the implication clearly, even in rejecting it. "This fellow is blaspheming!" they said.

Fearless, Jesus never backed away from a conflict. He took on hecklers and scoffers of every stripe. Once, he stood down a mob intent on stoning an adulterous woman. Another time, when guards went to seize him, they returned to the temple empty-handed: "No one ever spoke the way this man does," they said, awed by his presence. Jesus even gave direct orders to demons: "Be quiet!" "You deaf and dumb spirit, I command you, come out of him and never enter him again!" (Interestingly, the demons never failed to recognize him as the "holy one of God" or "son of the Most High"; it was human beings who questioned his identity.)

Jesus' statements about himself (I and the Father are one; I have the power to forgive sins; I will rebuild the temple in three days) were unprecedented and got him into constant trouble. Indeed, his teaching was so entwined with his person that many of his words could not have outlived him; the grand claims died with him on the cross. Disciples who had followed him as a master returned to their former lives, muttering sadly, "We had hoped that he was the one who was going to redeem Israel." It took the Resurrection to turn the proclaimer of truth into the one proclaimed.

I have placed myself on the edges of the crowd in Jesus' day, as a sincere seeker captivated by the rabbi but reluctant to commit to him. If I turn my attention from Jesus himself to the constellation of people surrounding me, I would see several groupings of onlookers forming concentric rings around him.

Farthest away, in the outer circle, are the groundlings, curiosity-seekers and others who, like me, are trying to figure out Jesus. The very presence of this multitude serves to protect Jesus: grumbling that "the whole world has gone after him," his enemies hesitate to seize him. In the early days especially, Jewish patriots hang out as well, eager for Jesus to announce a revolt against Rome. I note that Jesus never caters to this outer group. Yet he does preach to them, and that in itself distinguishes him from the Essenes and other sects, who reserve their meetings for initiates only.

Closer in, I spot a group of maybe a hundred sincere followers. Many of these traveling companions, I know, have joined up after John the Baptist's arrest—John's disciples complained that "everyone" was going over to Jesus. Spurning popularity, Jesus directs most of his comments not to the masses but to these serious seekers. He constantly pushes them toward a deeper level of commitment, with strong words that would bring anyone up short. You cannot serve two masters, he says. Forsake the love of money and the pleasures the world has to offer. Deny yourself. Serve others. Take up your cross.

That last phrase is no idle metaphor: along the roads of Palestine, Romans regularly nail up the worst criminals as an object lesson to the Jews. What kind of image could these words of "invitation" summon up in his followers' minds? Is he to lead a procession of martyrs? Apparently so. Jesus repeats one saying more than any other: "Whoever finds his life will lose it, and whoever loses his life for my sake will find it."

I have heard the closest ring of followers, the Twelve, boast that they welcome such a sacrifice. "You don't know what you are asking," Jesus replied. "Can you drink the cup I am going to drink?" "We can," they insist in their naïveté.

I sometimes ask myself if I would have wanted to join the Twelve. No matter. Unlike other rabbis, Jesus handpicked his inner circle of disciples, rather than letting them choose him. Such was Jesus' magnetism that it took only a few phrases to persuade them to leave their jobs and families to join him. Two sets of brothers—James and John, and Peter and Andrew—worked as partners on fishing boats, and when he called them they abandoned the business (ironically, after Jesus gave them their most successful fishing day ever). All but Judas Iscariot come from Jesus' home province of Galilee; Judas hails from Judea, which shows how Jesus' reputation has spread across the country.

I would have puzzled over the strange mixture represented by the Twelve. Simon the Zealot belongs to the party violently opposing Rome, while Matthew the tax collector has recently been employed by Rome's puppet ruler. No scholars like Nicodemus or wealthy patrons like Joseph of Arimethea have made it into the Twelve. One must look hard to detect any strong leadership abilities.

In my observation, in fact, the disciples' most obvious trait seems to be their denseness. "Are you so dull?" Jesus asks, and again, "How long shall I put up with you?" While he is trying to teach them servant leadership, they are squabbling about who deserves the most favored position. Their gnomic faith exasperates Jesus. After every miracle, they fret anxiously about the next. Can he feed five thousand—what about four thousand? Much of the time a fog of incomprehension separates the Twelve from Jesus.

Why does Jesus invest so much in these apparent losers? To answer that, I turn to Mark's written account, which mentions Jesus' motives in choosing the Twelve: "that they might be with him and that he might send them out to preach."

That they might be with him. Jesus never tried to hide his loneliness and his dependence on other people. He chose his disciples not as servants but as friends. He shared moments of joy and grief with them, and asked for them in times of need. They became his family, his substitute mother and brothers and sisters. They gave up everything for him, as he had given up everything for them. He loved them, plain and simple.

That he might send them out. From his very first invitation to the Twelve, Jesus had in mind what would transpire one day on Calvary. He knew his time on earth was short, and the ultimate success of his mission depended not just on what he accomplished in a few years but on what the Twelve—then eleven, soon to be thousands and then millions—would do after he had left.

Oddly, as I look back on Jesus' time from the present perspective, it is the very ordinariness of the disciples that gives me hope. Jesus does not seem to choose his followers on the basis of native talent or perfectibility or potential for greatness. When he lived on earth he surrounded himself with ordinary people who misunderstood him, failed to exercise much spiritual power, and sometimes behaved like churlish school-children. Three followers in particular (the brothers James and John, and Peter) Jesus singled out for his strongest reprimands—yet two of these would become the most prominent leaders of the early Christians.

I cannot avoid the impression that Jesus prefers working with unpromising recruits. Once, after he had sent out seventy-two disciples on a training mission, Jesus rejoiced at the successes they reported back. No passage in the Gospels shows him more exuberant. "At that time Jesus, full of joy through the Holy Spirit, said, 'I praise you, Father, Lord of heaven and earth, because you have hidden these things from the wise and learned, and revealed them to little children. Yes, Father, for this was your good pleasure.'" From such a ragtag band Jesus founded a church that has not stopped growing in nineteen centuries.

Part Two

Why He Came

6
Beatitudes: Lucky Are the Unlucky

A saint is one who exaggerates what the world neglects.

G. K. Chesterton

6
Beatitudes: Lucky Are the Unlucky

The Sermon on the Mount haunted my adolescence. I would read a book like Charles Sheldon's *In His Steps*, solemnly vow to act "as Jesus would act," and turn to Matthew 5–7 for guidance. What to make of such advice! Should I mutilate myself after a wet dream? Offer my body to be pummeled by the motorcycle-riding "hoods" in school? Tear out my tongue after speaking a harsh word to my brother?

Once, I became so convicted about my addiction to material things that I gave away to a friend my prized collection of 1,100 baseball cards, including an original 1947 Jackie Robinson and a Mickey Mantle rookie card. Anticipating a divine reward for this renunciation, instead I had to endure the monumental injustice of watching my friend auction off the entire collection at a huge profit. "Blessed are those who are persecuted because of righteousness," I consoled myself.

Now that I am an adult, the crisis of the Sermon on the Mount still has not gone away. Though I have tried at times to dismiss it as rhetorical excess, the more I study Jesus, the more I realize that the statements contained here lie at the heart of his message. If I fail to understand this teaching, I fail to understand him.

Jesus delivered the famous sermon at a time when his popularity was soaring. Crowds pursued him wherever he went, obsessed with one question: *Has the Messiah come at last?* On this unusual occasion

Jesus skipped the parables and granted his audience a full-blown "philosophy of life," somewhat like a candidate unveiling a new political platform. What a platform.

When time came to teach the Beatitudes to my class at LaSalle Street Church in Chicago, I followed my regular routine of previewing the movies about Jesus. Since I drew from fifteen different movies, the task of locating and viewing all the right portions consumed several hours of my time each week, much of it spent waiting for the VCR to fast-forward or reverse to the appropriate scenes. To relieve boredom while the VCR whirred and clicked its way to the right places, I had CNN playing on the TV monitor in the foreground. As the machine sped, say, to the eight-minute-twenty-second mark of Cecil B. DeMille's *King of Kings*, I caught up on news from around the world. Then I hit the "play" button and was transported back into first-century Palestine.

A lot was happening in the world in 1991 the week I taught the Beatitudes. In a ground campaign that lasted a scant one hundred hours, allied forces had achieved a stunning victory over Iraq in the Gulf War. Like most Americans, I could hardly believe the long-feared war had ended so quickly, with so few American casualties. As my VCR searched through the celluloid frames of Jesus in the background, various commentators on-screen were illustrating with charts and maps exactly what had transpired in Kuwait. Then came General Norman Schwarzkopf.

CNN announced an interruption in scheduled programming: they would shift to live coverage of the morning-after press conference by the commander of allied forces. For a time I tried to continue preparing for my class. I watched five minutes of Pasolini's version of Jesus delivering the Beatitudes, then several minutes of General Schwarzkopf's version of allied troops bearing down on Kuwait City. Soon I abandoned the VCR altogether—Stormin' Norman proved entirely too engaging. He told of the "end run" around Iraq's elite Republican Guard, of a decoy invasion by sea, of the allied capability of marching all the way to Baghdad unopposed. He credited the Kuwaitis, the British, the Saudis, and every other participant in the multinational force. A general confident in his mission and immensely proud of the soldiers who had carried it out, Schwarzkopf gave a bravura performance. I remember thinking, *That's exactly the person you want to lead a war.*

The briefing ended, CNN switched to commercials, and I returned to the VCR tapes. Max von Sydow, a blond, pasty Jesus, was giving an improbable rendition of the Sermon on the Mount in *The Greatest Story Ever Told.* "Blessed ... are ... the ... poor ... in spirit," he intoned in a slow, thick Scandinavian accent, "for ... theirs ... is ... the ... kingdom ... of ... heaven." I had to adjust to the languid pace of the movie compared to General Schwarzkopf's briefing, and it took a few seconds for the irony to sink in: I had just been watching the Beatitudes in reverse!

Blessed are the strong, was the general's message. Blessed are the triumphant. Blessed are the armies wealthy enough to possess smart bombs and Patriot missiles. Blessed are the liberators, the conquering soldiers.

The bizarre juxtaposition of two speeches gave me a feeling for the shock waves the Sermon on the Mount must have caused among its original audience, Jews in first-century Palestine. Instead of General Schwarzkopf, they had Jesus, and to a downtrodden people yearning for emancipation from Roman rule, Jesus gave startling and unwelcome advice. If an enemy soldier slaps you, turn the other cheek. Rejoice in persecution. Be grateful for your poverty.

The Iraqis, chastened on the battlefield, got a nasty measure of revenge by setting fire to Kuwait's oil fields; Jesus enjoined not revenge but love for one's enemies. How long would a kingdom founded on such principles survive against Rome?

"Happy are the bombed-out and the homeless," Jesus might as well have said. "Blessed are the losers and those grieving for fallen comrades. Blessed are the Kurds still suffering under Iraqi rule." Any Greek scholar will tell you the word "blessed" is far too sedate and beatific to carry the percussive force Jesus intended. The Greek word conveys something like a short cry of joy, "Oh, you lucky person!"

"How lucky are the unlucky!" Jesus said in effect.

* * *

A few years after the Gulf War episode, I received an invitation to the White House. President Bill Clinton, alarmed about his low standing among evangelical Christians, summoned twelve of us to a private breakfast in order to hear our concerns. Each of us would have five minutes to say whatever we wanted the president and vice-president to hear. The question, "What would Jesus say in such a setting?" crossed my mind, and I realized with a start that the only time Jesus met with powerful political leaders, his hands were tied and his back was clotted with blood. Church and state have had an uneasy relationship ever since.

I turned to the Beatitudes and found myself startled anew. What if I translated their message into contemporary terms?

> Mr. President, first I want to advise you to stop worrying so much about the economy and jobs. A lower Gross National Product is actually good for the country. Don't you understand that the poor are the fortunate ones? The more poor we have in the U.S., the more blessed we are. Theirs is the kingdom of heaven.
>
> And don't devote so much time to health care. You see, Mr. President, those who mourn are blessed too, for they'll be comforted.
>
> I know you've heard from the Religious Right about the increasing secularization of our country. Prayer is no longer allowed in schools, and protesters against abortion are subject to arrest. Relax, sir. Government oppression gives Christians an opportunity to be persecuted, and therefore blessed. Thank you for the expanded opportunities.

I did not deliver such a speech to President Clinton, choosing instead to represent the immediate concerns of American Christians, but I did come away from the experience puzzled afresh. What meaning can the Beatitudes have for a society that honors the self-assertive, confident, and rich? Blessed are the happy and the strong, we believe. Blessed are those who hunger and thirst for a good time, who look out for Number One.

Some psychologists and psychiatrists, following Freud's lead, point to the Beatitudes as proof of Jesus' imbalance. Said one distinguished British psychologist, in a speech prepared for the Royal Society of Medicine,

> The spirit of self-sacrifice which permeates Christianity, and is so highly prized in the Christian religious life, is masochism moderately indulged. A much stronger expression of it is to be found in Christ's teaching in the Sermon on the Mount. This blesses the poor, the meek, the persecuted; exhorts us not to resist evil but to offer the second cheek to the smiter; and to do good to them that hate you and forgive men their trespasses. All this breathes masochism.

Which is it, masochism or profound wisdom? Anyone who responds with a quick and easy answer probably has not taken the Beatitudes seriously enough.

To put the issue bluntly, are the Beatitudes true? If so, why doesn't the church encourage poverty and mourning and meekness and persecution instead of striving against them? What is the real meaning of the Beatitudes, this cryptic ethical core of Jesus' teaching?

If I had been sitting in the audience when Jesus first delivered the Beatitudes, I believe I would have left the event feeling confused or outraged, not comforted. Nineteen centuries later, I still struggle to make sense of them. Yet now, especially as I think back on my teenage days of frenzied legalism, I can see that my understanding has developed in stages.

I am not, and may never be, ready to declare, "This is what the Beatitudes mean." But gradually, almost osmotically, I have come to recognize them as important truths. To me, they apply on at least three levels.

Dangled Promises. In my first stage of understanding, I regarded the Beatitudes as a sop Jesus threw to the unfortunates: "Well, since you aren't rich, and your health is failing, and your face is wet with tears, I'll toss out a few nice phrases to make you feel better." Later, as cynicism faded and my faith strengthened, I came to see them as genuine promises central to Jesus' message.

Unlike medieval kings who threw coins to the masses (or modern politicians who make promises to the poor just before elections), Jesus had the ability to offer his audience lasting, even eternal rewards. Alone of all people on earth, Jesus had actually lived "on the other side," and he who came down from heaven knew well that the spoils of the kingdom of heaven can easily counterbalance whatever misery we might encounter in this life. Those who mourn *will be* comforted; the meek *will inherit the earth*; the hungry *will be filled*; the pure *will see God*. Jesus could make such promises with authority, for he had come to establish God's kingdom that would rule forever.

One summer I met with a group of Wycliffe Bible Translators at their austere headquarters in the Arizona desert. Many lived in mobile homes, and we convened in a concrete-block building with a metal roof. I was impressed with the dedication of these professional linguists who were preparing for a life of poverty and hardship in remote outposts. They loved to sing one song especially: "So send I you, to labor unrewarded, to serve unpaid, unloved, unsought, unknown. . . ." Listening to them, the thought occurred to me that the song has it slightly wrong: these missionaries were not planning to labor unrewarded. Rather, they endured certain hardships with the prospect of other rewards in mind. They served God, trusting in turn that God would make it worth their while—if not here, then in eternity.

In the mornings, before the sun rose too high above the hilltops, I went jogging along dirt roads that coiled among the stalky stands of saguaro cacti. Wary of rattlesnakes and scorpions, I mostly kept my head down looking at the road, but one morning on a new route I glanced up to see a shimmering resort looming before me, almost like a mirage. I jogged closer and discovered two Olympic swimming pools, aerobic workout rooms, a cinder jogging trail, lush gardens, a baseball diamond, soccer fields, and horse stables. The facilities, I learned, belonged to a famous eating disorder clinic that caters to movie stars and athletes. The clinic features the latest twelve-step program techniques, has a staff well stocked with Ph.D.'s and M.D.'s, and charges its clients about $300 per day.

I jogged slowly back to the jumble of houses and buildings at the Wycliffe base, keenly aware of their contrast to the gleaming architecture of the eating disorder clinic. One institution endeavored to save souls, to prepare people to serve God here and in eternity; the other endeavored to save bodies, to prepare people to enjoy this life. It seemed obvious which institution the world honors.

In the Beatitudes, Jesus honored people who may not enjoy many privileges in this life. To the poor, the mourners, the meek, the hungry, the persecuted, the poor in heart, he offered assurance that their service would not go unrecognized. They would receive ample reward. "Indeed," wrote C. S. Lewis, "if we consider the unblushing promises of reward and the staggering nature of the rewards promised in the Gospels, it would seem that Our Lord finds our desires, not too strong, but too weak. We are half-hearted creatures, fooling about with drink and sex and ambition when infinite joy is offered us, like an ignorant child who wants to go on making mud pies in a slum because he cannot imagine what is meant by the offer of a holiday at the sea."

I know that among many Christians an emphasis on future rewards has fallen out of fashion. My former pastor Bill Leslie used to observe, "As churches grow wealthier and more successful, their preference in hymns changes from 'This world is not my home, I'm just a passin' through' to 'This is my father's world.'" In the United States, at least, Christians have grown so comfortable that we no longer identify with the humble conditions Jesus addressed in the Beatitudes—which may explain why they sound so strange to our ears.

Yet, as C. S. Lewis reminds us, we dare not discount the value of future rewards. One need only listen to the songs composed by American slaves to realize this consolation of belief. "Swing low, sweet chariot, comin' for to carry me home." "When I get to heaven, goin' to put on my robe, goin' to shout all over God's heaven." "We'll soon be free, we'll soon be free, when the Lord will call us home." If the slave masters had written these songs for the slaves to sing, they would be an obscenity; rather, they come from the mouths of the slaves themselves, people who had little hope in this world but abiding hope in a world to come. For them, all hope centered in Jesus. "Nobody knows the trouble I see, nobody knows but Jesus." "I'm gonna' lay all my troubles on Jesus' shoulder."

I no longer scorn the eternal rewards mentioned in the Beatitudes as "pie in the sky." What good does it do to hope for future rewards? What good did it do Terry Waite to believe that he would not spend the rest of his life chained to a door in a filthy Beirut apartment, but that a world of family and friends and mercy and love and music and food and good books awaited him if he could just find the strength to hang on a little longer? What good did it do the slaves to believe that God was not satisfied with a world that included back-breaking labor and masters armed with bullwhips and lynching ropes? To believe in future rewards is to believe that the long arm of the Lord bends toward justice, to believe that one day the proud will be overthrown and the humble raised up and the hungry filled with good things.

The prospect of future rewards in no way cancels out our need to fight for justice now, in this life. Yet it is a plain fact of history that for convicts in the Soviet Gulag and slaves in America and Christians in Roman cages awaiting their turn with the wild beasts, the promise of reward was a source not of shame but of hope. It keeps you alive. It allows you to believe in a just God after all. Like a bell tolling from another world, Jesus' promise of rewards proclaims that no matter how things appear, there is no future in evil, only in good.

My wife, Janet, worked with senior citizens near a Chicago housing project judged the poorest community in the United States. About half her clients were white, half were black. All of them had lived through harsh times—two world wars, the Great Depression, social upheavals—and all of them, in their seventies and eighties, lived in awareness of death. Yet Janet noted a striking difference in the way the whites and the blacks faced death. There were exceptions, of course, but the trend was this: many of the whites became increasingly fearful and anxious. They complained about their lives, their families, and their deteriorating health. The blacks, in contrast, maintained a good humor and triumphant spirit even though they had more apparent reason for bitterness and despair.

What caused the difference in outlooks? Janet concluded the answer was hope, a hope that traced directly to the blacks' bedrock belief in heaven. If you want to hear contemporary images of heaven, attend a few black funerals. With characteristic eloquence, the preachers paint word pictures of a life so serene and sensuous that everyone in the congregation starts fidgeting to go there. The mourners feel grief, naturally, but in its proper place: as an interruption, a temporary setback in a battle whose end has already been determined.

I am convinced that for these neglected saints, who learned to anticipate and enjoy God in spite of the difficulties of their lives on earth, heaven will seem more like a long-awaited homecoming than a visit to a new place. In their lives, the Beatitudes have become true. To people who are trapped in pain, in broken homes, in economic chaos, in hatred and fear, in violence—to these, Jesus offers a promise of a time, far longer and more substantial than this time on earth, of health and wholeness and pleasure and peace. A time of reward.

The Great Reversal. Over time I learned to respect, and even long for, the rewards Jesus promised. Even so, these rewards lay somewhere in the future, and dangled promises do not satisfy immediate needs. Along the way, I have also come to believe that the Beatitudes describe the present as well as the future. They neatly contrast how to succeed in the kingdom of heaven as opposed to the kingdom of this world.

J. B. Phillips rendered the Beatitudes that apply in the kingdom of this world:

> Happy are the "pushers": for they get on in the world.
> Happy are the hard-boiled: for they never let life hurt them.
> Happy are they who complain: for they get their own way
> in the end.
> Happy are the blasé: for they never worry over their sins.
> Happy are the slave-drivers: for they get results.
> Happy are the knowledgeable men of the world: for they know
> their way around.
> Happy are the trouble-makers: for they make people take notice
> of them.*

---

*Indeed, it appears that Jesus adapted a form of proverbs common in his day to make the opposite point. According to Walter Kasper, Greek and Jewish wisdom

Modern society lives by the rules of survival of the fittest. "The one who dies with the most toys wins," reads one bumper sticker. So does the nation with the best weapons and the largest gross national product. The owner of the Chicago Bulls gave a compact summary of the rules governing the visible world on the occasion of Michael Jordan's (temporary) retirement. "He's living the American Dream," said Jerry Reinsdorf. "The American Dream is to reach a point in your life where you don't have to do anything you don't want to do and can do everything that you do want to do."

That may be the American Dream, but it decidedly is not Jesus' dream as revealed in the Beatitudes. The Beatitudes express quite plainly that God views this world through a different set of lenses. God seems to prefer the poor and those who mourn to the Fortune 500 and supermodels who frolic on the beach. Oddly, God may prefer South Central L. A. to Malibu Beach, and Rwanda to Monte Carlo. In fact, one could almost subtitle the Sermon on the Mount not "survival of the fittest" but "triumph of the victims."

Various scenes in the Gospels give a good picture of the kind of people who impressed Jesus. A widow who placed her last two cents in the offering. A dishonest tax collector so riddled with anxiety that he climbed a tree to get a better view of Jesus. A nameless, nondescript child. A woman with a string of five unhappy marriages. A blind beggar. An adulteress. A man with leprosy. Strength, good looks, connections, and the competitive instinct may bring a person success in a society like ours, but those very qualities may block entrance to the kingdom of heaven. Dependence, sorrow, repentance, a longing to change—these are the gates to God's kingdom.

"Blessed are the poor in spirit," said Jesus. One commentary translates that "Blessed are the desperate." With nowhere else to turn, the desperate just may turn to Jesus, the only one who can offer the deliverance they long for. Jesus really believed that a person who is poor in spirit, or mourning, or persecuted, or hungry and thirsty for righteousness has a peculiar "advantage" over the rest of us. Maybe,

---

literature describes as blessed the man who has obedient children, a good wife, faithful friends, is successful, and so forth. Jesus added a contrarian twist to what the audience expected.

just maybe, the desperate person will cry out to God for help. If so, that person is truly blessed.

Catholic scholars coined the phrase "God's preferential option for the poor" to describe a phenomenon they found throughout both the Old and New Testaments: God's partiality toward the poor and the disadvantaged. *Why would God single out the poor for special attention over any other group?* I used to wonder. What makes the poor deserving of God's concern? I received help on this issue from a writer named Monika Hellwig, who lists the following "advantages" to being poor:

1. The poor know they are in urgent need of redemption.
2. The poor know not only their dependence on God and on powerful people but also their interdependence with one another.
3. The poor rest their security not on things but on people.
4. The poor have no exaggerated sense of their own importance, and no exaggerated need of privacy.
5. The poor expect little from competition and much from cooperation.
6. The poor can distinguish between necessities and luxuries.
7. The poor can wait, because they have acquired a kind of dogged patience born of acknowledged dependence.
8. The fears of the poor are more realistic and less exaggerated, because they already know that one can survive great suffering and want.
9. When the poor have the Gospel preached to them, it sounds like good news and not like a threat or a scolding.
10. The poor can respond to the call of the Gospel with a certain abandonment and uncomplicated totality because they have so little to lose and are ready for anything.

In summary, through no choice of their own—they may urgently wish otherwise—poor people find themselves in a posture that befits the grace of God. In their state of neediness, dependence, and dissatisfaction with life, they may welcome God's free gift of love.

As an exercise I went back over Monika Hellwig's list, substituting the word "rich" for "poor," and changing each sentence to its opposite. "The rich do not know they are in urgent need of redemption.... The rich rest their security not on people but on things...." (Jesus did something similar in Luke's version of the Beatitudes, but that portion gets much less attention: "But woe to you who are rich, for you have already received your comfort....")

Next, I tried something far more threatening: I substituted the word "I." Reviewing each of the ten statements, I asked myself if my own attitudes more resembled those of the poor or of the rich. Do I easily acknowledge my needs? Do I readily depend on God and on other people? Where does my security rest? Am I more likely to compete or cooperate? Can I distinguish between necessities and luxuries? Am I patient? Do the Beatitudes sound to me like good news or like a scolding?

As I did this exercise I began to realize why so many saints voluntarily submit to the discipline of poverty. Dependence, humility, simplicity, cooperation, and a sense of abandon are qualities greatly prized in the spiritual life, but extremely elusive for people who live in comfort. There may be other ways to God but, oh, they are hard—as hard as a camel squeezing through the eye of a needle. In the Great Reversal of God's kingdom, prosperous saints are very rare.

I do not believe the poor to be more virtuous than anyone else (though I have found them more compassionate and often more generous), but they are less likely to *pretend* to be virtuous. They have not the arrogance of the middle class, who can skillfully disguise their problems under a facade of self-righteousness. They are more naturally dependent, because they have no choice; they must depend on others simply to survive.

I now view the Beatitudes not as patronizing slogans, but as profound insights into the mystery of human existence. God's kingdom turns the tables upside down. The poor, the hungry, the mourners, and the oppressed truly are blessed. Not because of their miserable states, of course—Jesus spent much of his life trying to remedy those miseries. Rather, they are blessed because of an innate advantage they hold over those more comfortable and self-sufficient. People who are rich, successful, and beautiful may well go through life relying on their natural gifts. People who lack such natural advantages, hence underqualified for success in the kingdom of this world, just might turn to God in their time of need.

Human beings do not readily admit desperation. When they do, the kingdom of heaven draws near.

Psychological Reality. More recently, I have come to see a third level of truth in the Beatitudes. Not only did Jesus offer an ideal for us to strive toward, with appropriate rewards in view; not only did he turn the tables on our success-addicted society; he also set forth a plain formula of psychological truth, the deepest level of truth that we can know on earth.

The Beatitudes reveal that what succeeds in the kingdom of heaven also benefits us most in this life here and now. It has taken me many years to recognize this fact, and only now am I beginning to understand the Beatitudes. They still jar me every time I read them, but they jar me because I recognize in them a richness that unmasks my own poverty.

Blessed are the poor in spirit ... Blessed are the meek. A book like Paul Johnson's *Intellectuals* sets out in convincing detail what all of us know to be true: the people we laud, strive to emulate, and feature on the covers of popular magazines are not the fulfilled, happy, balanced persons we might imagine. Although Johnson's subjects (Ernest Hemingway, Bertrand Russell, Jean-Paul Sartre, Edmund Wilson, Bertolt Brecht, et al.) would be judged successful by any modern standard, it would be difficult to assemble a more miserable, egomaniacal, abusive company.

My career as a journalist has afforded me opportunities to interview "stars," including NFL football greats, movie actors, music performers, best-selling authors, politicians, and TV personalities. These are the people who dominate the media. We fawn over them, poring over the minutiae of their lives: the clothes they wear, the food they eat, the aerobic routines they follow, the people they love, the toothpaste they use. Yet I must tell you that, in my limited experience, I have found Paul Johnson's principle to hold true: our "idols" are as miserable a group of people as I have ever met. Most have troubled or broken marriages. Nearly all are incurably dependent on psychotherapy. In a heavy irony, these larger-than-life heroes seem tormented by self-doubt.

I have also spent time with people I call "servants." Doctors and nurses who work among the ultimate outcasts, leprosy patients in rural India. A Princeton graduate who runs a hotel for the homeless in Chicago. Health workers who have left high-paying jobs to serve in a backwater town of Mississippi. Relief workers in Somalia, Sudan, Ethiopia, Bangladesh, and other repositories of human suffering. The Ph.D.s I met in Arizona, who are now scattered throughout jungles of South America translating the Bible into obscure languages.

I was prepared to honor and admire these servants, to hold them up as inspiring examples. I was not prepared to envy them. Yet as I now reflect on the two groups side by side, stars and servants, the servants clearly emerge as the favored ones, the graced ones. Without question, I would rather spend time among the servants than among the stars: they possess qualities of depth and richness and even joy that I have not found elsewhere. Servants work for low pay, long hours, and no applause, "wasting" their talents and skills among the poor and uneducated. Somehow, though, in the process of losing their lives they find them.

The poor in spirit and the meek are indeed blessed, I now believe. Theirs is the kingdom of heaven, and it is they who will inherit the earth.

Blessed are the pure in heart. During a period of my life when I was battling sexual temptation, I came across an article that referred me to a thin book, *What I Believe*, by the French Catholic writer François Mauriac. It surprised me that Mauriac, an old man, devoted considerable space to a discussion of his own lust. He explained, "Old age risks being a period of redoubled testing because the imagination in an old man is substituted in a horrible way for what nature refuses him."

I knew that Mauriac understood lust. *Viper's Tangle* and *A Kiss for the Leper*, novels which helped win him the Nobel prize in literature, portray lust, repression, and sexual anger as well as anything I have ever read. For Mauriac, sexual temptation was a familiar battleground.

Mauriac dismissed most of the arguments in favor of sexual purity that he had been taught in his Catholic upbringing. "Marriage will cure lust": it did not for Mauriac, as it has not for so many others, because lust involves the attraction of unknown creatures and the taste for adventure and chance meetings. "With self-discipline you can master lust": Mauriac found that sexual desire is like a tidal wave powerful enough to bear away all the best intentions. "True fulfillment can only be found in monogamy": this may be true, but it certainly does not *seem* true to someone who finds no slackening of sexual urges even in monogamy. Thus he weighed the traditional arguments for purity and found them wanting.

Mauriac concluded that self-discipline, repression, and rational argument are inadequate weapons to use in fighting the impulse toward impurity. In the end, he could find only one reason to be pure, and that is what Jesus presented in the Beatitudes: "Blessed are the pure in heart, for they will see God." In Mauriac's words, "Impurity separates us from God. The spiritual life obeys laws as verifiable as those of the physical world. . . . Purity is the condition for a higher love—for a possession superior to all possessions: that of God. Yes, this is what is at stake, and nothing less."

Reading François Mauriac's words did not end my struggle with lust. But I must say beyond all doubt that I have found his analysis to be true. The love God holds out to us requires that our faculties be cleansed and purified before we can receive a higher love, one attainable in no other way. That is the motive to stay pure. By harboring lust, I limit my own intimacy with God.

The pure in heart are truly blessed, for they will see God. It is as simple, and as difficult, as that.

Blessed are the merciful. I learned the truth of this Beatitude from Henri Nouwen, a priest who used to teach at Harvard University. At the height of his career, Nouwen moved from Harvard to a community called Daybreak, near Toronto, in order to take on the demanding chores required by his friendship with a man named Adam. Nouwen now ministers not to intellectuals but to a young man who is considered by many a useless person who should have been aborted.

Nouwen describes his friend:

> Adam is a 25-year-old man who cannot speak, cannot dress or undress himself, cannot walk alone, cannot eat without much help. He does not cry or laugh. Only occasionally does he make eye contact. His back is distorted. His arm and leg movements are twisted. He suffers from severe epilepsy and, despite heavy medication, sees few days without grand-mal seizures. Sometimes, as he grows suddenly rigid, he utters a howling groan. On a few occasions I've seen one big tear roll down his cheek.
>
> It takes me about an hour and a half to wake Adam up, give him his medication, carry him into his bath, wash him, shave him, clean his teeth, dress him, walk him to the kitchen, give him his breakfast, put him in his wheelchair and bring him to the place where he spends most of the day with therapeutic exercises.

On a visit to Nouwen in Toronto, I watched him perform that routine with Adam, and I must admit I had a fleeting doubt as to whether this was the best use of his time. I have heard Henri Nouwen speak, and have read many of his books. He has much to offer. Could not someone else take over the menial task of caring for Adam? When I cautiously broached the subject with Nouwen himself, he informed me that I had completely misinterpreted what was going on. "I am not giving up anything," he insisted. "It is *I*, not Adam, who gets the main benefit from our friendship."

Then Nouwen began listing for me all the benefits he has gained. The hours spent with Adam, he said, have given him an inner peace so fulfilling that it makes most of his other, more high-minded tasks seem boring and superficial by contrast. Early on, as he sat beside that helpless child-man, he realized how marked with rivalry and competition, how obsessive, was his drive for success in academia and Christian ministry. Adam taught him that "what makes us human is not our mind but our heart, not our ability to think but our ability to love." From Adam's simple nature, he had glimpsed the "emptiness" necessary before one can be filled by God—the kind of emptiness that desert monks achieved only after much searching and discipline.

All during the rest of our interview, Henri Nouwen circled back to my question, as if he could not believe I could ask such a thing. He kept thinking of other ways he had benefited from his relationship with Adam. Truly, he was enjoying a new kind of spiritual peace, acquired not within the stately quadrangles of Harvard, but by the bedside of incontinent Adam. I left Daybreak convicted of my own spiritual poverty, I who so carefully arrange my writer's life to make it efficient and single-focused. The merciful are indeed blessed, I learned, for they will be shown mercy.

Blessed are the peacemakers . . . Blessed are those who are persecuted for the sake of righteousness. This truth came to me in a roundabout way. The great novelist Leo Tolstoy tried to follow it, but his irascible temper kept getting in the way of peacemaking. Tolstoy did write eloquently about the Sermon on the Mount, however, and half a century later a Hindu ascetic named Mohandas Gandhi read *The Kingdom of God Is Within You* by Tolstoy and decided to live by the literal principles of the Sermon on the Mount.

The movie *Gandhi* contains a fine scene in which Gandhi tries to explain his philosophy to the Presbyterian missionary Charlie Andrews. Walking together in a South African city, the two suddenly find their way blocked by young thugs. The Reverend Andrews takes one look at the menacing gangsters and decides to run for it. Gandhi stops him. "Doesn't the New Testament say if an enemy strikes you on the right cheek you should offer him the left?" Andrews mumbles that he thought the phrase was used metaphorically. "I'm not so sure," Gandhi replies. "I suspect he meant you must show courage—be willing to take a blow, several blows, to show you will not strike back nor will you be turned aside. And when you do that it calls on something in human nature, something that makes his hatred decrease and his respect increase. I think Christ grasped that and I have seen it work."

Years later an American minister, Martin Luther King Jr., studied Gandhi's tactics and decided to put them into practice in the United States. Many blacks abandoned King over the issue of nonviolence and drifted toward "black power" rhetoric. After you've been hit on the head with a policeman's nightstick for the dozenth time and received yet another jolt from a jailer's cattle prod, you begin to question the effectiveness of nonviolence. But King himself never wavered.

As riots broke out in places like Los Angeles, Chicago, and Harlem, King traveled from city to city trying to cool tempers, forcefully reminding demonstrators that moral change is not accomplished through immoral means. He had learned that principle from the Sermon on the Mount and from Gandhi, and almost all his speeches reiterated the message. "Christianity," he said, "has always insisted that the cross we bear precedes the crown we wear. To be a Christian one must take up his cross, with all its difficulties and agonizing and tension-packed content, and carry it until that very cross leaves its mark upon us and redeems us to that more excellent way which comes only through suffering."

Martin Luther King Jr. had some weaknesses, but one thing he got right. Against all odds, against all instincts of self-preservation, he stayed true to the principle of peacemaking. He did not strike back. Where others called for revenge, he called for love. The civil rights marchers put their bodies on the line before sheriffs with nightsticks and fire hoses and snarling German shepherds. That, in fact, was what brought them the victory they had been seeking so long. Historians point to one event as the single moment in which the movement attained a critical mass of public support for its cause. It occurred on a bridge outside Selma, Alabama, when Sheriff Jim Clark turned his policemen loose on unarmed black demonstrators. The American public, horrified by the scene of violent injustice, at last gave assent to passage of a civil rights bill.

I grew up in Atlanta, across town from Martin Luther King Jr., and I confess with some shame that while he was leading marches in places like Selma and Montgomery and Memphis, I was on the side of the white sheriffs with the nightsticks and German shepherds. I was quick to pounce on his moral flaws and slow to recognize my own blind sin. But because he stayed faithful, by offering his body as a target but never as a weapon, he broke through my moral calluses.

The real goal, King used to say, was not to defeat the white man, but "to awaken a sense of shame within the oppressor and challenge his false sense of superiority.... The end is reconciliation; the end is redemption; the end is the creation of the beloved community." And that is what Martin Luther King Jr. finally set into motion, even in racists like me.

King, like Gandhi before him, died a martyr. After his death, more and more people began adopting the principle of nonviolent protest as a way to demand justice. In the Philippines, after Benigno Aquino's martyrdom, ordinary people brought down a government by gathering in the streets to pray; army tanks rolled to a stop before the kneeling Filipinos as if blocked by an invisible force. Later, in the remarkable year of 1989, in Poland, Hungary, Czechoslovakia, East Germany, Bulgaria, Yugoslavia, Romania, Mongolia, Albania, the Soviet Union, Nepal, and Chile, more than half a billion people threw off the yoke of oppression through nonviolent means. In many of these places, especially the nations of Eastern Europe, the Christian church led the way. Protesters marched through the streets carrying candles, singing hymns, and praying. As in Joshua's day, the walls came tumbling down.

Peacemakers will be called sons and daughters of God. Blessed also are those who are persecuted because of righteousness, for theirs is the kingdom of heaven.

Blessed are those who mourn. Because I have written books with titles like *Where Is God When It Hurts?* and *Disappointment with God*, I have spent time among mourners. They intimidated me at first. I had few answers for the questions they were asking, and I felt awkward in the presence of their grief. I remember especially one year when, at the invitation of a neighbor, I joined a therapy group at a nearby hospital. This group, called Make Today Count, consisted of people who were dying, and I accompanied my neighbor to their meetings for a year.

Certainly I cannot say that I "enjoyed" the gatherings; that would be the wrong word. Yet the meetings became for me one of the most meaningful events of each month. In contrast to a party, where participants try to impress each other with signs of status and power, in this group no one was trying to impress. Clothes, fashions, apartment furnishings, job titles, new cars—what do these things mean to people who are preparing to die? More than any other people I had met, the Make Today Count group members concentrated on ultimate issues. I found myself wishing that some of my shallow, hedonistic friends would attend a meeting.

Later, when I wrote about what I had learned from grieving and suffering people, I began hearing from strangers. I have three folders, each one several inches thick, filled with these letters. They are among my most precious possessions. One letter, twenty-six pages long, was written on blue-lined note paper by a mother sitting in a lounge outside a room where surgeons were operating on her four-year-old daughter's brain tumor. Another came from a quadriplegic who "wrote" by making puffs of air into a tube, which a computer translated into letters on a printer.

Many of the people who have written me have no happy endings to their stories. Some still feel abandoned by God. Few have found answers to the "Why?" questions. But I have seen enough grief that I have gained faith in Jesus' promise that those who mourn will be comforted.

I know two small-scale ministries, run from private homes, that have developed out of grief. The first came into being when a woman in California discovered that her son, the apple of her eye, was dying of AIDS. She got little sympathy and support from her church and community because of the young man's homosexuality. She felt so alone and needy that she decided to start a newsletter that now brings together a network of parents of gay people. Although she offers little professional help and promises no magic cures, now hundreds of other parents view this courageous woman as a lifesaver.

Another woman, in Wisconsin, lost her only son in a Marine Corps helicopter crash. For years she could not escape the dark cloud of grief. She kept her son's room intact just as he had left it. Eventually, she began to notice how frequently helicopter crashes were reported on the news. She kept thinking of other families facing tragedies like hers, and wondering whether she could do something to help. Now, whenever a military helicopter crashes, she sends a packet of letters and helpful materials to an officer in the Defense Department who forwards the packet on to the affected family. About half of them strike up a regular correspondence, and in her retirement this Wisconsin woman directs her own "community of suffering." The activity has not solved the grief for her son, of course, but it has given her a sense of meaning, and she no longer feels helpless against that grief.

There is no more effective healer, I have found, than what Henri Nouwen calls "a wounded healer." Blessed are those who mourn, for they will be comforted.

Blessed are those who hunger and thirst for righteousness. In a sense, everyone I have mentioned in this litany of the Beatitudes manifests this final promise of Jesus. The "servants" who invest their lives among the poor and needy, François Mauriac striving to stay pure, Henri Nouwen bathing and dressing Adam, Martin Luther King Jr. and the disciples of nonviolence, mothers of gay men and Marine pilots who reach out beyond their grief—all these are responding to pangs of hunger and thirst for righteousness. All of them have received a reward, not only in the life to come, but in this life as well.

An Albanian nun spent sixteen years in an exclusive convent teaching geography to the wealthiest Bengali and British daughters of Calcutta. One day, on a railway trip to the Himalayas, she heard a voice calling her to change paths and minister to the poorest of the poor. Can anyone really doubt that Mother Teresa has found more personal fulfillment in her latter occupation than in her former? I have seen this principle borne out in saints and in ordinary people so often that I now easily understand why the Gospels repeat the one saying of Jesus more than any other: "Whoever wants to save his life will lose it, but whoever loses his life for my sake will find it."

Jesus came, he told us, not to destroy life but that we may have it more abundantly, "life . . . to the full." Paradoxically, we get this abundant life in ways we may not have counted on. We get it by investing in others, by taking courageous stands for justice, by ministering to the weak and needy, by pursuing God and not self. I would not dare feel pity for any of the people I have just mentioned, though all have lived with hardship. For all their "sacrifices," they seem to me more fully alive, not less. Those who hunger and thirst for righteousness get filled.

In the Beatitudes, strange sayings that at first glance seem absurd, Jesus offers a paradoxical key to abundant life. The kingdom of heaven, he said elsewhere, is like a treasure of such value that any shrewd investor would "in his joy" sell all he has in order to buy it. It represents value far more real and permanent than anything the world has to offer, for this treasure will pay dividends both here on earth and also in the life to come. Jesus places the emphasis not on what we give up but on what we receive. Is it not in our own self-interest to pursue such a treasure?

When I first heard the Beatitudes, they sounded to me like impossible ideals given by some dreamy mystic. Now, though, I see them as truths proclaimed by a realist every bit as pragmatic as General Norman Schwarzkopf. Jesus knew how life works, in the kingdom of heaven as well as the kingdom of this world. In a life characterized by poverty, mourning, meekness, a hunger for righteousness, mercy, purity, peacemaking, and persecution, Jesus himself embodied the Beatitudes. Perhaps he even conceived the Beatitudes as a sermon to himself as well as to the rest of us, for he would have much opportunity to practice these hard truths.

7

Message:
A Sermon of Offense

The test of observance of Christ's teachings is our consciousness of our failure to attain an ideal perfection. The degree to which we draw near this perfection cannot be seen; all we can see is the extent of our deviation.

Leo Tolstoy

7
Message:
A Sermon of Offense

The Beatitudes represent only the first step toward understanding the Sermon on the Mount. Long after I came to recognize the enduring truth of the Beatitudes, I still brooded over the uncompromising harshness of the rest of Jesus' sermon. Its absolutist quality left me gasping. "Be perfect, therefore, as your heavenly Father is perfect," Jesus said, his statement tucked almost casually between commands to love enemies and give away money. Be perfect like God? Whatever did he mean?

I cannot easily dismiss this extremism, because it turns up elsewhere in the Gospels. When a rich man asked Jesus what he should do to ensure eternal life, Jesus told him to give his money away—not 10 percent or 18.5 percent or even 50 percent, but all of it. When a disciple asked if he should forgive his brother seven times, Jesus replied, "I tell you, not seven times, but seventy-seven times." Other religions taught variations of the "Golden Rule," but stated in a more limited, negative form: "Don't do to others what you wouldn't want them to do to you." Jesus expanded the Rule into its unbounded form, "In everything, do to others what you would have them do to you."

Has anyone ever lived a life as perfect as God's? Has anyone ever followed the Golden Rule? How can we even respond to such impossible ideals? We humans prefer common sense and balance, something closer to Aristotle's Golden Mean than Jesus' Golden Rule.

* * *

A friend of mine named Virginia Stem Owens assigned the Sermon on the Mount to her composition class at Texas A&M University, asking the students to write a short essay. She had expected them to have a basic respect for the text, since the Bible Belt extends right across Texas, but her students' reactions soon disabused her of that notion. "In my opinion religion is one big hoax," wrote one. "There is an old saying that 'you shouldn't believe everything you read' and it applies in this case," wrote another.

Virginia recalled her own introduction to the Sermon on the Mount in Sunday school, where pastel poster illustrations showed Jesus sitting on a green hillside surrounded by eager, pink children. It never occurred to her to react with anger or disgust. Her students thought otherwise:

> The stuff the churches preach is extremely strict and allows for almost no fun without thinking it is a sin or not.

> I did not like the essay "Sermon on the Mount." It was hard to read and made me feel like I had to be perfect and no one is.

> The things asked in this sermon are absurd. To look at a woman is adultery. That is the most extreme, stupid, unhuman statement that I have ever heard.

"At this point," Virginia wrote about the experience, "I began to be encouraged. There is something exquisitely innocent about not realizing you shouldn't call Jesus stupid.... This was the real thing, a pristine response to the gospel, unfiltered through a two-millennia cultural haze.... I find it strangely heartening that the Bible remains offensive to honest, ignorant ears, just as it was in the first century. For me, that somehow validates its significance. Whereas the scriptures almost lost their characteristically astringent flavor during the past century, the current widespread biblical illiteracy should catapult us into a situation more nearly approximating that of their original, first-century audience."

Offensive, astringent—yes, these are apt words to apply to the Sermon on the Mount. As I viewed fifteen movie treatments of the scene, only one seemed to capture anything like the offense of the original. A low-budget BBC production entitled *Son of Man* sets the Sermon on the Mount against a background of chaos and violence. Roman soldiers have just invaded a Galilean village to exact vengeance for some trespass against the empire. They have strung up Jewish men of fighting age, shoved their hysterical wives to the ground, even speared babies in order to "teach these Jews a lesson." Into that tumultuous scene of blood and tears and keening for the dead strides Jesus with eyes ablaze.

> I tell you: Love your enemies and pray for those that persecute you.
>
> An eye for an eye, a tooth for a tooth, right? So our forefathers said. Love your kinsmen, hate your enemies, right? But I say it's easy to love your own brother, to love those who love you. Even tax collectors do that! You want me to congratulate you for loving your own kinsmen? No, Love your *enemy*.
>
> Love the man who would kick you and spit at you. Love the soldier who would drive his sword in your belly. Love the brigand who robs and tortures you.
>
> Listen to me! Love your enemy! If a Roman soldiers hits you on the left cheek, offer him the right one. If a man in authority orders you to walk one mile, walk two miles. If a man sues you for your coat, give him the shirt off your back.
>
> Listen! I tell you, it is hard to follow me. What I'm saying to you hasn't been said since the world began!

You can imagine the villagers' response to such unwelcome advice. The Sermon on the Mount did not puzzle them; it infuriated them.

Early in the Sermon on the Mount, Jesus addressed head-on a question that worried most of his listeners: Was he a revolutionary or an authentic Jewish prophet? Here is Jesus' own description of his relationship to the Torah:

> Do not think that I have come to abolish the Law or the Prophets; I have not come to abolish them but to fulfill them....

For I tell you that unless your righteousness surpasses that of the Pharisees and the teachers of the law, you will certainly not enter the kingdom of heaven.

That last statement surely made the crowd sit up and take notice. Pharisees and teachers of the law competed with one another in strictness. They had atomized God's law into 613 rules—248 commands and 365 prohibitions—and bolstered these rules with 1,521 emendations. To avoid breaking the third commandment, "You shall not misuse the name of the LORD," they refused to pronounce God's name at all. To avoid sexual temptation they had a practice of lowering their heads and not even looking at women (the most scrupulous of these were known as "bleeding Pharisees" because of frequent collisions with walls and other obstacles). To avoid defiling the Sabbath they outlawed thirty-nine activities that might be construed as "work." How could an ordinary person's righteousness ever *surpass* that of such professional holy men?

The Sermon on the Mount details exactly what Jesus meant, and this explication is what seemed so absurd to twentieth-century students at Texas A&M as well as first-century Jews in Palestine. Using the Torah as a starting point, Jesus pushed the law in the same direction, further than any Pharisee had dared push it, further than any monk has dared live it. The Sermon on the Mount introduced a new moon in the moral universe that has exerted its own force of gravity ever since.

Jesus made the law impossible for anyone to keep and then charged us to keep it. Consider some examples.

Every human society in history has had a law against murder. There are variations, of course: the U.S. allows killing in self-defense or in unusual circumstances such as spouse abuse. But no society has come up with anything like Jesus' enlarged definition of murder: "I tell you that anyone who is angry with his brother will be subject to judgment. . . . anyone who says 'You fool!' will be in danger of the fire of hell." Growing up with an older brother, I fretted over this verse. Can two brothers weather the storms of adolescence without relying on words such as "stupid" and "fool"?

Every society also has taboos against sexual promiscuity. Today at least one college requires male students to ask females' permission for each stage of sexual contact. Meanwhile, some feminist groups are trying to forge a legal link between pornography and crimes against women. But no society has ever proposed a rule as strict as Jesus': "I tell you that anyone who looks at a woman lustfully has already committed adultery with her in his heart. If your right eye causes you to sin, gouge it out and throw it away. It is better for you to lose one part of your body than for your whole body to be thrown into hell."

I have heard calls for castration of serial rapists, but never have I heard a proposal for facial mutilation on account of lust. Indeed, lust in America is an established national pastime, celebrated in ads for blue jeans and beer, in the annual *Sports Illustrated* swimming suit issue, and in the twenty million copies of pornographic magazines sold each month. When presidential candidate Jimmy Carter tried to explain this verse in a *Playboy* magazine interview, the press reacted with what John Updike described as "nervous hilarity." "How strangely on modern ears," said Updike, "falls the notion that lust—sexual desire that wells up in us as involuntarily as saliva—in itself is wicked!"

As for divorce, in Jesus' day the Pharisees heatedly debated how to interpret the Old Testament rules. The prominent rabbi Hillel taught that a man could divorce his wife if she did anything at all to displease him, even something as trivial as burning his food; a husband needed only to pronounce "I divorce you" three times to make the divorce final. Jesus countered, "I tell you that anyone who divorces his wife, except for marital unfaithfulness, causes her to become an adulteress, and anyone who marries the divorced woman commits adultery."

Finally, Jesus spelled out the principle of nonviolence. Who could even survive with the rule Jesus laid down: "Do not resist an evil person. If someone strikes you on the right cheek, turn to him the other also. And if someone wants to sue you and take your tunic, let him have your cloak as well."

I stare at these and the other strict commands of the Sermon on the Mount and ask myself how to respond. Does Jesus really expect me to give to every panhandler who crosses my path? Should I abandon all insistence on consumer rights? Cancel my insurance policies and trust God for the future? Discard my television to avoid temptations to lust? How can I possibly translate such ethical ideals into my everyday life?

* * *

I once went on a reading binge in search of the "key" to understanding the Sermon on the Mount, and it brought some consolation to learn I was not the first to flounder over its high ideals. Throughout church history, people have found canny ways to reconcile Jesus' absolute demands with the grim reality of human delinquency.

Thomas Aquinas divided Jesus' teaching into Precepts and Counsels, which in more modern language we might rename Requirements and Suggestions. Precepts encompassed universal moral laws like the Ten Commandments. But for the more idealistic commands, such as Jesus' statements about anger and lust, Aquinas applied a different standard: though we should accept them as a good model and strive to fulfill them, they have not the moral force of Precepts. The Roman Catholic Church later codified Aquinas's distinctions into lists of "mortal" and "venial" sins.

Martin Luther interpreted the Sermon on the Mount in light of Jesus' formula "Give to Caesar what is Caesar's and to God what is God's." Christians maintain a dual citizenship, he said: one in the kingdom of Christ and one in the kingdom of the world. The extremism in the Sermon on the Mount applies absolutely to Christ's kingdom, but not to the world's. Take the commands to "Love your enemies" and "Do not resist an evil person"; of course these do not apply to the state! In order to prevent anarchy, a government must resist evil and repel enemies. Therefore, a Christian should learn to separate the office from the person: a Christian soldier, say, must carry out orders to fight and kill even while following Christ's law of love for enemies in his heart.

In Luther's day, various Anabaptist movements chose a radically different approach. All such attempts to water down Jesus' straightforward commands are misguided, they said. Had not the early church cited Christ's command to "love your enemies" more often than any other during its first four centuries? Simply read the Sermon on the Mount. Jesus does not differentiate between Precepts and Counsels, or the office and the person. He says don't resist an evil person, don't take oaths, give to the needy, love your enemies. We should follow his commands in the most literal way possible. For this reason some groups vowed to hold no personal property. Others, like the Quakers, refused to take oaths or doff their hats to a public official, and opposed having an army or even a police force. Subsequently, thousands of Anabaptists were killed in Europe, England, and Russia; many of the survivors made their way across the ocean to America, where they attempted to found colonies and communes based on the principles of the Sermon on the Mount.*

In nineteenth-century America a theological movement emerged with a new spin on the Sermon on the Mount. Dispensationalism explained such teaching as the last vestige of the age of Law, soon to be displaced by the age of Grace after Jesus' death and resurrection. Hence we need not follow its strict commands. The popular Scofield Bible described the sermon as "pure law" but with "beautiful moral application to the Christian."

Still another interpretation came from Albert Schweitzer, who saw the Sermon on the Mount as a set of interim demands for unusual times. Convinced that the world would soon end in the apocalypse, Jesus was setting into motion a kind of "martial law." Since the world did not end, we must now view his instructions differently.

Assiduously I studied all these movements, trying to understand the Sermon on the Mount from their vantage point—and, I must admit, trying to find a way to wriggle out from under its stern demands. Each school of thought contributed important insights, yet each also seemed to have a blind spot. Like most of the good doctor's elucidations, Aquinas's categories of Precepts and Counsels made fine common sense, but his was not a distinction Jesus made. Jesus seemed rather to equate the Precept "Do not commit adultery" with the Counsel " . . . anyone who looks at a woman lustfully has already committed adultery with her in his heart." Luther's solution seemed ingenious and wise, but World War II demonstrated the schizophrenic abuse it may allow. Many Lutheran Christians served in Hitler's army with a clear conscience: "just following orders," they carried out the office of the state while maintaining an inner allegiance to Christ.

---

*In response to Anabaptists, Luther scornfully wrote about a Christian who let lice nibble on him because he would not kill the vermin and thus risk defying the command "Resist not evil."

As for Anabaptists and other literalists, their nonviolent response to persecution stands as one of the shining moments in church history. Yet they themselves admitted their failure to fulfill literally every command in the Sermon on the Mount. Quakers, for example, found ways to circumvent the rules in order to help the cause of the American Revolution. And what of Jesus' unbending statements against anger and lust? Origen had taken the warning against lust to its literal extreme many centuries before, but the church, horrified, then banned his solution of castration.

Dispensationalists and apocalyptists found clever ways to dodge the harder requirements of Jesus' sermon, but they seemed to me just that: ways to dodge. Jesus himself gave no indication that his commands applied only for a short period or in special circumstances. He delivered them with authority ("But I say unto you . . .") and severity ("Anyone who breaks one of the least of these commandments and teaches others to do the same will be called least in the kingdom of heaven . . .").

No matter how hard I tried, I could not find an easy way around or through the Sermon on the Mount. Like a low-grade case of depression, my cognitive dissonance over Jesus' words kept me in a state of spiritual restlessness. If the Sermon on the Mount sets forth God's standard of holiness, I concluded, then I may as well resign from the start. The Sermon on the Mount did not help me improve; it simply revealed all the ways I had not.

Ultimately I found a key to understanding the Sermon on the Mount, not in the writings of great theologians but in a more unlikely place: the writings of two nineteenth-century Russian novelists. From them I have gained my own view of the Sermon on the Mount and its mosaic of law and grace, consisting of one-half Tolstoy and one-half Dostoevsky.*

*In the early 1970s Malcolm Muggeridge was surprised to hear that members of the intellectual elite in the Soviet Union were experiencing a spiritual revival. Anatoli Kuznetsov, living in exile in England, told him there was scarcely a single

From Tolstoy I learned a deep respect for God's inflexible, absolute Ideal. The ethical ideals Tolstoy encountered in the Gospels attracted him like a flame, though his failure to live up to those ideals ultimately consumed him. Like the Anabaptists, Tolstoy strove to follow the Sermon on the Mount literally, and his intensity soon caused his family to feel like victims of his quest for holiness. For instance, after reading Jesus' command to the rich man to give away everything, Tolstoy decided to free serfs, give away his copyrights, and dispose of his vast estate. He wore peasant clothes, made his own shoes, and began working in the fields. His wife, Sonya, seeing the family's financial security about to vaporize, protested petulantly until he made some concessions.

As I read Tolstoy's diaries, I see flashbacks of my own lunges toward perfectionism. The diaries record many struggles between Tolstoy and his family, but many more between Tolstoy and himself. In an attempt to reach perfection he kept devising new lists of rules. He gave up hunting, smoking, drinking, and meat. He drafted "Rules for developing the emotional will. Rules for developing lofty feelings and eliminating base ones." Yet he could never achieve the self-discipline necessary to keep the rules. More than once, Tolstoy took a public vow of chastity and asked for separate bedrooms. He could never keep the vow for long, and much to his shame, Sonya's sixteen pregnancies broadcast to the world that inability.

Sometimes Tolstoy managed to accomplish great good. For example, after a long hiatus he wrote one last novel, *Resurrection*, at the age of seventy-one, in support of the Doukhobors—an Anabaptist group undergoing persecution by the tsar—donating all proceeds to finance their emigration to Canada. And, as I have mentioned, Tolstoy's philosophy of nonviolence, lifted directly from the Sermon on the Mount, had an impact that long outlived him, in ideological descendants like Gandhi and Martin Luther King Jr.

---

writer or artist or musician in the U.S.S.R. who was not exploring spiritual issues. Muggeridge said, "I asked him [Kuznetsov] how this could have happened, given the enormous anti-religious brainwashing job done on the citizenry, and the absence of all Christian literature, including the Gospels. His reply was memorable; the authorities, he said, forgot to suppress the works of Tolstoy and Dostoevsky, the most perfect expositions of the Christian faith of modern times."

For every Gandhi stirred by such high-minded ideals, though, there is a critic or biographer repelled by how miserably Tolstoy himself failed to meet those ideals. Frankly, he failed to practice what he preached. His wife put it well (in an obviously biased account):

> There is so little genuine warmth about him; his kindness does not come from his heart, but merely from his principles. His biographies will tell of how he helped the laborers to carry buckets of water, but no one will ever know that he never gave his wife a rest and never—in all these thirty-two years—gave his child a drink of water or spent five minutes by his bedside to give me a chance to rest a little from all my labors.

Tolstoy's ardent strides toward perfection never resulted in any semblance of peace or serenity. Up to the moment of his death the diaries and letters kept circling back to the rueful theme of failure. When he wrote about his religious faith, or attempted to live out that faith, the antagonism between the real and the ideal haunted him like a dybbuk. Too honest for self-deception, he could not silence the conscience that convicted him because he knew his conscience to be true.

Leo Tolstoy was a deeply unhappy man. He fulminated against the corrupt Russian Orthodox Church of his day and earned their excommunication. His schemes for self-improvement all foundered. He had to hide all the ropes on his estate and put away his guns in order to resist the temptation toward suicide. In the end, Tolstoy fled from his fame, his family, his estate, his identity; he died like a vagrant in a rural railroad station.

What, then, do I learn from the tragic life of Leo Tolstoy? I have read many of his religious writings, and without fail I come away inspired by his penetrating insight into God's Ideal. I have learned that, contrary to those who say the gospel solves our problems, in many ways—justice issues, money issues, race issues—the gospel actually adds to our burdens. Tolstoy saw this, and never lowered the ideals of the gospel. A man willing to free his serfs and give away his possessions in simple obedience to Christ's command is not easy to dismiss. If only he could live up to those ideals—if only I could live up to them.

To his critics Tolstoy replied, Don't judge God's holy ideals by my inability to meet them. Don't judge Christ by those of us who imperfectly bear his name. One passage especially, taken from a personal letter, shows how Tolstoy responded to such critics toward the end of his life. It stands as a summary of his spiritual pilgrimage, at once a ringing affirmation of the truth that he believed with all his heart and a plangent appeal for grace that he never fully realized.

"What about you, Lev Nikolayevich, you preach very well, but do you carry out what you preach?" This is the most natural of questions and one that is always asked of me; it is usually asked victoriously, as though it were a way of stopping my mouth. "You preach, but how do you live?" And I answer that I do not preach, that I am not able to preach, although I passionately wish to. I can preach only through my actions, and my actions are vile.... And I answer that I am guilty, and vile, and worthy of contempt for my failure to carry them out.

At the same time, not in order to justify, but simply in order to explain my lack of consistency, I say: "Look at my present life and then at my former life, and you will see that I do attempt to carry them out. It is true that I have not fulfilled one thousandth part of them [Christian precepts], and I am ashamed of this, but I have failed to fulfill them not because I did not wish to, but because I was unable to. Teach me how to escape from the net of temptations that surrounds me, help me and I will fulfill them; even without help I wish and hope to fulfill them.

"Attack me, I do this myself, but attack *me* rather than the path I follow and which I point out to anyone who asks me where I think it lies. If I know the way home and am walking along it drunkenly, is it any less the right way because I am staggering from side to side! If it is not the right way, then show me another way; but if I stagger and lose the way, you must help me, you must keep me on the true path, just as I am ready to support you. Do not mislead me, do not be glad that I have got lost, do not shout out joyfully: 'Look at him! He said he was going home, but there he is crawling into a bog!' No, do not gloat, but give me your help and support."

I feel sad as I read Tolstoy's religious writings. The X-ray vision into the human heart that made him a great novelist also made him a tortured Christian. Like a spawning salmon, he fought upstream all his life, in the end collapsing from moral exhaustion.

Yet I also feel grateful to Tolstoy, for his relentless pursuit of authentic faith has made an indelible impression upon me. I first came across his novels during a period when I was suffering the delayed effects of "biblical child abuse." The churches I grew up in contained too many frauds, or at least that is how I saw it in the arrogance of youth. When I observed the huge gap between the ideals of the gospel and the flaws of its followers, I was sorely tempted to abandon those ideals as hopelessly unattainable.

Then I discovered Tolstoy. He was the first author who, for me, accomplished that most difficult of tasks: to make Good as believable and appealing as Evil. I found in his novels, fables, and short stories a Vesuvian source of moral power. Unfailingly, he raised my sights.

A. N. Wilson, a biographer of Tolstoy, remarks that Tolstoy suffered from a "fundamental theological inability to understand the Incarnation. His religion was ultimately a thing of Law rather than of Grace, a scheme for human betterment rather than a vision of God penetrating a fallen world." With crystalline clarity Tolstoy could see his own inadequacy in the light of God's Ideal. But he could not take the further step of trusting God's grace to overcome that inadequacy.

Shortly after reading Tolstoy I discovered his countryman Fyodor Dostoevsky. These two, the most famous and accomplished of all Russian writers, lived and worked during the same period of history. Oddly, they never met, and perhaps it was just as well—they were opposites in every way. Where Tolstoy wrote bright, sunny novels, Dostoevsky wrote dark and brooding ones. Where Tolstoy worked out ascetic schemes for self-improvement, Dostoevsky periodically squandered his health and fortune on alcohol and gambling. Dostoevsky got many things wrong, but he got one thing right: His novels communicate grace and forgiveness with a Tolstoyan force.

Early in his life, Dostoevsky underwent a virtual resurrection. He had been arrested for belonging to a group judged treasonous by Tsar

Nicholas I, who, to impress upon the young parlor radicals the gravity of their errors, sentenced them to death and staged a mock execution. The conspirators were dressed in white death gowns and led to a public square where a firing squad awaited them. Blindfolded, robed in white burial shrouds, hands bound tightly behind them, they were paraded before a gawking crowd and then tied to posts. At the very last instant, as the order, "Ready, aim!" was heard and rifles were cocked and lifted upward, a horseman galloped up with a pre-arranged message from the tsar: he would mercifully commute their sentences to hard labor.

Dostoevsky never recovered from this experience. He had peered into the jaws of death, and from that moment life became for him precious beyond all calculation. "Now my life will change," he said; "I shall be born again in a new form." As he boarded the convict train toward Siberia, a devout woman handed him a New Testament, the only book allowed in prison. Believing that God had given him a second chance to fulfill his calling, Dostoevsky pored over that New Testament during his confinement. After ten years he emerged from exile with unshakable Christian convictions, as expressed in one famous passage, "If anyone proved to me that Christ was outside the truth . . . then I would prefer to remain with Christ than with the truth."

Prison offered Dostoevsky another opportunity as well. It forced him to live at close quarters with thieves, murderers, and drunken peasants. His shared life with these people later led to unmatched characterizations in his novels, such as that of the murderer Raskolnikov in *Crime and Punishment*. Dostoevsky's liberal view of the inherent goodness in humanity shattered in collision with the granitic evil he found in his cellmates. Yet over time he also glimpsed the image of God in even the lowest of prisoners. He came to believe that only through being loved is a human being capable of love; "We love because he [God] first loved us," as the apostle John says.

I encountered grace in the novels of Dostoevsky. *Crime and Punishment* portrays a despicable human being who commits a despicable crime. Yet grace enters Raskolnikov's life as well, through the person of the converted prostitute Sonia, who follows him all the way to Siberia and leads him to redemption. *The Brothers Karamazov*, perhaps the greatest novel ever written, draws a contrast between Ivan the brilliant agnostic and his devout brother Alyosha. Ivan can critique the failures of humankind and every political system devised to deal with those failures, but he can offer no solutions. Alyosha has no solutions for the intellectual problems Ivan raises, but he has a solution for humanity: love. "I do not know the answer to the problem of evil," said Alyosha, "but I do know love." Finally, in the magical novel *The Idiot*, Dostoevsky presents a Christ figure in the form of an epileptic prince. Quietly, mysteriously, Prince Myshkin moves among the circles of Russia's upper class, exposing their hypocrisy while also illuminating their lives with goodness and truth.

Taken together, these two Russians became for me, at a crucial time in my Christian pilgrimage, spiritual directors. They helped me come to terms with a central paradox of the Christian life. From Tolstoy I learned the need to look inside, to the kingdom of God that is within me. I saw how miserably I had failed the high ideals of the gospel. But from Dostoevsky I learned the full extent of grace. Not only the kingdom of God is within me; Christ himself dwells there. "Where sin increased, grace increased all the more," is how Paul expressed it in Romans.

There is only one way for any of us to resolve the tension between the high ideals of the gospel and the grim reality of ourselves: to accept that we will never measure up, but that we do not have to. We are judged by the righteousness of the Christ who lives within, not our own. Tolstoy got it halfway right: anything that makes me feel comfort with God's moral standard, anything that makes me feel, "At last I have arrived," is a cruel deception. But Dostoevsky got the other half right: anything that makes me feel discomfort with God's forgiving love is also a cruel deception. "There is now no condemnation for those who are in Christ Jesus": that message, Leo Tolstoy never fully grasped.

Absolute ideals and absolute grace: after learning that dual message from Russian novelists, I returned to Jesus and found that it suffuses his teaching throughout the Gospels and especially in the Sermon on the Mount. In his response to the rich young ruler, in the parable of the Good Samaritan, in his comments about divorce, money, or any other moral issue, Jesus never lowered God's Ideal. "Be perfect, therefore, as your heavenly Father is perfect," he said. "Love the Lord your God with all your heart and with all your soul and with all your mind." Not Tolstoy, not Francis of Assisi, not Mother Teresa, not anyone has completely fulfilled those commands.

Yet the same Jesus tenderly offered absolute grace. Jesus forgave an adulteress, a thief on the cross, a disciple who had denied ever knowing him. He tapped that traitorous disciple, Peter, to found his church and for the next advance turned to a man named Saul, who had made his mark persecuting Christians. Grace is absolute, inflexible, all-encompassing. It extends even to the people who nailed Jesus to the cross: "Father, forgive them, for they do not know what they are doing" were among the last words Jesus spoke on earth.

For years I had felt so unworthy before the absolute ideals of the Sermon on the Mount that I had missed in it any notion of grace. Once I understood the dual message, however, I went back and found that the message of grace gusts through the entire speech. It begins with the Beatitudes—Blessed are the poor in spirit, those who mourn, the meek; blessed are the desperate—and it moves toward the Lord's Prayer: "Forgive us our debts ... deliver us from the evil one." Jesus began this great sermon with gentle words for those in need and continued on with a prayer that has formed a model for all twelve-step groups. "One day at a time," say the alcoholics in AA; "Give us this day our daily bread," say the Christians. Grace is for the desperate, the needy, the broken, those who cannot make it on their own. Grace is for all of us.

For years I had thought of the Sermon on the Mount as a blueprint for human behavior that no one could possibly follow. Reading it again, I found that Jesus gave these words not to cumber us, but to tell us what *God* is like. The character of God is the urtext of the Sermon on the Mount. Why should we love our enemies? Because our clement Father causes his sun to rise on the evil and the good. Why be perfect? Because God is perfect. Why store up treasures in heaven? Because the Father lives there and will lavishly reward us. Why live without fear and worry? Because the same God who clothes the lilies and the grass of the field has promised to take care of us. Why pray?

If an earthly father gives his son bread or fish, how much more will the Father in heaven give good gifts to those who ask him.

How could I have missed it? Jesus did not proclaim the Sermon on the Mount so that we would, Tolstoy-like, furrow our brows in despair over our failure to achieve perfection. He gave it to impart to us God's Ideal toward which we should never stop striving, but also to show that none of us will ever reach that Ideal. The Sermon on the Mount forces us to recognize the great distance between God and us, and any attempt to reduce that distance by somehow moderating its demands misses the point altogether.

The worst tragedy would be to turn the Sermon on the Mount into another form of legalism; it should rather put an end to all legalism. Legalism like the Pharisees' will always fail, not because it is too strict but because it is not strict enough. Thunderously, inarguably, the Sermon on the Mount proves that before God we all stand on level ground: murderers and temper-throwers, adulterers and lusters, thieves and coveters. We are all desperate, and that is in fact the only state appropriate to a human being who wants to know God. Having fallen from the absolute Ideal, we have nowhere to land but in the safety net of absolute grace.

8
Mission:
A Revolution of Grace

The quality of mercy is not strained.
It droppeth as the gentle rain from heaven ...
And earthly power doth then show likest God's
When mercy seasons justice.

Shakespeare, The Merchant of Venice

8

Mission:
A Revolution of Grace

As my class in Chicago read the Gospels and watched movies about Jesus' life, we noticed a striking pattern: the more unsavory the characters, the more at ease they seemed to feel around Jesus. People like these found Jesus appealing: a Samaritan social outcast, a military officer of the tyrant Herod, a quisling tax collector, a recent hostess to seven demons.

In contrast, Jesus got a chilly response from more respectable types. Pious Pharisees thought him uncouth and worldly, a rich young ruler walked away shaking his head, and even the open-minded Nicodemus sought a meeting under the cover of darkness.

I remarked to the class how strange this pattern seemed, since the Christian church now attracts respectable types who closely resemble the people most suspicious of Jesus on earth. What has happened to reverse the pattern of Jesus' day? Why don't sinners *like* being around us?

I recounted a story told me by a friend who works with the down-and-out in Chicago. A prostitute came to him in wretched straits, homeless, her health failing, unable to buy food for her two-year-old daughter. Her eyes awash with tears, she confessed that she had been renting out her daughter—two years old!—to men interested in kinky sex, in order to support her own drug habit. My friend could hardly bear hearing the sordid details of her story. He sat in silence, not knowing what to say. At last he asked if she had ever thought of going to a church for help. "I will never forget the look of pure astonishment that crossed her face," he later told me. "'Church!' she cried. 'Why would I ever go there? They'd just make me feel even worse than I already do!'"

Somehow we have created a community of respectability in the church, I told my class. The down-and-out, who flocked to Jesus when he lived on earth, no longer feel welcome. How did Jesus, the only perfect person in history, manage to attract the notoriously imperfect? And what keeps us from following in his steps today?

Someone in the class suggested that legalism in the church had created a barrier of strict rules that made non-Christians feel uncomfortable. The class discussion abruptly lurched in a new direction, as survivors of Christian colleges and fundamentalist churches began swapping war stories. I told of my own bemusement in the early seventies when the redoubtable Moody Bible Institute, located just four blocks down the street from our church, was banning all beards, mustaches, and hair below the ears of male students—though each day students filed past a large oil painting of Dwight L. Moody, hirsute breaker of all three rules.

Everyone laughed. Everyone except Greg, that is, who fidgeted in his seat and smoldered. I could see his face flush red, then blanch with anger. Finally Greg raised his hand, and rage and indignation spilled out. He was almost stammering. "I feel like walking out of this place," he said, and all of a sudden the room hushed. "You criticize others for being Pharisees. I'll tell you who the real Pharisees are. They're *you* [he pointed at me] and the rest of you people in this class. You think you're so high and mighty and mature. I became a Christian because of Moody Church. You find a group to look down on, to feel more spiritual than, and you talk about them behind their backs. That's what a Pharisee does. You're all Pharisees."

All eyes in the class turned to me for a reply, but I had none to offer. Greg had caught us red-handed. In a twist of spiritual arrogance, we were now looking down on other people for being Pharisees. I glanced at the clock, hoping for a reprieve. No such luck: It showed fifteen minutes of class time remaining. I waited for a flash of inspiration, but none came. The silence grew louder. I felt embarrassed and trapped.

Then Bob raised his hand. Bob was new to the class, and until the day I die I will always be grateful to him for rescuing me. He began softly, disarmingly, "I'm glad you didn't walk out, Greg. We need you here. I'm glad you're here, and I'd like to tell you why I come to this church.

"Frankly, I identify with the Chicago prostitute Philip mentioned. I was addicted to drugs, and in a million years it wouldn't have occurred to me to approach a church for help. Every Tuesday, though, this church lets an Alcoholics Anonymous chapter meet in the basement room we're sitting in right now. I started attending that group, and after a while I decided a church that welcomes an AA group— cigarette butts, coffee spills, and all—can't be too bad, so I made a point to visit a service.

"I've got to tell you, the people upstairs were threatening to me at first. They seemed like they had it all together while I was barely hanging on. People here dress pretty casually, I guess, but the best clothes I owned were blue jeans and T-shirts. I managed to swallow my pride, though, and started coming on Sunday mornings as well as Tuesday nights. People didn't shun me. They reached out to me. It's here that I met Jesus."

As if someone had opened an air lock, all tension discharged from the room during Bob's speech of simple eloquence. Greg relaxed, I mumbled an apology for my own Pharisaism, and the class ended on a note of unity. Bob had brought us back to common ground, as sinners equally desperate in our need of God.

What would it take, I asked in closing, for church to become a place where prostitutes, tax collectors, and even guilt-tinged Pharisees would gladly gather?

Jesus was the friend of sinners. They liked being around him and longed for his company. Meanwhile, legalists found him shocking, even revolting. What was Jesus' secret that we have lost?

"You can know a person by the company he keeps," the proverb goes. Imagine the consternation of people in first-century Palestine who tried to apply that principle to Jesus of Nazareth. The Gospels mention eight occasions when Jesus accepted an invitation to dinner. Three of these (the wedding at Cana, hospitality by Mary and Martha, and the interrupted meal in Emmaus after his resurrection) were normal social occasions among friends. The other five, however, defy all rules of social propriety.

Once, Jesus dined with Simon the Leper. Because of my work with Dr. Paul Brand, a leprosy specialist, I too have dined with leprosy patients, and I can tell you that two thousand years of medical progress have done little to lessen the social stigma of the disease. One refined, educated man in India told me of the day he sat weeping in a car outside a church as his daughter got married within. He dared not show his disfigured face, lest all the guests leave. Nor could he host the traditional wedding banquet, for who would enter the home of a leper?

In Palestine, stern laws enforced the stigma against leprosy: the afflicted had to live outside city walls and yell "Unclean!" when they approached anyone. Yet Jesus ignored those rules and reclined at the table of a man who wore that stigma as part of his name. To make matters worse, during the course of the meal a disreputable woman poured expensive perfume on Jesus' head. According to Mark, Judas Iscariot left the meal in disgust and went straight to the chief priests to betray Jesus.

In a different scene with some striking parallels, Jesus shared a meal with another man named Simon, and here too a woman anointed Jesus with perfume, wiping his feet with her hair and her tears. This Simon, though, being a proper Pharisee, recoiled at the indiscretion. Jesus gave a searing reply that helps explain why he preferred the company of "sinners and tax collectors" over outstanding citizens like Simon:

> Do you see this woman? I came into your house. You did not give me any water for my feet, but she wet my feet with her tears and wiped them with her hair. You did not give me a kiss, but this woman, from the time I entered, has not stopped kissing my feet. You did not put oil on my head, but she has poured perfume on my feet. Therefore, I tell you, her many sins have been forgiven—for she loved much. But he who has been forgiven little loves little.

At least one other time Jesus accepted hospitality from a prominent Pharisee. Like double agents, the religious leaders were following him around and inviting him to meals while scrutinizing his every move. Provocatively, despite it being the Sabbath, Jesus healed a man from dropsy, and then he drew a stinging contrast between the social-climbing banquets of the Pharisees and God's banquet spread for "the poor, the crippled, the blind and the lame." The Gospels record no other meals with prominent citizens, and I can easily understand why: Jesus hardly made for a soothing dinner guest.*

The last two meals we know about took place in the homes of "publicans," or tax collectors, a class of people unpopular in any age but especially so in Jesus' day. They collected taxes on a commission basis, pocketing whatever profits they could extort from the locals, and most Jews viewed them as traitors serving the Roman Empire. The word *publican* became synonymous with robber, brigand, murderer, and reprobate. Jewish courts considered a tax collector's evidence as invalid, and his money could not be accepted as alms for the poor or used in exchange since it had been acquired by such despicable means.

Pointedly, Jesus invited himself to the homes of both tax collectors. When he noticed the ostracized Zacchaeus, so short he had to climb a tree to see Jesus, he called the man down and asked to stay at his house. The crowd muttered disapproval, but Jesus shrugged off their complaints: "For the Son of Man came to seek and to save what was lost." Another such reprobate, Levi, Jesus met at a booth in the very act of collecting the hated taxes. "It is not the healthy who need a doctor, but the sick," he told the crowd that time.

Reading about Jesus' assorted dinner companions, I search for a clue that might explain why Jesus made one group (sinners) feel so comfortable and the other group (pious) feel so uncomfortable. I find such a clue in one more scene from the Gospels that brings together Pharisees and a blatant sinner simultaneously. The Pharisees have

---

*Pharisees thought of their dining table as a kind of "little temple," which explains why they refused to dine with Gentiles or sinners. Perhaps Jesus understood his dining table as a little temple as well, which explains why he ate with such a motley assortment of dining companions. The great banquet, he proclaimed, is now open to all, not merely those who have been through proper purification.

caught a woman in the very act of adultery, a crime that calls for the death penalty. What would Jesus have them do? they ask, hoping to trap him in a conflict between morality and mercy.

Jesus pauses, writes on the ground for a moment, then says to the accusers, "If any one of you is without sin, let him be the first to throw a stone at her." When all of them have filed away, Jesus turns to the cringing woman. "Where are they? Has no one condemned you?" he asks. "Then neither do I condemn you. Go now and leave your life of sin."

This tense scene reveals a clear principle in Jesus' life: he brings to the surface repressed sin, yet forgives any freely acknowledged sin. The adulteress went away forgiven, with a new lease on life; the Pharisees slunk away, stabbed to the heart.

Perhaps prostitutes, tax collectors, and other known sinners responded to Jesus so readily because at some level they knew they were wrong and to them God's forgiveness looked very appealing. As C. S. Lewis has said, "Prostitutes are in no danger of finding their present life so satisfactory that they cannot turn to God: the proud, the avaricious, the self-righteous, are in that danger."

Jesus' message met a mixed response among first-century Jews, many of whom preferred the style of John the Baptist, with his insect diet and his stern message of judgment and wrath, to Jesus' message of grace and a banquet spread for all. I can understand this odd preference for the law because of the legalistic environment I grew up in. Grace was slippery, evanescent, hard to get my mind around. Sin was concrete, visible, an easy target to pounce on. Under law, I always knew where I ranked.

Wendy Kaminer, a modern Jew trying to comprehend Christianity, confesses that "as an article of faith, this doctrine of salvation by grace and grace alone is remarkably unappealing to me. It takes, I think, remarkable disregard for justice to idealize a God who so values belief over action. I prefer the God who looks down upon us (in a very old joke) and says, 'I wish they'd stop worrying about whether or not I exist and start obeying my commandments.'"

In truth we Christians, too, may find it easier to follow a God who simply says, "Start obeying my commandments."

Jews in Jesus' day envisioned a ladder reaching higher and higher towards God, a hierarchy expressed in the very architecture of the temple. Gentiles and "half-breeds" like the Samaritans were permitted only in the outer Court of the Gentiles; a wall separated them from the next partition, which admitted Jewish women. Jewish men could proceed one stage further, but only priests could enter the sacred areas. Finally, only one priest, the high priest, could enter the Most Holy Place, and that just once a year on the day of Yom Kippur.

The society was, in effect, a religious caste system based on steps toward holiness, and the Pharisees' scrupulosity reinforced the system daily. All their rules on washing hands and avoiding defilement were an attempt to make themselves acceptable to God. Had not God set forth lists of desirable (spotless) and undesirable (flawed, unclean) animals for use in sacrifice? Had not God banned sinners, menstruating women, the physically deformed, and other "undesirables" from the temple? The Qumram community of the Essenes made a firm rule, "No madman, or lunatic, or simpleton, or fool, no blind man, or maimed, or lame, or deaf man, and no minor, shall enter into the Community."

In the midst of this religious caste system, Jesus appeared. To the Pharisees' dismay he had no qualms about socializing with children or sinners or even Samaritans. He touched, or was touched by, the "unclean": those with leprosy, the deformed, a hemorrhaging woman, the lunatic and possessed. Although Levitical laws prescribed a day of purification after touching a sick person, Jesus conducted mass healings in which he touched scores of sick people; he never concerned himself with the rules of defilement after contact with the sick or even the dead.

To take just one example of the revolutionary changes Jesus set in motion, consider Jesus' attitude toward women. In those days, at every synagogue service Jewish men prayed, "Blessed art thou, O Lord, who hast not made me a woman." Women sat in a separate section, were not counted in quorums, and were rarely taught the Torah. In social life, few women would talk to men outside of their families, and a woman was to touch no man but her spouse. Yet Jesus associated freely with women and taught some as his disciples. A Samaritan woman who had been through five husbands, Jesus tapped to lead a spiritual revival (notably, he began the conversation by asking *her* for help). A prostitute's anointing, he accepted with gratitude. Women traveled with his band of followers, no doubt stirring up much gossip. Women populated Jesus' parables and illustrations, and frequently he did miracles on their behalf. According to biblical scholar Walter Wink, Jesus violated the mores of his time in every single encounter with women recorded in the four Gospels. Truly, as Paul would later say, in Christ "There is neither Jew nor Greek, slave nor free, male nor female. ..."*

Indeed, for women and other oppressed people, Jesus turned upside down the accepted wisdom of the day. Pharisees believed that touching an unclean person polluted the one who touched. But when Jesus touched a person with leprosy, Jesus did not become soiled—the leprous became clean. When an immoral woman washed Jesus' feet, *she* went away forgiven and transformed. When he defied custom to enter a pagan's house, the pagan's servant was healed. In word and in deed Jesus was proclaiming a radically new gospel of grace: to get clean a person did not have to journey to Jerusalem, offer sacrifices, and undergo purification rituals. All a person had to do was follow Jesus. As Walter Wink puts it, "The contagion of holiness overcomes the contagion of uncleanness."

---

*Dorothy Sayers expands the point: "Perhaps it is no wonder that the women were first at the Cradle and last at the Cross. They had never known a man like this Man—there had never been such another. A prophet and teacher who never nagged at them, who never flattered or coaxed or patronized; who never made arch jokes about them, never treated them either as 'The women, God help us!' or 'The ladies, God bless them!'; who rebuked without querulousness and praised without condescension; who took their questions and arguments seriously, who never mapped out their sphere for them, never urged them to be feminine or jeered at them for being female; who had no ax to grind and no uneasy male dignity to defend; who took them as he found them and was completely unselfconscious.

"There is no act, no sermon, no parable in the whole Gospel that borrows its pungency from female perversity; nobody could possibly guess from the words of Jesus that there was anything 'funny' about woman's nature.

"But we might easily deduce it from His contemporaries, and from His prophets before Him, and from His Church to this day."

In short, Jesus moved the emphasis from God's holiness (exclusive) to God's mercy (inclusive). Instead of the message "No undesirables allowed," he proclaimed, "In God's kingdom there are no undesirables." By going out of his way to meet with Gentiles, eat with sinners, and touch the sick, he extended the realm of God's mercy. To Jewish leaders, Jesus' actions jeopardized the very existence of their religious caste system—no wonder the Gospels mention more than twenty occasions when they conspired against Jesus.

One of Jesus' stories, contrasting a pious Pharisee with a remorseful tax collector, captures the inclusive gospel of grace in a nutshell. The Pharisee, who fasted twice a week and tithed on schedule, piously thanked God that he was above robbers, evildoers, and adulterers—and far above the tax collector standing to the side. The tax collector, too humiliated even to raise his eyes to heaven, prayed the simplest prayer possible, "God, have mercy on me, a sinner." Jesus drew the conclusion, "I tell you that this man, rather than the other, went home justified before God."

Can we infer from Jesus' story that behavior does not matter, that there is no moral difference between a disciplined legalist and a robber, evildoer, and adulterer. Of course not. Behavior matters in many ways; it simply is not how to get accepted by God. The skeptic A. N. Wilson comments on Jesus' parable of the Pharisee and tax collector, "It is a shocking, morally anarchic story. All that matters in the story appears to be God's capacity to forgive." Precisely.

In his own social interactions, Jesus was putting into practice "the great reversal" heralded in the Beatitudes. Normally in this world we look up to the rich, the beautiful, the successful. Grace, however, introduces a world of new logic. Because God loves the poor, the suffering, the persecuted, so should we. Because God sees no undesirables, neither should we. By his own example, Jesus challenged us to look at the world through what Irenaeus would call "grace-healed eyes."

Jesus' parables underscored that mission, for often he made the poor and oppressed the heroes of his stories. One such story featured a poor man, Lazarus—the only named person in Jesus' parables—who was being exploited by a rich man. At first the rich man enjoyed sumptuous clothes and food while the beggar Lazarus, covered with scars, lay outside his gate with the dogs. Death, though, stunningly reversed their fortunes. The rich man heard from Abraham, "Son, remember that in your lifetime you received your good things, while Lazarus received bad things, but now he is comforted here and you are in agony."

That trenchant story sank deep into the consciousness of early Christians, many of whom belonged to lower economic classes. Rich and poor Christians struck a bargain: the rich agreed to fund charities in exchange for the poor praying for their souls. Surely God was more inclined toward the prayers of the poor, they reasoned. (Even today at funerals Benedictine monks pray that "Lazarus will know" their fallen colleague, following the tradition that Lazarus, not Peter, guards the entrance into heaven.)

For a while, the church worked hard to follow this new logic, and as a result, early Christians were renowned within the Roman Empire for their support of the poor and suffering. The Christians, unlike their pagan neighbors, readily ransomed their friends from barbarian captors, and when plague hit, the Christians tended their sufferers whereas the pagans abandoned the sick at the first symptoms. For the first few centuries, at least, the church took literally Christ's commands to receive strangers, clothe the naked, feed the hungry, and visit those in prison.*

As I read the stories of Jesus and study the history of the early church, I feel both inspired and troubled. The question I first raised with my class in Chicago returns to convict me. In view of Jesus' clear example, how is it that the church has now become a community of respectability, where the down-and-out no longer feel welcome?

I presently live in Colorado, where I attend a church in which most people come from the same race (white) and the same social class (middle). It startles me to open the New Testament and see in what mixed soil the early church took root. The middle-class church many

---

*According to church historians, this good work continued until the triumph of Constantine, who legalized the faith and established an official imperial church. From that point on the church tended to spiritualize poverty and leave "welfare" to the emperor. Over time the church itself became part of the wealthy establishment.

of us know today bears little resemblance to the diverse group of social rejects described in the Gospels and the book of Acts.

Projecting myself back into Jesus' time, I try to picture the scene. The poor, the sick, the tax collectors, sinners, and prostitutes crowd around Jesus, stirred by his message of healing and forgiveness. The rich and powerful stand on the sidelines, testing him, spying, trying to entrap him. I know these facts about Jesus' time, and yet, from the comfort of a middle-class church in a wealthy country like the U.S., I easily lose sight of the radical core of Jesus' message.

To help correct my vision, I have read sermons that come out of the Christian base communities in the Third World. The gospel through Third World eyes looks very different from the gospel as preached in many U.S. churches. The poor and the unlearned cannot always identify Jesus' mission statement (" . . . he has anointed me to preach good news to the poor . . . to proclaim freedom for the captives and release for the prisoners . . .") as a quotation from Isaiah, but they hear it as good news indeed. They understand the great reversal not as an abstraction but as God's promise of defiant hope and Jesus' challenge to his followers. Regardless of how the world treats them, the poor and the sick have assurance, because of Jesus, that God knows no undesirables.

It took the writings of a Japanese novelist named Shusaku Endo to impress on me that the phenomenon of reversal lay at the very heart of Jesus' mission.

In a country where the church comprises less than one percent of the population, Endo was raised by a devout Christian mother and baptized at the age of eleven. Growing up as a Christian in prewar Japan, he felt a constant sense of alienation and was sometimes bullied by classmates for his association with a "Western" religion. After World War II ended he traveled to France, hoping there to find spiritual soulmates. Again he faced persecution, this time on account of race, not religion. As one of the first Japanese exchange students in an

Allied country, Endo found himself the target of racial abuse. "Slanty-eyed gook," some called him.

Rejected in his homeland, rejected in his spiritual homeland, Endo underwent a grave crisis of faith. He began visiting Palestine to research the life of Jesus, and while there he made a transforming discovery: Jesus too knew rejection. More, Jesus' life was *defined* by rejection. His neighbors laughed at him, his family questioned his sanity, his closest friends betrayed him, and his countrymen traded his life for that of a terrorist. Throughout his ministry, Jesus gravitated toward the poor and the rejected ones, the riffraff.

This new insight into Jesus hit Endo with the force of revelation. From his faraway vantage point in Japan he had viewed Christianity as a triumphant, Constantinian faith. He had studied the Holy Roman Empire and the glittering Crusades, had admired photos of the grand cathedrals of Europe, had dreamed of living in a nation where one could be a Christian without disgrace. Now, as he studied the Bible, he saw that Christ himself had not avoided "dis-grace." Jesus was the Suffering Servant, as depicted by Isaiah: "despised and rejected by men, a man of sorrows, and familiar with suffering. Like one from whom men hide their faces. ..." Endo felt that surely this Jesus, if anyone, could understand the rejection he himself was going through.

As Shusaku Endo sees it, Jesus brought the message of mother-love to balance the father-love of the Old Testament.* Of course mercy appears in the Old Testament as well, but it easily gets lost amid the overwhelming emphasis on judgment and law. Addressing a culture raised on those strict demands of the Torah, Jesus told of a God who prefers the pleas of an ordinary sinner to the supplications of a religious professional. He likened God to a shepherd who leaves ninety-nine sheep inside the fence and hunts frantically for one stray; to a father who can't stop thinking about his rebellious ingrate of a son though he has another who's

---

*Therapist Erich Fromm says that a child from a balanced family receives two kinds of love. Mother-love tends to be unconditional, accepting the child no matter what, regardless of behavior. Father-love tends to be more provisional, bestowing approval as the child meets certain standards of behavior. Ideally, says Fromm, a child should receive and internalize both kinds of love. According to Endo, Japan, a nation of authoritarian fathers, has understood the father-love of God, but not the mother-love.

respectful and obedient; to a rich host who opens the doors of the banquet hall to a menagerie of bag ladies and bums.

Jesus was often "moved by compassion," and in New Testament times that very word was used maternally to express what a mother feels for her child in her womb. Jesus went out of his way to embrace the unloved and unworthy, the folks who matter not at all to the rest of society—they embarrass us, we wish they'd go away—to prove that even "nobodies" matter infinitely to God. One unclean woman, too shy and full of shame to approach Jesus face-to-face, grabbed his robe, hoping he would not notice. He did notice. She learned, like so many other "nobodies," that you cannot easily escape Jesus' gaze.

Jesus proved in person that God loves people not as a race or species, but as individuals. We *matter* to God. "By loving the unlovable," said Augustine, "You made me lovable."

At times, I do not find it easy to believe in the love of God. I do not live in poverty, like the Christians in the Third World. Nor have I known a life of rejection, like Shusaku Endo. But I have known my share of suffering, a fact of life that cuts across all racial and economic boundaries. Suffering people also need grace-healed eyes.

One terrible week two people called me on successive days to talk about one of my books. The first, a youth pastor in Colorado, had just learned his wife and baby daughter were dying of AIDS. "How can I possibly talk to my youth group about a loving God after what has happened to me?" he asked. The next day I heard from a blind man who, several months before, had invited a recovering drug addict into his home as an act of mercy. Recently he had discovered that the recovering addict was carrying on an affair with his wife, under his own roof. "Why is God punishing me for trying to serve him?" he asked. Just then he ran out of quarters, the phone went dead, and I never heard from the man again.

I have learned not even to attempt an answer to the "Why?" questions. Why did the youth pastor's wife happen to get the one tainted bottle of blood? Why do some good people get persecuted for their deeds while some evil people live to healthy old age? Why do so few of the millions of prayers for physical healing get answered? I do not know.

One question, however, no longer gnaws at me as it once did, a question that I believe lurks behind most of our issues with God: "Does God care?" I know of only one way to answer that question, and it has come through my study of the life of Jesus. In Jesus, God gave us a face, and I can read directly in that face how God feels about people like the youth pastor and the blind man who never gave me his name. By no means did Jesus eliminate all suffering—he healed only a few in one small patch of the globe—but he did signify an answer to the question of whether God cares.

Three times that we know of, suffering drove Jesus to tears. He wept when his friend Lazarus died. I remember one dreadful year when three of my friends died in quick succession. Grief, I found, is not something you get used to. My experience of the first two deaths did nothing to prepare me for the third. Grief hit like a freight train, flattening me. It left me gasping for breath, and I could do nothing but cry. Somehow, I find it comforting that Jesus felt something similar when his friend Lazarus died. That gives a startling clue into how God must have felt about my three friends, whom he also loved.

Another time, tears came to Jesus when he looked out over Jerusalem and realized the fate awaiting that fabled city. He let out a cry of what Shusaku Endo has called mother-love: "O Jerusalem, Jerusalem, you who kill the prophets and stone those sent to you, how often I have longed to gather your children together, as a hen gathers her chicks under her wings, but you were not willing." I sense in that spasm of emotional pain something akin to what a parent feels when a son or daughter goes astray, flaunting freedom, rejecting everything he or she was brought up to believe. Or the pain of a man or woman who has just learned a spouse has left—the pain of a jilted lover. It is a helpless, crushing pain of futility, and it staggers me to realize that the Son of God himself emitted a cry of helplessness in the face of human freedom. Not even God, with all his power, can force a human being to love.

Finally, Hebrews tells us, Jesus "offered up ... loud cries and tears to the one who could save him from death." But of course he was not saved from death. Is it too much to say that Jesus himself asked the question that haunts me, that haunts most of us at one time or another: Does God care? What else can be the meaning of his quotation from that dark psalm, "My God, my God, why have you forsaken me?"

Again, I find it strangely comforting that when Jesus faced pain he responded much as I do. He did not pray in the garden, "Oh, Lord, I am so grateful that you have chosen me to suffer on your behalf. I rejoice in the privilege!" No, he experienced sorrow, fear, abandonment, and something approaching even desperation. Still, he endured because he knew that at the center of the universe lived his Father, a God of love he could trust regardless of how things appeared at the time.

Jesus' response to suffering people and to "nobodies" provides a glimpse into the heart of God. God is not the unmoved Absolute, but rather the Loving One who draws near. God looks on me in all my weakness, I believe, as Jesus looked on the widow standing by her son's bier, and on Simon the Leper, and on another Simon, Peter, who cursed him yet even so was commissioned to found and lead his church, a community that need always find a place for rejects.

9

Miracles: Snapshots of the Supernatural

The genuine realist, if he is an unbeliever, will always find strength and ability to disbelieve in the miraculous, and if he is confronted with a miracle as an irrefutable fact he would rather disbelieve his own senses than admit the fact. Faith does not ... spring from the miracle, but the miracle from faith.

Fyodor Dostoevsky

9
Miracles: Snapshots of the Supernatural

The atmosphere I grew up in was humid with miracles. Most Sundays people in our church would testify about marvelous answers to prayer they had received the preceding week. God found parking places for mothers who drove their children to the doctor. Lost fountain pens mysteriously reappeared. Tumors shrank away the day before scheduled surgery.

In those days I envisioned Jesus as the Great Magician and, fittingly, the story of his walking on water especially impressed me. If only I could pull off such a stunt in my school, just once! How I would love to fly through the room like an angel, silencing with levitation all who scoffed at me and other religious types. How I would love to walk unscathed through the bullies at the bus stop, as Jesus had walked through an angry crowd in his hometown.

I never managed to fly through the classroom, though, and bullies continued to torment me no matter how hard I prayed. Even the "answers to prayer" confused me. Sometimes, after all, parking places did not open up and fountain pens stayed lost. Sometimes church people lost their jobs. Sometimes they died. A great shadow darkened my own life: my father had died of polio just after my first birthday, despite a round-the-clock prayer vigil involving hundreds of dedicated Christians. Where was God then?

I have spent much of my adult life coming to terms with questions first stirred up during my youth. Prayer, I have found, does not work like a vending machine: insert request, receive answer. Miracles are just that, *miracles*, not "ordinaries" common to daily experience. My view of Jesus too has changed. As I now reflect on his life, miracles play a less prominent role than what I had imagined as a child. Superman, he was not.

Yes, Jesus performed miracles—around three dozen, depending on how you count them—but the Gospels actually downplay them. Often Jesus asked those who had seen a miracle not to tell anyone else. Some miracles, such as the Transfiguration or the raising of a twelve-year-old dead girl, he let only his closest disciples watch, with strict orders to keep things quiet. Though he never denied someone who asked for physical healing, he always turned down requests for a demonstration to amaze the crowds and impress important people. Jesus recognized early on that the excitement generated by miracles did not readily convert into life-changing faith.

Some skeptics, of course, have no place for miracles, and for them any account of a supernatural event must by definition be discarded. The Smithsonian museum in Washington displays a leather-bound book in which Thomas Jefferson pasted all the passages from the Gospels that contain no miraculous element. This was the Bible he read every day toward the end of his life, a more palatable gospel of Jesus the teacher but not the miracle worker.

Thomas Jefferson's approach is a historical echo of what happened in Jesus' own day. Then too rationalists pondered Jesus' teaching and scrutinized his miracles. Sometimes they denied the plain evidence in front of them and sometimes they sought alternative explanations (magic, the Devil's power). Rarely did people find it easy to believe in miracles; they seemed as peculiar in the first century as they would seem if performed today. Then, as now, miracles aroused suspicion, contempt, and only occasionally faith.

Because I accept Jesus as God's Son, who came to earth "trailing clouds of glory," I accept the miracles he performed as a natural complement to his work. Even so, the miracles raise big questions for me. Why are there so few? Why any at all? Why these particular miracles and not others? I am a journalist, not a theologian, so in my search for clues I look at the miracles not in systematic categories but rather as individual scenes, impressionistic snapshots from the life of Jesus.

Jesus' first miracle was perhaps the strangest of all. He never repeated anything quite like it, and the miracle seemed to take Jesus by surprise as much as anyone else.

At the age of thirty or so Jesus showed up at a wedding with his newly formed band of disciples. His mother came too, probably accompanied by other members of the family. In the village life of Galilee, a wedding brought celebration into an otherwise drab existence. The bridegroom and his men made a gala procession through the streets to fetch the bride's party by torchlight, then everyone rushed to the groom's house for a feast worthy of royalty. Think of happy scenes from *Fiddler on the Roof*: of peasant Jewish families dancing across the courtyard in their finest embroidered clothes, of music and laughter, of banquet tables laden with clay platters of food and jugs of wine. The feast might go on for as long as a week, as long as the food and wine and good cheer held out. Truly a wedding was a time of high joy.

Jesus' disciples must have blinked in disbelief at the raucous scene, especially those who had come over to him from John the Baptist with his desert diet and animal-skin clothes. Did these ascetics now dance with the Jewish girls and gorge themselves on culinary delights? Did townsfolk quiz them about the Baptist, the closest thing to a prophet Israel had seen in four hundred years? John's gospel does not say. It only tells us that in a moment of social crisis the whole feast nearly ground to a halt. The wine ran out.

As emergencies go, this one falls well down the list. It caused embarrassment, to be sure, but need a Messiah who had come to heal the sick and liberate the captives concern himself with a social *faux pas*? "Dear woman, why do you involve me?" Jesus replied when his mother mentioned the problem. "My time has not yet come."

We can only guess what went through Jesus' mind during those next few seconds as he weighed Mary's request. If he acted, that would mean his time *had* come, and from that moment on life would change. If word of his powers leaked, he would soon hear pleas from needy people from Tyre to Jerusalem. Crowds would flock: epileptics, paralytics, deaf-mutes, the demon-possessed, not to mention any street beggar who wanted a free glass of wine. Investigators would be dispatched from the capital. A clock would start ticking that would not stop until Calvary.

Then Jesus, the same person who while fasting in the desert a scant time before had rebuffed Satan's challenge to turn stones into bread, reached a decision. For the first but surely not the last time in his public life, he changed his plans to accommodate someone else. "Fill the jars with water," he told the servants. Water went in and miraculously wine—the best wine, the choice wine usually served early on when palates are most discriminating and guests most impressionable—flowed out. The feast kicked into gear again, the host relaxed, the bridal party returned to serious celebrating.

John gives no indication that the guests or even the host knew about the little drama behind the scenes. Mary knew, of course, as did the servants. And Jesus' disciples knew: "He thus revealed his glory and his disciples put their faith in him."

What can we learn from this odd incident? The writers George MacDonald and C. S. Lewis see in it a reminder of God's common grace, focused in this instance in a narrow beam like solar rays through a magnifying glass. Jesus' miracles, they note, do not usually contradict natural law, but rather replicate the normal activity of creation at a different speed and on a smaller scale. "Some of the miracles do locally what God has already done universally," writes Lewis. "God creates the vine and teaches it to draw up water by its roots and, with the aid of the sun, to turn that water into a juice which will ferment and take on certain qualities. Thus every year, from Noah's time till ours, God turns water into wine." Similarly, antibodies and antigens conduct miracles of healing in our bodies every day, but in a slower, less sensational manner than the kinds of healings Jesus would go on to perform.

Yes, but what about the underlying meaning? What did this strange first miracle signify? In a departure from custom, John fails to interpret for us the miraculous "sign," which for him almost always means a symbol, a kind of acted parable. Some commentators see in it a preview of the Last Supper, when Jesus transforms not water into wine but wine into blood, his blood, shed for all humanity. Maybe.

I prefer a more whimsical interpretation. Tellingly, John notes that the wine came from huge (twenty- to thirty-gallon) jugs that stood full of water at the front of the house, vessels that were used by observant Jews to fulfill the rules on ceremonial washing. Even a wedding feast had to honor the burdensome rituals of cleansing. Jesus, perhaps with a twinkle in his eye, transformed those jugs, ponderous symbols of the old way, into wineskins, harbingers of the new. From purified water of the Pharisees came the choice new wine of a whole new era. The time for ritual cleansing had passed; the time for celebration had begun.

Prophets like John the Baptist preached judgment, and indeed many miracles of the Old Testament expressed that sense of stern judgment. Jesus' first miracle, though, was one of tender mercy. The lesson was not lost on the disciples who joined him at the wedding that night in Cana—especially the recent recruits from the Baptist.

The miracle of changing water into wine, a one-time event, occurred out of the spotlight in an obscure town whose location archaeologists cannot even agree on. Before long, though, Jesus was exercising miraculous powers in broad daylight before enthusiastic crowds. As is true today, the miracles of physical healing captured the most attention, and John 9 tells of one such miracle in Jerusalem, the capital city and heart of opposition to Jesus. John devotes an entire chapter to the story, sketching a classic portrayal of what happens when Jesus disturbs the accepted order.

The story starts where many sick people start, with the question of cause. *Why me? What is God trying to tell me?* In Jesus' day people assumed that tragedy hit people who deserved it.* "There is no death

_____

*I have noticed a remarkable change since Jesus' time in how people think about calamity. Nowadays we tend to blame God, both for the cataclysmic (which insurance companies call "acts of God") and for the trivial. At the 1994 Winter

without sin, and there is no suffering without iniquity," taught the Pharisees, who saw the hand of punishment in natural disasters, birth defects, and such long-term conditions as blindness and paralysis. Here is where "the man blind from birth" entered the picture. Steeped in good Jewish tradition, Jesus' disciples debated what could account for such a birth defect. Had the man somehow sinned *in utero*? Or was he suffering the consequences of his parents' sin—a prospect easier to imagine but patently unfair.

Jesus responded by overturning common notions about how God views sick and disabled people. He denied that the man's blindness came from any sin, just as he dismissed the common opinion that tragedies happen to those who deserve them (see Luke 13:1–5). Jesus wanted the sick to know they are especially loved, not cursed, by God. Every one of his miracles of healing, in fact, undercut the rabbinic tradition of "You deserved it."

The disciples were looking backward, to find out "Why?" Jesus redirected their attention forward, answering a different question: "To what end?" His answer: "Neither this man nor his parents sinned, but this happened so that the work of God might be displayed in his life."

What began as a tragic tale of one man's blindness ends as a surreal tale of everyone else's blindness. The man's neighbors make him prove his identity, the Pharisees subject him to formal interrogations, and his own parents (who had been callous enough to let him lead a life of begging, after all) waffle under all the pressure. As for the once-blind man, he has little time for such theoretical musings: "Whether he is a sinner or not, I don't know," he testifies about Jesus. "One thing I do know. I was blind but now I see!"

In Jerusalem, where Jesus had been censured as a heretic, a clear-cut miracle, especially one performed on the Sabbath, posed a grave threat to official doctrine. Although the Pharisees could not disprove

---

Olympics, when speed-skater Dan Janssen scraped the ice and lost the 500-meter race once again, his wife, Robin, cried out instinctively, "Why, God, again? God can't be that cruel!" A few months later a young woman wrote Dr. James Dobson this letter, "Four years ago, I was dating a man and became pregnant. I was devastated! I asked God, 'Why have You allowed this to happen to me?'" Exactly what role, I cannot help but wonder, did God play in an ice-skater losing control on a turn and a young couple losing control on a date?

the miracle—a blind beggar was now looking them in the eye and taunting them in open court—in the end they clung to their time-worn theories of punishment. "You were steeped in sin at birth; how dare you lecture us!" they snapped at the man. Theological blinders do not easily fall off.

The response to this miracle, as well as most of the others reported in the Gospels, bears out a striking principle of faith: Although faith may produce miracles, miracles do not necessarily produce faith.

You can view disease as a mechanical breakdown of bodily cells, or you can view it in a broader sense as a state of dis-ease involving body, mind, and soul. I learned this from the patients of Dr. Paul Brand, the leprosy specialist whose books I have coauthored. Except in very early stages, the leprosy patient does not feel physical pain. That, in fact, is the problem: after leprosy bacilli deaden nerve cells, patients no longer alert to danger proceed to damage their own bodies. A leprosy patient may walk all day on a sharp metal screw, or use a splintery hammer, or scratch an infected spot on the eyeball. Each of these acts destroys tissue and may eventually lead to loss of limb or vision, but at no point does the leprosy patient *hurt*.

Though they may not hurt, leprosy patients surely *suffer*, as much as any people I have ever known. Almost all the pain they feel comes from outside, the pain of rejection imposed on them by the surrounding community. Dr. Brand told me of one bright young man he was treating in India. In the course of the examination Brand laid his hand on the patient's shoulder and informed him through a translator of the treatment that lay ahead. To his surprise the man began to shake with muffled sobs. "Have I said something wrong?" Brand asked his translator. She quizzed the patient in a spurt of Tamil and reported, "No, doctor. He says he is crying because you put your hand around his shoulder. Until he came here no one had touched him for many years."

In modern Western countries, where leprosy is rare, a new disease has taken over much of its moral and social stigma. "AIDS is the modern-day leprosy," says former Surgeon General C. Everett Koop. "There are people who have the same attitude toward AIDS patients today that many people had toward leprosy patients one hundred years ago." I know of one AIDS patient who traveled eleven hundred miles to be with his family in Michigan for Thanksgiving dinner. He had not seen them in seven years. The parents welcomed him warily, and when dinner was served everyone got a heaping portion of turkey and all the trimmings on the best Wedgewood china plates—except for their son the AIDS patient, who was served on Chinette, with plastic utensils.

Jesus knew all about the social stigma that accompanies a disease like AIDS or leprosy. Levitical laws decreed that a person with leprosy live outside the town, keep a six-foot distance from everyone else, and wear the clothes of a mourner going to a burial service. I can easily imagine indignation rippling through the crowd when one such outcast walked through them, no doubt given a wide berth, and threw himself at the feet of Jesus. "Lord, if you are willing, you can make me clean," he said.

Matthew, Mark, and Luke give varying accounts of the scene, but all three include the same explosive sentence: "Jesus reached out his hand and touched the man." The crowd must have gasped—had not Moses' law forbidden such an act? The leprosy victim may have flinched. For how many months or years had he been deprived of the sensation of warm human flesh against his own? That one touch from Jesus brought his state of dis-ease to an end. Shalom was restored.

Jesus' response to dis-ease set a pattern for the church that formed around him, and Christians proceeded to follow his example of caring for the sick, the poor, and the outcast. In the case of leprosy, although the church sometimes added to the misery with its "curse of God" message, at the same time individuals rose up to lead the way in treatment. Religious orders dedicated themselves to the care of leprosy, and scientific breakthroughs on the disease tended to come from missionaries because they were the only ones willing to work with leprosy patients.* Similarly,

---

*A bizarre belief in the Middle Ages spurred the church's outreach to leprosy patients. Due to a mistranslation by Jerome, church leaders came to believe that Isaiah's description of the Suffering Servant as "afflicted," or "familiar with suffering"

Christians are now involved in ministries to AIDS patients and in hospice, a modern movement devoted to those who have little hope of physical healing but much need for love and care.

Mother Teresa, whose sisters in Calcutta run both a hospice and a clinic for leprosy patients, once said, "We have drugs for people with diseases like leprosy. But these drugs do not treat the main problem, the disease of being *unwanted*. That's what my sisters hope to provide." The sick and the poor, she said, suffer even more from rejection than material want. "An alcoholic in Australia told me that when he is walking along the street he hears the footsteps of everyone coming toward him or passing him becoming faster. Loneliness and the feeling of being unwanted is the most terrible poverty." One need not be a doctor or a miracle worker to meet that need.

A delightful story that directly follows the leprosy healing in the Gospels shows the difference friends can make for an afflicted person. A paralyzed man, who by necessity had to rely on others for food, bathing, and even help with sanitation, now needed assistance in acting on his faith.

I remember my destructive impulses being aroused the first time I heard the story in Sunday school. This paralytic wanted so desperately to meet Jesus that he talked four friends into digging up a roof and lowering him through the hole! The man who had spent his life horizontal would have one moment of vertical fame. Biblical commentators take pains to mention that the thatch and tile roofs of Palestine were much easier to disassemble and repair than the roofs that adorn our houses today. They miss the point: a hole in the roof is hardly the normal way to

---

meant he was actually stricken with leprosy. Thus in the twelfth and thirteenth centuries people jumped to the conclusion that Jesus must have had leprosy. This belief led to a complete reversal of how leprosy was regarded: no longer a curse of God, it was now a "Holy Disease." Crusaders who returned with leprosy were treated with great reverence, and "lazar houses" to treat the disease (named for Lazarus the beggar) sprang up everywhere, nearly two thousand in France alone. This historical movement stands as a novel example of the church following literally Jesus' command to treat "the least of these brothers of mine" as they would treat Christ himself.

enter a house. Moreover, no matter how flimsy the roof, ripping a hole in it will surely disrupt what goes on underneath. Dust flies, bits of straw and clay fall on the guests, noise and chaos interrupt the meeting.*

The crowd whose very presence had created the accessibility problem had two rude shocks. First was the messy way the paralytics' friends solved it. Then came Jesus' completely unexpected reaction. When Jesus saw *their* faith—plural, emphasizing the four friends' role in the healing—he said, "Take heart, son; your sins are forgiven." "Son, be of good cheer," the *King James Version* translates that first phrase. Literally, "Cheer up!"

Apparently, Jesus rather enjoyed the interruption. Outstanding faith never failed to impress him, and certainly the four-man demolition crew had demonstrated that. Yet his response baffled the observers. Who said anything about sins? And who was Jesus to forgive them? In typical fashion, the religious experts started arguing about Jesus' right to forgive sins, all the while ignoring the disabled man lying in the debris.

Jesus hushed the debate with enigmatic words that seem to sum up his general attitude toward physical healing: "Which is easier, to say to the paralytic, 'Your sins are forgiven,' or to say, 'Get up, take your mat and walk'?" Although he let the question hang there for the moment, his entire ministry provides an answer. Physical healing was far easier, without question. As if to prove the point, Jesus merely gave a word and the paralyzed man stood to his feet, rolled up his mat, and walked—or perhaps skipped—home.

Jesus never met a disease he could not cure, a birth defect he could not reverse, a demon he could not exorcise. But he did meet skeptics he could not convince and sinners he could not convert. Forgiveness of sins requires an act of will on the receiver's part, and some

---

*A priest named Donald Senior made an observation about this story that I had never before noticed, concerning the issue of accessibility for the disabled. Senior writes, "Any disabled person can supply lots of stories like this one—entering a church through the sacristy (or, worse, having to be carried up the front steps like a child), coming into a lecture hall by means of a freight elevator and then through the kitchen or utility room before being able to join the 'normal' people who come in the front door."

who heard Jesus' strongest words about grace and forgiveness turned away unrepentant.

"But that you may know that the Son of Man has authority on earth to forgive sins . . ." Jesus announced to the skeptics as he healed the man, a clear illustration of the "lower" serving the "higher." Jesus knew that spiritual dis-ease has a more devastating effect than any mere physical ailment. Every healed person ultimately dies—then what? He had not come primarily to heal the world's cells, but to heal its souls.

How easily do we who live in material bodies devalue the world of spirit. It occurs to me that although Jesus spent much time on issues such as hypocrisy, legalism, and pride, I know of no television ministries devoted to healing those "spiritual" problems; yet I know of many that center on physical ailments. Just as I begin feeling smug, however, I remember how easily I feel tormented by the slightest bout with physical suffering, and how seldom I feel tormented by sin.

When it comes to miracles, Jesus has a different set of priorities than most of his followers.

Only one miracle made it into all four Gospels. It transpired on the grassy hills by the shores of the Sea of Galilee at a time when Jesus' popularity—and also his vulnerability—was cresting. Wherever he went, a throng that included many deranged and afflicted trailed behind.

The day before the big miracle, Jesus crossed the lake to elude the masses. Herod had just executed John the Baptist, Jesus' relative, his forerunner and friend, and Jesus needed time alone to grieve. Doubtless, John's death provoked somber thoughts of the fate awaiting him.

Alas, there would be no secluded retreat. A huge swarm of yesterday's multitude made the ten-mile journey around the lake and soon hundreds, even thousands of people clamored around Jesus. "He had compassion on them," says Mark, "because they were like sheep without a shepherd." Instead of spending the day renewing his spirit, Jesus spent it healing the sick, always an energy drain, and speaking to a crowd large enough to fill a modern basketball arena.

The issue of food came up. *What to do? There are at least five thousand men, not to mention the women and children!* Send them away, suggested one disciple. Buy them dinner, said Jesus. *What? Is he kidding? We're talking eight months' wages!*

Then Jesus took command in a way none of them had seen before. Have the people sit down in groups of fifty, he said. It was like a political rally—festive, orderly, hierarchical—exactly what one might expect from a Messiah figure.

Unavoidably, we moderns read Jesus' life backwards, knowing how it turns out. That day, no one but Jesus had a clue. Murmurs rustled through the groups on the packed hillside. *Is he the one? Could it be?* In the wilderness, Satan had dangled before Jesus the prospects of a crowd-pleasing miracle. Now, not to please a crowd but merely to settle their stomachs, Jesus took two salted fish and five small loaves of bread and performed the miracle everyone was waiting for.

Three of the Gospels leave it at that. "They all ate and were satisfied, and the disciples picked up twelve basketfuls of broken pieces of bread and fish," reports Mark with masterful understatement. Only John tells what happened next. Jesus got his time alone, at last. As the disciples rowed back across the lake, fighting a storm all the way, Jesus spent the night on a mountain, alone in prayer. Later that night he rejoined them by walking across the water.

The next morning, in a near-comic chase scene, the crowd commandeered boats and sailed in hot pursuit, like a shoal of fish chasing a curiosity around the lake. After a day to savor one miracle, they were spoiling for more. Jesus detected the mob's true intent: to seize him by force and crown him king. *All the kingdoms of the world I will give you*, Satan had promised.

A conversation ensued between two parties who might as well have been speaking different languages. Jesus was unusually brusque, accusing the crowd of greedy motives, of desiring only food for their bellies. He made provocative statements, such as "I am the bread of life" and "I have come down from heaven." He said incomprehensible things like, " . . . unless you eat the flesh of the Son of Man and drink his blood, you have no life in you."

Like a Greek chorus, the audience gave a dramatic response to each of these tough words. They grumbled. They argued. Not easily would they give up their dream, however. An old Jewish tradition taught that the Messiah would renew Moses' practice of serving manna, and had not Jesus done that very thing the day before? With yesterday's miracle still digesting in their bellies, they asked for yet another miraculous sign. They were addicted.

In the end, Jesus "won" the argument. He was not their kind of Messiah after all: he would not provide bread and circuses on demand. The large, restless crowd filed away, and Jesus' own disciples began grumbling among themselves. "This is a hard teaching. Who can accept it?" they said. Many deserted him, a breakup of disciples mentioned only by John. "You do not want to leave too, do you?" Jesus sadly asked the Twelve.

The feeding of the five thousand illustrates why Jesus, with all the supernatural powers at his command, showed such ambivalence toward miracles. They attracted crowds and applause, yes, but rarely encouraged repentance and long-term faith. He was bringing a hard message of obedience and sacrifice, not a sideshow for gawkers and sensation-seekers.

From that day on, Jesus' teaching had a different twist. As if the back-to-back scenes of acclamation and rejection had clarified his future, he began to talk much more openly about his death. The odd figures of speech he had used against the crowd began to make more sense. The bread of life was not magic, like manna; it came down from heaven in order to be broken, and mixed with blood. He was talking about his own body. In the words of Robert Farrar Capon, "the Messiah was not going to save the world by miraculous, Band-Aid interventions: a storm calmed here, a crowd fed there, a mother-in-law cured back down the road. Rather, it was going to be saved by means of a deeper, darker, left-handed mystery, at the center of which lay his own death."

Jesus passed a kind of test that day on the grassy knoll by the lake. Satan had given him a preview in the desert, but that temptation was more theoretical. This was the real thing, a test of proffered kingship to which he had every right—and which he declined, in favor of a harder, humbler way.

"A wicked and adulterous generation asks for a miraculous sign!" Jesus would say when someone else asked for a display of his powers.

And in Jerusalem, the capital, though many people saw the miracles he did and believed in him, "he would not entrust himself to them," for he knew what was in their hearts.

A sign is not the same thing as proof; a sign is merely a marker for someone who is looking in the right direction.

The last great "sign" in John appears in the exact center of his book, chapter 11, and forms a narrative hinge for all that precedes and follows. John points to the miracle involving Lazarus as the event that turned the religious establishment fatally against Jesus. His account also offers a neat summary of what miracles did, and did not, accomplish in Jesus' time on earth.

The story of Lazarus has a unique "staged" quality about it. Usually when Jesus got word of a sick person he responded immediately, sometimes changing plans in order to accommodate the request. This time, after receiving word of the illness of one of his good friends, he lingered in another town for two more days. He did so intentionally, in full knowledge that the delay would result in Lazarus's death. John includes Jesus' cryptic explanation to his disciples, "Lazarus is dead, and for your sake I am glad I was not there, so that you may believe." Deliberately, he let Lazarus die and his family grieve.

In another context Luke contrasts the personality types of Lazarus's two sisters: Martha, the obsessive hostess who scurries about the kitchen, and Mary the contemplative, content to sit at the feet of Jesus. In a time of tragedy, the personality types held true. Martha rushed down the road to meet Jesus' party outside the village. "Lord," she chided him, "if you had been here, my brother would not have died." Some time later Mary caught up and, poignantly, said exactly the same words: "Lord, if you had been here, my brother would not have died."

The sisters' words carry the tone of accusation, the indictment of a God who did not answer prayer. No matter how hard we try, those of us who grieve cannot avoid words like "if only." *If only he had missed that flight. If only she had quit smoking. If only I had taken time to say "Good-bye."*

In this case, Mary and Martha had a clear target for their "if onlys": the Son of God himself, their friend, who could have prevented the death.

Lack of faith was not to blame. Martha assured Jesus that she believed in the afterlife, and, remarkably, she even proclaimed Jesus the Messiah, the Son of God. That childlike faith lay at the heart of the issue: Why had Jesus not honored it? Friends and relatives asked curtly, "Could not he who opened the eyes of the blind man have kept this man from dying?"

Martha was crying. Mary was crying. All the mourners were crying. Finally, Jesus himself, "deeply moved in spirit and troubled," broke into tears. John does not say why Jesus wept. Since he had already revealed his plans to raise Lazarus from the dead, he surely did not feel the same grief as the devastated mourners. Still, something got to him. As he approached the tomb, again he felt a spasm, "groaning in spirit" as some translations have it.

Death had never bothered Jesus before. Effortlessly he restored a son to the widow of Nain, stopping a funeral prosession in its tracks. He returned Jairus's daughter to life with an almost playful command, "My child, get up!"—like a parent announcing the end of nap time. With Lazarus's family, though, he seemed troubled, affected, distressed.

Jesus' prayer at the tombside gives a clue: "Father, I thank you that you have heard me. I knew that you always hear me, but I said this for the benefit of the people standing here, that they may believe that you sent me." Nowhere else had Jesus prayed with an over-the-shoulder audience in mind, like a Shakespearean actor who turns to the crowd to deliver an aside. At this moment Jesus seemed self-consciously aware of his dual identity, simultaneously the One who came down from heaven and the Son of Man born on earth.

The public prayer, the loud voice, the gestures—these have all the marks of a spiritual battle under way. Jesus was making a point, working out a "sign" in full public view, and here as nowhere else he acknowledged the in-between state of God's creation. Jesus knew, of course, that Lazarus was now whole and content, in every way better for having shuffled off this mortal coil. Martha and Mary knew as much too, theoretically. But unlike Jesus and unlike Lazarus, they had never heard the sounds of laughter from the other side of death. Belief in God's power and love was for the moment overwhelmed by grief. All they knew was loss, all they felt was pain.

That in-between state of loss and pain perhaps explains the source of Jesus' tears. Greek scholars say that the word translated "deeply moved" conveys more than distress; it implies anger, even rage. At that very moment Jesus himself hung between two worlds. Standing before a tomb stinking of death gave a portent of what lay before him in this damned—literally damned—world. That his own death would also end in resurrection did not reduce the fear or the pain. He was human: he had to pass through Golgotha to reach the other side.

Lazarus's story, seen in full cycle, gives not only a preview of Jesus' future but also a compressed view of the entire planet. All of us live out our days in the in-between time, the interval of chaos and confusion between Lazarus's death and reappearance. Although such a time may be temporary, and may pale into insignificance alongside the glorious future that awaits us, right now it is all we know, and that is enough to bring tears to our eyes—enough to bring tears to Jesus' eyes.

The resurrection of one man, Lazarus, would not solve the dilemma of planet earth. For that, it would take one man's death. John adds the startling, ironic detail that the miracle of Lazarus sealed Jesus' fate. "So from that day on they plotted to take his life." And from that day on, significantly, Jesus' signs and wonders ceased.

As I now read the accounts of selected miracles from Jesus' time, I find in them a very different message.

As a child, I saw the miracles as absolute proofs of Jesus' claims. In the Gospels, however, miracles never offered such certitude even to those who saw the wonders in person. "If they do not listen to Moses and the Prophets, they will not be convinced even if someone rises from the dead," Jesus said of skeptics. Probably Jesus had his own resurrection in mind, but the sequel to Lazarus's story proves the same point: bizarrely, the chief priests sought to cover up the miracle by killing off poor Lazarus again! With hard evidence of a spectacular miracle walking around free in the person of Lazarus, they balefully conspired to destroy that evidence. In no event did the miracles bowl people over and "steam-roller" them into belief. Otherwise, there would be no room for faith.

As a child, I saw the miracles as guarantees of personal safety. Did not Jesus promise, " ... not one [sparrow] will fall to the ground apart from the will of your Father"? Later, I learned that this promise appears in the midst of a series of dire warnings to the twelve disciples, in which Jesus predicts their arrest, persecution, and death. According to tradition, the eleven disciples who survived Judas all died martyrs' deaths. Jesus suffered, as did the apostle Paul and most early Christian leaders. Faith is not an insurance policy. Or, as Eddie Askew suggests, maybe it is: insurance does not prevent accidents, but rather gives a secure base from which to face their consequences.

As a child, I strove for ever more faith. Adults urged me to develop faith, and I had few clues as to how to proceed. Reading all the healing stories together, I now detect in the Gospels a kind of "ladder of faith." At the top of the ladder stand those people who impressed Jesus with bold, unshakable faith: a centurion, an impertinent blind beggar, a persistent Canaanite woman. These stories of gristly faith threaten me, because seldom do I have such faith. I am easily discouraged by the silence of God. When my prayers are not answered, I am tempted to give up and not ask again. For this reason, I look down the ladder to find people of lesser faith, and it heartens me to learn that Jesus seemed willing to work with whatever tiny glimmer of faith came to light. I cling to the tender accounts of how Jesus treated the disciples who forsook and then doubted him. The same Jesus who praised the bold faith of those high up the ladder also gently quickened the flagging faith of his disciples. And I take special comfort in the confession of the father of a demon-possessed boy who said to Jesus, "I do believe; help me overcome my unbelief!" Even that wavering man got his request granted.

As a child, I saw miracles everywhere. Now I see them rarely, and they seem ambiguous, susceptible to different interpretations. My childlike vision has doubtless grown cloudy with age, and I feel this as a loss. Yet surely the baffling selectivity of miracles was no easier to understand in Jesus' day than it is today. A man who could walk on water did it only once. What self-restraint! Yes, he brought Lazarus back from death and dried the tears of his sisters—but what about the many other sisters and wives and daughters and mothers who were grieving that day for their own loved ones? When Jesus himself discussed miracles directly, he stressed their *infrequency*.

As a child, I saw miracles as magic. Now, I see them as signs. When John the Baptist languished in prison, Jesus sent him reports of healings and resurrections to prove that he was "the one"; a short time later, though, John himself died at an executioner's hand. Jesus' message to John did nothing to alleviate his physical condition, and we do not know what effect it might have had on his faith. Regardless, the message did express the character of the kingdom Jesus had come to set in motion. It was a kingdom of liberation in which the blind would see, the lame would leap, the deaf would hear, the leprous would be cleansed, and the poor set free. For some (in three dozen miraculous instances that we know of), liberation occurred while Jesus walked the roads of Galilee and Judea. Others have realized liberation through the dedicated service of Jesus' followers. But others, John the Baptist among them, did not achieve such liberation on earth at all.

Why, then, any miracles? Did they make any difference? I readily concede that Jesus, with a few dozen healings and a handful of resurrections from the dead, did little to solve the problem of pain on this planet. That is not why he came. Nevertheless, it was in Jesus' nature to counteract the effects of the fallen world during his time on earth. As he strode through life Jesus used supernatural power to set right what was wrong. Every physical healing pointed back to a time in Eden when physical bodies did not go blind, get crippled, or bleed nonstop for twelve years—and also pointed forward to a time of re-creation to come. The miracles he did perform, breaking as they did the chains of sickness and death, give me a glimpse of what the world was meant to be and instill hope that one day God will right its wrongs. To put it mildly, God is no more satisfied with this earth than we are; Jesus' miracles offer a hint of what God intends to do about it.

Some see miracles as an implausible suspension of the laws of the physical universe. As signs, though, they serve just the opposite function. Death, decay, entropy, and destruction are the true suspensions of God's laws; miracles are the early glimpses of restoration. In the words of Jürgen Moltmann, "Jesus' healings are not supernatural miracles in a natural world. They are the only truly 'natural' things in a world that is unnatural, demonized and wounded."

10
Death:
The Final Week

Why did Providence hide its face "at the most critical moment" . . .
as though voluntarily submitting to the blind, dumb, pitiless laws
of nature?

Fyodor Dostoevsky

10
Death:
The Final Week

The church I grew up in skipped past the events of Holy Week in a rush to hear the cymbal sounds of Easter. We never held a service on Good Friday. We celebrated the Lord's Supper only once per quarter, an awkward ceremony in which solemn ushers monitored the progress of trays bearing thimble-cups and broken Saltine crackers.

Roman Catholics did not believe in the Resurrection, I was told, which explained why Catholic girls wore crosses "with the little man on them." Mass, I learned, they celebrated with burning candles in a kind of cultic ritual, a symptom of their fixation with death. We Protestants were different. We saved our best clothes, our rousing hymns, and our few sanctuary decorations for Easter.

When I began to study theology and church history I found that my church was wrong about the Catholics, who believed in Easter as strongly as we did and in fact wrote many of the creeds best expressing that belief. From the Gospels I also learned that, unlike my church, the biblical record slows down rather than speeds up when it gets to Holy Week. The Gospels, said one early Christian commentator, are chronicles of Jesus' final week with increasingly longer introductions.

Of the biographies I have read, few devote more than ten percent of their pages to the subject's death—including biographies of men like Martin Luther King Jr. and Mahatma Gandhi, who died violent and politically significant deaths. The Gospels, though, devote nearly a third of their length to the climactic last week of Jesus' life. Matthew, Mark, Luke, and John saw death as the central mystery of Jesus.

Only two of the Gospels mention the events of his birth, and all four offer only a few pages on his resurrection, but each chronicler gives a detailed account of the events leading to Jesus' death. Nothing remotely like it had happened before. Celestial beings had slipped in and out of our dimension prior to the Incarnation (remember Jacob's wrestler and Abraham's visitors), and a few humans had even waked from the dead. But when the Son of God died on planet earth—how could it be that a Messiah should face defeat, a God get crucified? Nature itself convulsed at the deed: the ground shook, rocks cracked open, the sky went black.

For several years, as Holy Week approaches, I have read all the gospel accounts together, sometimes back-to-back, sometimes interwoven in a "harmony of the Gospels" format. Each time I feel swept away by the sheer drama. The simple, unadorned rendering has a grinding power, and I can almost hear a bass drum beating dolefully in the background. No miracles break in, no supernatural rescue attempts. This is tragedy beyond Sophocles or Shakespeare.

The might of the world, the most sophisticated religious system of its time allied with the most powerful political empire, arrays itself against a solitary figure, the only perfect man who has ever lived. Though he is mocked by the powers and abandoned by his friends, yet the Gospels give the strong, ironic sense that he himself is overseeing the whole long process. He has resolutely set his face for Jerusalem, knowing the fate that awaits him. The cross has been his goal all along. Now, as death nears, he calls the shots.

One year I came to the gospel narratives just after reading the entire Old Testament. Working my way through the books of history, poetry, and prophecy, I had got to know a God of muscular power. Heads rolled, empires toppled, entire nations disappeared from the earth. Every year the Jews paused as a nation to remember God's great feat of deliverance from Egypt, an event replete with miracles. I felt aftershocks of the Exodus all through the psalms and prophets, cues to a beleaguered tribe that the God who had answered their prayers once might do so again.

With those accounts still ringing in my ears, I arrived at Matthew's scene-by-scene description of Jesus' final week. Once more Jews had gathered in Jerusalem to remember the Exodus and celebrate the Passover. Once more hope sprang eternal: *Messiah has come!* ran one rumor. And then, like an arrow shot into the heart of hope, came Jesus' betrayal, trial, and death.

How can we who know the outcome in advance ever recapture the dire end-of-the-world feeling that descended upon Jesus' followers? Over the centuries the story has grown familiar, and I cannot comprehend, much less re-create, the impact of that final week on those who lived through it. I will merely record what stands out to me as I review the Passion story one more time.

Triumphal Entry. All four Gospels mention this event, which at first glance seems the one departure from Jesus' aversion to acclaim. Crowds spread clothes and tree branches across the road to show their adoration. "Blessed is the king who comes in the name of the Lord!" they cried. Though Jesus usually recoiled from such displays of fanaticism, this time he let them yell. To indignant Pharisees he explained, "I tell you, if they keep quiet, the stones will cry out."

Was the prophet from Galilee now being vindicated in Jerusalem? "Look how the whole world has gone after him!" exclaimed the Pharisees in alarm. At that moment, with several hundred thousand pilgrims assembled in Jerusalem, it looked for all the world as if the King had arrived in force to claim his rightful throne.

I remember as a child riding home from Palm Sunday service, absentmindedly tearing apart the palm fronds, skimming ahead in the Sunday school quarterly to the next week's topic. It made no sense. With such a throng throwing themselves at his feet one week, how did Jesus get arrested and killed the next?

Now when I read the Gospels I see undercurrents that help explain the shift. On Palm Sunday a group from Bethany surrounded him, still exultant over the miracle of Lazarus. No doubt pilgrims from Galilee, who knew him well, comprised another large portion of the crowd. Matthew points out that further support came from the blind, the lame, and the children. Beyond that constituency, however, lurked danger. Religious authorities resented Jesus, and Roman legions brought in to control the festival crowds would heed the Sanhedrin's assessment of who might present a threat to order.

Jesus himself had mixed feelings during the clamorous parade. Luke reports that as he approached the city he began to weep. He knew how easily a mob could turn. Voices who shout "Hosanna!" one week can shriek "Crucify him!" the next.

The triumphal entry has about it an aura of ambivalence, and as I read all the accounts together, what stands out to me now is the slapstick nature of the affair. I imagine a Roman officer galloping up to check on the disturbance. He has attended processions in Rome, where they do it right. The conquering general sits in a chariot of gold, with stallions straining at the reins and wheel spikes flashing in the sunlight. Behind him, officers in polished armor display the banners captured from vanquished armies. At the rear comes a ragtag procession of slaves and prisoners in chains, living proof of what happens to those who defy Rome.

In Jesus' triumphal entry, the adoring crowd makes up the ragtag procession: the lame, the blind, the children, the peasants from Galilee and Bethany. When the officer looks for the object of their attention he spies a forlorn figure, *weeping*, riding on no stallion or chariot but on the back of a baby donkey, a borrowed coat draped across its backbone serving as his saddle.

Yes, there was a whiff of triumph on Palm Sunday, but not the kind of triumph that might impress Rome and not the kind that impressed crowds in Jerusalem for long either. What manner of king was this?

The Last Supper. Every time I read John's account I am startled by its "modern" tone. Here, as nowhere else, a writer of the Gospels provides a realistic, slow-motion portrayal. John quotes long stretches of dialogue and notes the emotional interplay between Jesus and his disciples. We have, in John 13–17, an intimate memoir of Jesus' most anguished night on earth.

There were many surprises in store for the disciples that evening as they moved through the Passover ritual, laden with symbolism. When Jesus read aloud the story of the Exodus, the disciples' minds may have understandably substituted "Rome" for "Egypt." What better plan than for God to duplicate that tour de force at such a moment, with all the pilgrims congregated in Jerusalem. Jesus' sweeping pronouncement excited their wildest dreams: "I confer on you a kingdom," he said magisterially, and "I have overcome the world."

As I read John's account, I keep coming back to a peculiar incident that interrupts the progress of the meal. "Jesus knew that the Father had put all things under his power," John begins with a flourish and then adds this incongruous completion: "so he got up from the meal, took off his outer clothing, and wrapped a towel around his waist." In the garb of a slave, he then bent over and washed the grime of Jerusalem from the disciples' feet.

What a strange way for the guest of honor to act during a final meal with his friends. What incomprehensible behavior from a ruler who would momentarily announce, "I confer on you a kingdom." In those days, foot washing was considered so degrading that a master could not require it of a Jewish slave. Peter blanched at the provocation.

The scene of the foot washing stands out to author M. Scott Peck as one of the most significant events of Jesus' life. "Until that moment the whole point of things had been for someone to get on top, and once he had gotten on top to stay on top or else attempt to get farther up. But here this man already on top—who was rabbi, teacher, master—suddenly got down on the bottom and began to wash the feet of his followers. In that one act Jesus symbolically overturned the whole social order. Hardly comprehending what was happening, even his own disciples were almost horrified by his behavior."

Jesus asked us his followers to do three things to remember him. He asked us to baptize others, just as he had been baptized by John. He asked to us remember the meal he shared that very evening with the disciples. Finally, he asked us to wash one another's feet. The church has always honored two of those commands, although with much dispute about what they mean and how best to fulfill them. But today we tend to associate the third, foot washing, with small denominations tucked away in the hills of Appalachia. Only a few denominations carry on the practice of foot washing; for the rest, the whole notion seems primitive, rural, unsophisticated. One can debate about whether Jesus intended his command only for the twelve disciples or for all of us to come, but there is no evidence that the Twelve followed instructions either.

Later that same evening a dispute arose among the disciples as to which of them was considered to be greatest. Pointedly, Jesus did not deny the human instinct of competition and ambition. He simply redirected it: "the greatest among you should be like the youngest, and the one who rules like the one who serves." That is when he proclaimed, "I confer on you a kingdom"—a kingdom, in other words, based on service and humility. In the foot washing, the disciples had seen a living tableau of what he meant. Following that example has not gotten any easier in two thousand years.

Betrayal. In the midst of this intimate evening with his closest friends, Jesus dropped a bombshell: One of the twelve men gathered around him would, that night, betray him to the authorities. The disciples "stared at one another, at a loss to know which of them he meant," and began to interrogate each other.

Jesus had hit a nerve. "Surely not I?" the disciples responded in turn, exposing their underlying doubts. Betrayal was no new thought. In conspiratorial Jerusalem, who knows how many disciples had been approached by Jesus' enemies, probing for access. The Last Supper itself was shrouded in danger, the upstairs room arranged clandestinely with a mystery man carrying a jar of water.

A few moments after Jesus' bombshell, Judas quietly left the room, arousing no suspicion. Naturally the group's treasurer may have to excuse himself to purchase supplies or perhaps run an errand of charity.

The name "Judas," once common, has all but disappeared. No parent wants to name a child after the most notorious traitor in history. And yet now, to my own surprise, as I read the gospel accounts it is Judas's *ordinariness*, not his villainy, that stands out. He, like other disciples, had been handpicked by Jesus after a long night of prayer. As treasurer, he obviously held the others' trust. Even at the Last Supper he sat in an honored place near Jesus. The Gospels contain no hint that Judas had been a "mole" infiltrating the inner circle to plan this perfidy.

How, then, could Judas betray the Son of God? Even as I ask the question I think of the remaining disciples fleeing from Jesus in Gethsemane and of Peter swearing, "I don't know the man!" when pressured in a courtyard and of the Eleven stubbornly refusing to believe reports of Jesus' resurrection. Judas's act of betrayal differed in degree, but not in kind, from many other disloyalties.

Curious as to how Hollywood would render the act of betrayal, I watched fifteen movie treatments of Judas. Theories abounded. According to some, he was money hungry. Others showed him as fearful, deciding to strike a deal as Jesus' enemies closed in. Some portrayed him as disillusioned—why did Jesus cleanse the sacred temple with a whip instead of raising an army against Rome? Perhaps he had grown annoyed at Jesus' "softness": like militants in modern Palestine or Northern Ireland, Judas had no patience for a slow, nonviolent revolution. Or, on the contrary, was he hoping to force Jesus' hand? If Judas arranged an arrest, surely that would prompt Jesus to declare himself and install his kingdom.

Hollywood prefers casting Judas as a complex, heroic rebel; the Bible states simply, "Satan entered into him" as he left the table to do the deed. In any event, Judas's disenchantment differed, again, only in degree from what other disciples had felt. When it became clear that Jesus' kind of kingdom led to a cross, not a throne, each one of them slunk away into the darkness.

Judas was not the first or the last person to betray Jesus, merely the most famous. Shusaku Endo, the Christian novelist in Japan, centered many of his novels on the theme of betrayal. *Silence*, his best known, tells of Japanese Christians who recanted their faith under persecution by the shoguns. Endo had read many thrilling stories about the Christian martyrs, but none about the Christian traitors. How could he? None had been written. Yet, to Endo, the most powerful message of Jesus was his unquenchable love even for—*especially for*—people who betrayed him. When Judas led a lynch mob into the garden, Jesus addressed him as "Friend." The other disciples deserted him but still he loved them. His nation had him executed; yet while stretched out naked in the posture of ultimate disgrace, Jesus roused himself for the cry, "Father, forgive them. . . ."

I know of no more poignant contrast between two human destinies than that of Peter and Judas. Both assumed leadership within the group of Jesus' disciples. Both saw and heard wondrous things. Both went through the same dithery cycle of hope, fear, and disillusionment. As the stakes increased, both denied their Master. There, the similarity breaks off. Judas, remorseful but apparently unrepentant, accepted the logical consequences of his deed, took his own life, and went down as the greatest traitor in history. He died unwilling to receive what Jesus had come to offer him. Peter, humiliated but still open to Jesus' message of grace and forgiveness, went on to lead a revival in Jerusalem and did not stop until he had reached Rome.

Gethsemane. From an upstairs room in Jerusalem, stuffy with the smells of lamb, bitter herbs, and sweaty bodies, Jesus and his band of eleven arose and headed for the cool, spacious olive groves in a garden called Gethsemane. Spring was in full bloom, the night air fragrant with blossoms. Reclining under the moon and stars in a peaceful setting outside the bustle of the city, the disciples quickly drifted asleep.

Jesus, however, felt no such peace. "He began to be sorrowful and troubled," says Matthew. He felt "deeply distressed," adds Mark. Both writers record his plaintive words to the disciples: "My soul is overwhelmed with sorrow to the point of death. Stay here and keep watch with me." Often Jesus had gone off by himself to pray, sometimes sending the disciples away in a boat so he could spend the night alone with the Father. This night, though, he needed their presence.

By instinct, we humans want someone by our side in the hospital the night before surgery, in the nursing home as death looms near, in any great moment of crisis. We need the reassuring touch of human presence—solitary confinement is the worst punishment our species has devised. I detect in the Gospels' account of Gethsemane a profound depth of loneliness that Jesus had never before encountered.

Perhaps if women had been included in the Last Supper, Jesus would not have spent those hours alone. Jesus' mother, presciently, had come to Jerusalem—her first mention in the Gospels since early in her son's ministry. The same women who would stand by the cross, and wrap his stiff body, and hurry to the tomb at daybreak surely would have sat with him in the garden, held his head, wiped away his tears. But only male friends accompanied Jesus. Drowsy with dinner and wine, they slept while Jesus endured the crucible, alone.

When the disciples failed him, Jesus did not try to conceal the hurt: "Could you not keep watch for one hour?" His words suggest something more ominous than loneliness. Is it possible that for the first time ever he did not want to be alone with the Father?

A great struggle was under way, and the Gospels describe Jesus' torment in a way quite unlike Jewish and Christian stories of martyrdom. "Take this cup from me," he pled. These were no pious, formal prayers: "being in anguish, he prayed more earnestly, and his sweat was like drops of blood falling to the ground." What was the struggle, exactly? Fear of pain and death? Of course. Jesus no more relished the prospects than you or I do. But there was more at work as well, a new experience for Jesus that can only be called God-forsakenness. At its core Gethsemane depicts, after all, the story of an unanswered prayer. The cup of suffering was not removed.

The world had rejected Jesus: proof came in the torchlight parade then snaking through the pathways of the garden. Soon the disciples would forsake him. During the prayers, the anguished prayers that met a stone wall of no response, it surely must have felt as if God, too, had turned away.

John Howard Yoder speculates on what might have happened if God had intervened to grant the request "Take this cup from me." Jesus was by no means powerless. If he had insisted on his will and not the

Father's, he could have called down twelve legions of angels (72,000) to fight a Holy War on his behalf. In Gethsemane, Jesus relived Satan's temptation in the desert. Either time he could have solved the problem of evil by force, with a quick stab of the accuser in the desert or a fierce battle in the garden. There would be no church history—no church, for that matter—as all human history would come to a halt and the present age would end. All this lay within Jesus' power if he merely said the word, skipped the personal sacrifice, and traded away the messy future of redemption. No kingdom would advance like a mustard seed; the kingdom would rather descend like a hailstorm.

Yet, as Yoder reminds us, the cross, the "cup" that now seemed so terrifying, was the very reason Jesus had come to earth. "Here at the cross is the man who loves his enemies, the man whose righteousness is greater than that of the Pharisees, who being rich became poor, who gives his robe to those who took his cloak, who prays for those who despitefully use him. The cross is not a detour or a hurdle on the way to the kingdom, nor is it even the way to the kingdom; it is the kingdom come."

After several hours of torturous prayer, Jesus came to a resolution. His will and the Father's converged. "Did not the Christ have to suffer these things?" is how he would later put it. He woke his slumberous friends one last time and marched boldly through the darkness toward the ones intent on killing him.

The Trials. These days television programs and best-selling novels make familiar the once-arcane world of legal procedure. For those who desire greater realism, a cable channel broadcasts live the grisliest murder trials and sexiest harassment cases. Time after time the American public has watched with fascination as lawyers craft clever defenses to get famous people off the hook when everyone watching knows the defendants are guilty as sin.

In a span of less than twenty-four hours, Jesus faced as many as six interrogations, some conducted by the Jews and some by the Romans. In the end an exasperated governor pronounced the harshest verdict permitted under Roman law. As I read the trial transcripts, Jesus' *defense-lessness* stands out. Not a single witness rose to his defense. No leader had the nerve to speak out against injustice. Not even Jesus tried to defend himself. Throughout, God the Father said not a word.

The trial sequence has a "pass-the-buck" quality. No one seems willing to accept full responsibility for executing Jesus, yet everyone wants him disposed of. Scholars have written thousands of words to determine precisely what share of the blame for Jesus' death belongs to Rome and what share to the Jews.* In fact, both parties participated in the decision. Focusing on all the irregularities in the trials risks missing the main point: Jesus posed a genuine threat to the establishment in Jerusalem.

As a charismatic leader with a large following, Jesus had long aroused the suspicion of Herod in Galilee and the Sanhedrin in Jerusalem. They misunderstood the nature of his kingdom, it is true, but shortly before his arrest Jesus had indeed used force to drive moneychangers out of the temple. To a puppet Sanhedrin government intent on keeping "peace at any cost" for their Roman masters, such an event raised alarm. In addition, a rumor had spread that Jesus claimed he could destroy the temple and rebuild it in three days. Jewish leaders had trouble getting witnesses to agree on the exact wording of Jesus' statement, but their alarm is understandable. Imagine the reaction today if an Arab ran through the streets of New York City shouting, "The World Trade Center will blow up, and I can rebuild it in three days."

---

*To hold the Jewish race as a whole responsible for Jesus' death is one of the great slanders of history. No one thinks of holding modern Italians responsible for what *their* forebears did nineteen centuries ago. Joseph Klausner writes, "The Jews, *as a nation*, were far less guilty of the death of Jesus than the Greeks, as a nation, were guilty of the death of Socrates; but who now would think of avenging the blood of Socrates the Greek upon his countrymen, the present Greek race? Yet these nineteen hundred years past, the world has gone on avenging the blood of Jesus the Jew upon his countrymen, the Jews, who have already paid the penalty, and still go on paying the penalty in rivers and torrents of blood." This despite the fact that Jesus said he had come to "the lost sheep of Israel," and despite the fact that almost all of the first Christians were Jews.

To the priests and the pious, these political threats paled before the reports of Jesus' religious claims. The Pharisees had often blanched at Jesus' boldness in unilaterally forgiving sins and in calling God his own Father. His seeming disregard for the Sabbath scandalized them; Moses' law made Sabbath-breaking a capital offense. Jesus represented a threat to the Law, the sacrificial system, the temple, kosher food regulations, and the many distinctions between clean and unclean.

Finally, at the trial, the high priest appealed to the solemn Oath of the Testimony—"I charge you under oath by the living God"—to ask a question that Jesus as the defendant was required by law to answer. "Tell us if you are the Christ [Messiah], the Son of God." At last Jesus broke his silence: "Yes, it is as you say."

The accused went on to speak in exalted terms of the Son of Man coming on the clouds of heaven. It was too much. To a faithful Jew, Jesus' words sounded blasphemous by any stretch of justice. "Why do we need any more witnesses?" said the high priest, tearing his clothes.

There was only one alternative to blasphemy and the death sentence it carried: that Jesus' words were true and he really was the Messiah. How could that be? Bound, surrounded by armed guards, the very picture of helplessness, Jesus looked to be the least Messiah-like figure in all of Israel.

Blasphemy meant little to the Romans, though, who preferred to stay aloof from local religious disputes. On the way to the Roman judges, the implications of the *Messiah* claim changed from blasphemy to sedition. The word did mean king, after all, and Rome had no tolerance for any agitator who professed such a title.

Before Herod, the same ruler who had hacked off the head of John the Baptist and had long wanted to examine Jesus in person, Jesus maintained a serene silence. Only Pilate could get any kind of confession out of him. "Are you the king of the Jews?" Pilate asked. Once again Jesus, hands tied behind his back, face puffy with sleeplessness, soldiers' palm prints impressed on his cheeks, replied simply, "Yes, it is as you say."

Many times before, Jesus had turned down the chance to declare himself. When healed people, disciples, and even demons recognized him as Messiah, he had hushed them up. In the days of popularity, when crowds chased him around the lake like fanatics pursuing a celebrity, he had fled. When these fans caught him, eager to coronate him on the spot, he preached a sermon so troublesome that all but a few turned away.

Only on this day, first before the religious establishment and then before the political, only when his claims would seem the height of absurdity, did he admit to who he was. "The Son of God," he told the religious powers, who had him in their grasp. "A king," he told a Roman governor, who must have laughed aloud. A pitiful specimen, he probably reminded Pilate of one of Rome's deranged who claimed to be Caesar.

Weak, rejected, doomed, utterly alone—only then did Jesus think it safe to reveal himself and accept the title "Christ." As Karl Barth comments, "He does not confess his Messiahship until the moment when the danger of founding a religion is finally past."

Such a notion was an offense, Paul would later say. A stumbling block—the kind of rock tossed aside as useless, a nuisance on the construction site. But such a rock can form, with God's kind of power, the cornerstone of a new kingdom.

Calvary. In a memoir of the years before World War II, Pierre Van Paassen tells of an act of humiliation by Nazi storm troopers who had seized an elderly Jewish rabbi and dragged him to headquarters. In the far end of the same room, two colleagues were beating another Jew to death, but the captors of the rabbi decided to have some fun with him. They stripped him naked and commanded that he preach the sermon he had prepared for the coming Sabbath in the synagogue. The rabbi asked if he could wear his yarmulke, and the Nazis, grinning, agreed. It added to the joke. The trembling rabbi proceeded to deliver in a raspy voice his sermon on what it means to walk humbly before God, all the while being poked and prodded by the hooting Nazis, and all the while hearing the last cries of his neighbor at the end of the room.

When I read the gospel accounts of the imprisonment, torture, and execution of Jesus, I think of that naked rabbi standing humiliated in a police station. Even after watching scores of movies on the subject, and reading the Gospels over and over, I still cannot fathom the indignity, the *shame* endured by God's Son on earth, stripped naked, flogged, spat on, struck in the face, garlanded with thorns.

Jewish leaders as well as Romans intended the mockery to parody the crime for which the victim had been condemned. *Messiah, huh? Great, let's hear a prophecy.* Wham. *Who hit you, huh?* Thunk. *C'mon, tell us, spit it out, Mr. Prophet. For a Messiah, you don't know much, do you?*

You say you're a king? Hey, Captain, get a load of this. We have us a regular king here, don't we. Well, then, let's all kneel down before hizzoner. What's this? A king without a crown? Oh, that will never do. Here, Mr. King, we'll fix you a crown, we will. Crunch. *How's that? A little crooked? I'll fix that. Hey, hold still! My, look how modest we are. Well, how about a robe then—something to cover that bloody mess on your back. What happened, did your majesty have a little tumble?*

It went like that all day long, from the bullying game of Blind Man's Bluff in the high priest's courtyard, to the professional thuggery of Pilate's and Herod's guards, to the catcalls of spectators turned out to jeer the criminals stumbling up the long road to Calvary, and finally to the cross itself where Jesus heard a stream of taunts from the ground below and even from the cross alongside. *You call yourself a Messiah? Well, then come down from that cross. How you gonna save us if you can't even save yourself?*

I have marveled at, and sometimes openly questioned, the self-restraint God has shown throughout history, allowing the Genghis Khans and the Hitlers and the Stalins to have their way. But nothing—nothing—compares to the self-restraint shown that dark Friday in Jerusalem. With every lash of the whip, every fibrous crunch of fist against flesh, Jesus must have mentally replayed the Temptation in the wilderness and in Gethsemane. Legions of angels awaited his command. One word, and the ordeal would end.

"The idea of the cross should never come near the bodies of Roman citizens," said Cicero; "it should never pass through their thoughts, eyes or ears." For the Romans, crucifixion was the cruelest form of capital punishment, reserved for murder, slave revolts, and other heinous crimes in the colonies. Roman citizens were beheaded, not crucified. Jews shared their revulsion—"anyone who is hung on a tree is under God's curse," said Deuteronomy—and preferred stoning when they had authority to carry out executions.

Evangelists, archaeologists, and medical experts have described the grim details of crucifixion so thoroughly that I see no need to iterate them here. Besides, if the "seven last words of Christ" are any indication, Jesus himself had other things on his mind than the pain. The closest to a physical complaint was his cry, "I thirst!" and even then he turned down the vinegar wine offered as an anesthetic. (The irony of one who had made gallons of wine for a wedding party, who had spoken of living water that would quench all thirst forever, dying with a swollen tongue and the sour smell of spilled vinegar on his beard.)

As always, Jesus was thinking about others. He forgave the men who had done the deed. He arranged care for his mother. He welcomed a shriven thief into paradise.

The Gospels record different snatches of conversation from Calvary, and only two agree on Jesus' very last words. Luke has him saying, "Father, into your hands I commit my spirit," a final act of trust before he died. John has the cryptic summation of his entire mission to earth, "It is finished." But Matthew and Mark have the most mysterious saying of all, the woeful quotation, "My God, my God, why have you forsaken me?"*

This time only, of all his prayers in the Gospels, Jesus used the formal, distant word "God" rather than "Abba" or "Father." He was quoting from a psalm, of course, but he was also expressing a grave sense of estrangement. Some inconceivable split had opened up in the Godhead. The Son felt abandoned by the Father.

"The 'hiddenness' of God perhaps presses most painfully on those who are in another way nearest to Him, and therefore God Himself, made man, will of all men be by God most forsaken," wrote C. S. Lewis. No doubt he is right. It matters little if I am rebuffed by the checkout girl at the supermarket or even by a neighbor two blocks down the street. But if my wife, with whom I've spent my entire adult life, suddenly cuts off all communication with me—that matters.

No theologian can adequately explain the nature of what took place within the Trinity on that day at Calvary. All we have is a cry of pain from a child who felt forsaken. Did it help that Jesus had antici-

---

*Commentators have observed that the record in Matthew and Mark is one of the strongest proofs that we have an authentic account of what took place on Calvary. For what reason would the founders of a new religion put such despairing words in the mouth of their dying hero—unless that's precisely what he said.

pated that his mission on earth would include such a death? Did it help Isaac to know his father Abraham was just following orders when he tied him to the altar? What if no angel had appeared and Abraham had plunged a knife into the heart of his son, his only son, whom he loved? What then? That is what happened on Calvary, and to the Son it felt like abandonment.

We are not told what God the Father cried out at that moment. We can only imagine. The Son became "a curse for us," said Paul in Galatians, and "God made him who had no sin to be sin for us," he wrote the Corinthians. We know how God feels about sin; the sense of abandonment likely cut both ways.

Dorothy Sayers writes, "He is the only God who has a date in history.... There is no more astonishing collocation of phrases than that which, in the Nicene Creed, sets these two statements flatly side by side: 'Very God of Very God ... He suffered under Pontius Pilate.' All over the world, thousands of times a day, Christians recite the name of a rather undistinguished Roman proconsul ... merely because that name fixes within a few years the date of the death of God."

Despite the shame and sadness of it all, somehow what took place on a hill called Calvary became arguably the most important fact of Jesus' life—for the writers of the Gospels and Epistles, for the church, and, as far as we can speculate on such matters, for God as well.

It took time for the church to come to terms with the ignominy of the cross. Church fathers forbade its depiction in art until the reign of the Roman emperor Constantine, who had seen a vision of the cross and who also banned it as a method of execution.* Thus not until the fourth century did the cross become a symbol of the faith. (As C. S.

*According to historian Michael Grant, Constantine had little interest in the person of Jesus himself and found the crucifixion an embarrassment. In a remarkable irony, seeing "the Cross not so much as an emblem of suffering but as a magic totem confirming his own victoriousness," Constantine transformed the cross from a symbol of sacrificial love and humiliation into a symbol of triumph: he had it painted on the shields of his soldiers.

Lewis points out, the crucifixion did not become common in art until all who had seen a real one died off.)

Now, though, the symbol is everywhere: artists beat gold into the shape of the Roman execution device, baseball players cross themselves before batting, and candy confectioners even make chocolate crosses for the faithful to eat during Holy Week. Strange as it may seem, Christianity has become a religion of the cross—the gallows, the electric chair, the gas chamber, in modern terms.

Normally we think of someone who dies a criminal's death as a failure. Yet the apostle Paul would later reflect about Jesus, "Having disarmed the powers and authorities, he made a public spectacle of them, triumphing over them by the cross." What could he mean?

On one level I think of individuals in our own time who disarm the powers. The racist sheriffs who locked Martin Luther King Jr. in jail cells, the Soviets who deported Solzhenitsyn, the Czechs who imprisoned Václav Havel, the Filipinos who murdered Benigno Aquino, the South African authorities who imprisoned Nelson Mandela—all these thought they were solving a problem, yet instead all ended up unmasking their own violence and injustice. Moral power can have a disarming effect.

When Jesus died, even a gruff Roman soldier was moved to exclaim, "Surely this man was the Son of God!" He saw the contrast all too clearly between his brutish colleagues and their victim, who forgave them in his dying gasp. The pale figure nailed to a crossbeam revealed the ruling powers of the world as false gods who broke their own lofty promises of piety and justice. Religion, not irreligion, accused Jesus; the law, not lawlessness, had him executed. By their rigged trials, their scourgings, their violent opposition to Jesus, the political and religious authorities of that day exposed themselves for what they were: upholders of the status quo, defenders of their own power only. Each assault on Jesus laid bare their illegitimacy.

Thieves crucified on either side of Jesus showed two possible responses. One mocked Jesus' powerlessness: *A Messiah who can't even save himself?* The other recognized a different kind of power. Taking the risk of faith, he asked Jesus to "remember me when you come into your kingdom." No one else, except in mockery, had addressed Jesus as a king. The dying thief saw more clearly than anyone else the nature of Jesus' kingdom.

In a sense, the paired thieves present the choice that all history has had to decide about the cross. Do we look at Jesus' powerlessness as an example of God's impotence or as proof of God's love? The Romans, bred on power deities like Jupiter, could recognize little godlikeness in a crumpled corpse hanging on a tree. Devout Jews, bred on stories of a power Jehovah, saw little to be admired in this god who died in weakness and in shame. As Justin Martyr's "Dialogue with the Jew Tryphon" shows, Jesus' death on a cross made a decisive case against his Messiahship for the Jews; crucifixion had fulfilled the curse of the law.

Even so, over time it was the cross on the hill that changed the moral landscape of the world. M. Scott Peck writes,

> I cannot be any more specific about the methodology of love than to quote these words of an old priest who spent many years in the battle: "There are dozens of ways to deal with evil and several ways to conquer it. All of them are facets of the truth that the only ultimate way to conquer evil is to let it be smothered within a willing, living human being. When it is absorbed there like blood in a sponge or a spear into one's heart, it loses its power and goes no further."
>
> The healing of evil—scientifically or otherwise—can be accomplished only by the love of individuals. A willing sacrifice is required ... I do not know how this occurs. But I know that it does ... Whenever this happens there is a slight shift in the balance of power in the world.

The balance of power shifted more than slightly that day on Calvary because of who it was that absorbed the evil. If Jesus of Nazareth had been one more innocent victim, like King, Mandela, Havel, and Solzhenitsyn, he would have made his mark in history and faded from the scene. No religion would have sprung up around him. What changed history was the disciples' dawning awareness (it took the Resurrection to convince them) that God himself had chosen the way of weakness. The cross redefines God as One who was willing to relinquish power for the sake of love. Jesus became, in Dorothy Sölle's phrase, "God's unilateral disarmament."

Power, no matter how well-intentioned, tends to cause suffering. Love, being vulnerable, absorbs it. In a point of convergence on a hill called Calvary, God renounced the one for the sake of the other.

11
Resurrection: A Morning Beyond Belief

I find that Holy Week is draining; no matter how many times I have
lived through his crucifixion, my anxiety about his resurrection
is undiminished—I am terrified that, this year, it won't happen; that,
that year, it didn't. Anyone can be sentimental about the Nativity;
any fool can feel like a Christian at Christmas. But Easter
is the main event; if you don't believe in the resurrection,
you're not a believer.

John Irving, A Prayer for Owen Meany

11
Resurrection: A Morning Beyond Belief

In early childhood I associated Easter with death, not resurrection, because of what happened one sunny Easter Sunday to the only cat I ever owned. Boots was a six-week-old kitten, solid black except for white "boots" on each of her legs, as if she had daintily stepped in a shallow dish of paint. She lived in a cardboard box on the screened porch and slept on a pillow stuffed with cedar shavings. My mother, insisting that Boots must learn to defend herself before sampling the huge outdoors, had fixed a firm date of Easter Sunday for the kitten's big test.

At last the day arrived. Georgia sunshine had already coaxed spring into full bloom. Boots sniffed her first blade of grass that day, batted at her first daffodil, and stalked her first butterfly, leaping high in the air and missing. She kept us joyously entertained until neighbor kids came over for an Easter egg hunt.

When our next-door playmates arrived, the unthinkable happened. Their pet Boston terrier Pugs, following them into our yard, spied Boots, let out a low growl, and charged. I screamed, and we all ran toward Boots. Already Pugs had the tiny kitten in its mouth, shaking it like a sock. We kids encircled the scene, shrieking and jumping up and down to scare Pugs off. Helpless, we watched a whirl of flashing teeth and flying tufts of fur. Finally Pugs dropped the limp kitten on the grass and trotted off.

I could not have articulated it at the time, but what I learned that Easter under the noonday sun was the ugly word *irreversible*. All afternoon I prayed for a miracle. *No! It can't be! Tell me it's not true!* Maybe Boots would come back—hadn't the Sunday school teacher told such a story about Jesus? Or maybe the whole morning could somehow be erased, rewound, and played over again minus that horrid scene. We could keep Boots on the screen porch forever, never allowing her outside. Or we could talk our neighbors into building a fence for Pugs. A thousand schemes ran through my mind over the next days until reality won out and I accepted at last that Boots was dead. Irreversibly dead.

From then on, Easter Sundays in my childhood were stained by the memory of that death in the grass. As the years increased, I would learn much more about the word irreversible.

Not so long ago, as I have mentioned, three of my friends died in quick succession. One, a retired man in excellent health, fell over dead in a parking lot after dining out with his wife. Another, a young woman of forty, died in flames on the way to a church missions conference when a tanker truck rear-ended her car in the fog. A third, my friend Bob, died scuba diving at the bottom of Lake Michigan. Life came to a halt three times that year. I spoke at all three funerals, and each time as I struggled with what to say the old, ugly word *irreversible* came flooding back, with greater force than I had ever known. Nothing I could say, nothing I could do would accomplish what I wanted above all else: to get my friends back.

On the day Bob made his last dive I was sitting, oblivious, in a café at the University of Chicago, reading *My Quest for Beauty* by Rollo May. In that book the famous therapist recalls scenes from his lifelong search for beauty, especially a visit to Mt. Athos, a peninsula of monasteries attached to Greece. There, he happened to stumble upon an all-night celebration of Greek Orthodox Easter. Incense hung in the air. The only light came from candles. At the climax of that service, the priest gave everyone three Easter eggs, splendidly decorated and wrapped in a veil. "Christos Anesti!" he said—"Christ is Risen!" Each person present, including Rollo May, replied according to custom, "He is risen indeed!"

Rollo May writes, "I was seized then by a moment of spiritual reality: what would it mean for our world if He had truly risen?" I read that passage just before returning home to learn that Bob had died, and Rollo May's question kept floating around in my mind, hauntingly, after I heard the terrible news. What did it mean for our world that Christ had risen?

In the cloud of grief over Bob's death, I began to see the meaning of Easter in a new light. As a five-year-old on Easter Sunday I had learned the harsh lesson of irreversibility. Now, as an adult, I saw that Easter actually held out the awesome promise of reversibility. Nothing—no, not even death—was final. Even that could be reversed.

When I spoke at Bob's funeral, I rephrased Rollo May's question in the terms of our particular grief. What would it mean for us if Bob rose again? We were sitting in a chapel, numbed by three days of sorrow, death bearing down upon us like a crushing weight. How would it be to walk outside to the parking lot and there, to our utter astonishment, find Bob. *Bob!* With his bounding walk, his crooked grin, his clear gray eyes. It could be no one else but Bob, alive again!

That image gave me a hint of what Jesus' disciples felt on the first Easter. They too had grieved for three days. On Sunday they heard a new, euphonious sound, clear as a bell struck in mountain air. Easter hits a new note of hope and faith that what God did once in a graveyard in Jerusalem, he can and will repeat on grand scale. For Bob. For us. For the world. Against all odds, the irreversible will be reversed.

The first Christians staked everything on the Resurrection, so much so that the apostle Paul told the Corinthians, "And if Christ has not been raised, our preaching is useless and so is your faith." Did it really happen, this event apart from which our faith is useless? How can we be sure?

People who discount the resurrection of Jesus tend to portray the disciples in one of two ways: either as gullible rubes with a weakness for ghost stories, or as shrewd conspirators who conceived a resurrection plot as a way to jump-start their new religion. The Bible paints a distinctly different picture.

As for the first theory, the Gospels portray Jesus' followers themselves as the ones most leery of rumors about a risen Jesus. One disciple especially, "doubting Thomas," has gained the reputation as a skeptic, but in truth all the disciples showed a lack of faith. None of them believed the wild report the women brought back from the empty tomb; "nonsense" they called it. Even after Jesus appeared to them in person, says Matthew, "some doubted." The eleven, whom Jesus had to rebuke for a stubborn refusal to believe, can hardly be called gullible.

The alternative, a conspiracy theory, falls apart on close examination for, if the disciples had set out to concoct a seamless cover-up story, they failed miserably. Chuck Colson, who participated in a feckless conspiracy after the Watergate break-in, says that cover-ups only work if all participants maintain a unified front of assurance and competence. That, the disciples surely did not do.

The Gospels show the disciples cringing in locked rooms, terrified that the same thing that happened to Jesus might happen to them. Too afraid even to attend Jesus' burial, they left it to a couple of women to care for his body. (Ironically, for Jesus had fought Sabbath restrictions against works of mercy, the dutiful women waited until Sunday morning to finish the embalming process.) The disciples seemed utterly incapable of faking a resurrection or risking their lives by stealing a body; nor did it occur to them in their state of despair.

According to all four Gospels, women were the first witnesses of the resurrection, a fact that no conspirator in the first century would have invented. Jewish courts did not even accept the testimony of female witnesses. A deliberate cover-up would have put Peter or John or, better yet, Nicodemus in the spotlight, not built its case around reports from women. Since the Gospels were written several decades after the events, the authors had plenty of time to straighten out such an anomaly—unless, of course, they were not concocting a legend but recording the plain facts.

A conspiracy also would have tidied up the first witnesses' stories. Were there two white-clad figures or just one? Why did Mary Magdalene mistake Jesus for a gardener? Was she alone or with

Salome and another Mary? Accounts of the discovery of the empty tomb sound breathless and fragmentary. The women were "afraid yet filled with joy," says Matthew; "trembling and bewildered," says Mark. Jesus makes no dramatic, well-orchestrated entrance to quell all doubts; the early reports seem wispy, mysterious, confused. Surely conspirators could have done a neater job of depicting what they would later claim to be the hinge event of history.

In short, the Gospels do not present the resurrection of Jesus in the manner of apologetics, with arguments arranged to prove each main point, but rather as a shocking intrusion that no one was expecting, least of all Jesus' timorous disciples. The first witnesses reacted as any of us would react—as I would react if I answered the doorbell and suddenly saw my friend Bob standing on my front porch: with fear and great joy. Fear is the reflexive human response to an encounter with the supernatural. The fear, though, was overpowered by joy because the news they heard was news too good to be true yet news so good it had to be true. Jesus was alive! Dreams of a Messiah came surging back as the women ran, on legs of fear and joy, to tell the disciples the news.

There actually was a conspiracy, of course, one set in motion not by Jesus' disciples but by the authorities who had to deal with the embarrassing fact of the empty tomb. They could have put a stop to all the wild rumors about a resurrection merely by pointing to a sealed tomb or producing a body. But the seal was broken and the body missing, hence the need for an official plot. Even as the women ran to report their discovery, soldiers were rehearsing an alibi, their role in the scheme of damage-control.

Soldiers standing guard outside Jesus' tomb were the only eyewitnesses of the greatest miracle in history. Matthew says that when the earth quaked and an angel appeared, bright as lightning, they shook and became like dead men.* But here is an astounding fact: later

---

*The Resurrection actually constituted an act of civil disobedience, since it involved breaking Pilate's seal and striking down the official guards. In this case, triumphing over the powers meant active resistance.

The apocryphal Gospel of Peter gives a fanciful version of what took place at the tomb. Two figures descended in a cloud of light, so luminous that many eyewitnesses gathered round to watch. The stone rolled away all by itself, and the two that afternoon the soldiers who had seen proof of the resurrection with their own eyes changed their story to a lie, parroting the priests' line that "His disciples came during the night and stole him away while we were asleep." The alibi had obvious weaknesses (a huge stone rolled away without disturbing sleep? And how could they identify the disciples if asleep?), but at least it kept the guards out of trouble.

Like everything else in Jesus' life, the resurrection drew forth contrasting responses. Those who believed were transformed; infused with hope and courage, they went out to change the world. Those who did not believe found ways to ignore strong evidence. Jesus had predicted as much: "If they do not listen to Moses and the Prophets, they will not be convinced even if someone rises from the dead."

We who read the Gospels from the other side of Easter, who have the day printed on our calendars, forget how *hard* it was for the disciples to believe. In itself the empty tomb did not convince them: that fact only demonstrated "He is not here," not "He is risen." Convincing these skeptics would require intimate, personal encounters with the one who had been their Master for three years, and over the next six weeks Jesus provided exactly that.

Author Frederick Buechner is struck by the unglamorous quality of Jesus' appearances after resurrection Sunday. There were no angels in the sky singing choruses, no kings from afar bearing gifts. Jesus showed up in the most ordinary circumstances: a private dinner, two men walking along a road, a woman weeping in a garden, some fishermen working a lake.

I see in the appearances a whimsical quality, as if Jesus is enjoying the bird-like freedom of his resurrection body. Luke, for example, gives a touching account of Jesus' sudden arrival alongside two forlorn followers on a road to Emmaus. They know about the women's

glowing figures emerged from the tomb supporting a third figure, followed by a magical cross. The heads of the two "reached into heaven . . . but of him that was led by them . . . it overpassed the heavens." It is this kind of sensationalism that the authentic Gospels conspicuously avoid.

discovery of the empty tomb, and Peter's eyewitness confirmation. But who can believe such rumors? Is not death by definition irreversible? "We had hoped that he was the one who was going to redeem Israel," one of them says with obvious disappointment.

A short time later, at mealtime, the stranger makes a riveting gesture, breaking bread, and a link snaps into pace. It is Jesus who has been walking beside them and now sits at their table! Most strangely, the instant they recognize their guest, he disappears.

When the two rush back to Jerusalem, they find the Eleven meeting behind locked doors. They spill out their incredible story, which corroborates what Peter has already learned: Jesus is out there somewhere, alive. Without warning, even as the doubters argue the point, Jesus himself shows up in their midst. *I am no ghost*, he declares. *Touch my scars. It is I myself!* Even then the doubts persist, until Jesus volunteers to eat a piece of broiled fish. Ghosts don't eat fish; a mirage cannot cause food to disappear.

Life continues in that vein for nearly six weeks: Jesus is there, then he's gone. The appearances are not spectral, but flesh-and-blood encounters. Jesus can always prove his identity—no other living person bears the scars of crucifixion—yet often the disciples fail to recognize him right away. Painstakingly, he condescends to meet the level of their skepticism. For suspicious Thomas, it means a personal invitation to finger the scars. For the humiliated Peter, it means a bittersweet scene of rehabilitation in front of six friends.

The appearances, approximately a dozen, show a definite pattern: Jesus visited small groups of people in a remote area or closeted indoors. Although these private rendezvous bolstered the faith of those who already believed in Jesus, as far as we know not a single unbeliever saw Jesus after his death.

Reading the accounts of execution and resurrection back-to-back, I have sometimes wondered why Jesus did not make even more appearances. Why limit visitations to his friends? Why not reappear on Pilate's porch or before the Sanhedrin, this time with a withering blast against those who had condemned him? Perhaps a clue to strategy can be found in his words to Thomas, on the day Thomas's skepticism melted away forever. "Because you have seen me, you have believed; blessed are those who have not seen and yet have believed."

In the six-week interlude between Resurrection and Ascension, Jesus, if one may use such language, "broke his own rules" about faith. He made his identity so obvious that no disciple could ever deny him again (and none did). In a word, Jesus overwhelmed the witnesses' faith: anyone who saw the resurrected Jesus lost the freedom of choice to believe or disbelieve. Jesus was now irrefutable. Even Jesus' brother James, always a holdout, capitulated after one of the appearances— enough so that he became a leader of the church in Jerusalem and, according to Josephus, died as one of the early Christian martyrs.

"Because you have seen me, you have believed," said Jesus. These privileged few could hardly disbelieve. But what about the others? Very soon, as Jesus well knew, his personal appearances would come to a halt, leaving only "those who have not seen." The church would stand or fall based on how persuasive these eyewitnesses would be for all—including us today—who have not seen. Jesus had six weeks in which to establish his identity for all time.

That Jesus succeeded in changing a snuffling band of unreliable followers into fearless evangelists, that eleven men who had deserted him at death now went to martyrs' graves avowing their faith in a resurrected Christ, that these few witnesses managed to set loose a force that would overcome violent opposition first in Jerusalem and then in Rome—this remarkable sequence of transformation offers the most convincing evidence for the Resurrection. What else explains the whiplash change in men known for their cowardice and instability?

Others—at least fifteen Jews within a hundred years of Jesus—had made Messiah claims, only to flare and then fade like a dying star. Fanatic loyalty to Jesus, though, did not end with his death. Something had happened, something beyond all precedent. Surely the disciples would not lay down their lives for the sake of a cobbled-together conspiracy theory. Surely it would have been easier, and more natural, to honor a dead Jesus as one of the martyr-prophets whose tombs were so venerated by the Jews.

One need only read the Gospels' descriptions of disciples huddling behind locked doors and then proceed to the descriptions in Acts of the same men proclaiming Christ openly in the streets and in jail cells to perceive the seismic significance of what took place on Easter Sunday. The Resurrection is the epicenter of belief. It is, says C. H. Dodd, "not a belief that grew up within the church; it is the belief around which the church itself grew up, and the 'given' upon which its faith was based." Novelist John Updike states the same truth more poetically:

> Make no mistake: if He rose at all
> it was as His body;
> if the cells' dissolution did not reverse, the molecules
> reknit, the amino acids rekindle,
> the Church will fall.

"Blessed are those who have not seen and yet have believed," Jesus said to doubting Thomas after silencing his doubts with tangible proof of the Easter miracle. Except for the five hundred or so people to whom the resurrected Jesus appeared, every Christian who has ever lived falls into the category of "blessed." I ask myself, *Why do I believe?*—I, who resemble Thomas more than any other disciple in my skepticism and slowness to accept what cannot be proved beyond doubt.

I have weighed the arguments in favor of the resurrection, and they are indeed impressive. The English journalist Frank Morison dealt with most of these arguments in the classic *Who Moved the Stone?* Although Morison had set out to discount the resurrection as a myth, the evidence convinced him otherwise. Yet I also know that many intelligent people have looked at the same evidence and found it impossible to believe. Although much about the Resurrection invites belief, nothing compels it. Faith requires the possibility of rejection, or it is not faith. What, then, gives me Easter faith?

One reason I am open to belief, I admit, is that at a very deep level I want the Easter story to be true. Faith grows out of a subsoil of yearning, and something primal in human beings cries out against the reign of death. Whether hope takes the form of Egyptian pharaohs stashing their jewels and chariots in pyramids, or the modern American obsession with keeping bodies alive until the last possible nanosecond and then preserving them with embalming fluids in double-sealed caskets, we humans resist the idea of death having a final say. We want to believe otherwise.

I remember the year I lost my three friends. Above all else, I want Easter to be true because of its promise that someday I will get my friends back. I want to abolish that word *irreversible* forever.

I suppose you could say I want to believe in fairy tales. I am not alone. Has any age not produced fairy tales? We first hear them in our cribs from parents and grandparents, and repeat them to our children who will tell them to their children, and on it goes. Even in this scientific age, some of the highest-grossing movies are variations of fairy tales: *Star Wars*, *Aladdin*, *The Lion King*. Astonishingly in light of human history, most fairy tales have a happy ending. That old instinct, hope, billows up. Like life, fairy tales include much struggle and pain, yet even so they manage to resolve in a way that replaces tears with smiles. Easter does that too, and for this as well as many other reasons, it rings true.*

The crowd at Jesus' crucifixion challenged him to prove himself by climbing down from the cross, but not one person thought of what actually would happen: that he would die and then come back. Once the scenario played out, though, to those who knew Jesus best it made perfect sense. The style fit God's pattern and character. God has always chosen the slow and difficult way, respecting human freedom regardless of cost. "God did not abolish the fact of evil: He transformed it," wrote Dorothy Sayers. "He did not stop the crucifixion: He rose from the dead." The hero bore all consequences, yet somehow triumphed.

I believe in the Resurrection primarily because I have gotten to know God. I know that God is love, and I also know that we human beings want to keep alive those whom we love. I do not let my friends die; they live on in my memory and my heart long after I have stopped seeing them. For whatever reason—human freedom lies at the core, I

---

*J. R. R. Tolkien, perhaps this century's greatest creator of fairy tales, often faced the charge that fantasy is an "escapist" way of shifting attention away from the pressures of the "real world." His reply was simple: Everything depends on that from which one is escaping. We view the flight of a deserter and the escape of a prisoner very differently. "Why should a man be scorned if, finding himself in prison, he tries to get out and go home?"

imagine—God allows a planet where a man dies scuba diving in the prime of life and a woman dies in a fiery crash on the way to a church missions conference. But I believe—if I did not believe this, I would not believe in a loving God—that God is not satisfied with such a blighted planet. Divine love will find a way to overcome. "Death, be not proud," wrote John Donne: God will not let death win.

One detail in the Easter stories has always intrigued me: Why did Jesus keep the scars from his crucifixion? Presumably he could have had any resurrected body he wanted, and yet he chose one identifiable mainly by scars that could be seen and touched. Why?

I believe the story of Easter would be incomplete without those scars on the hands, the feet, and the side of Jesus. When human beings fantasize, we dream of pearly straight teeth and wrinkle-free skin and sexy ideal shapes. We dream of an unnatural state: the perfect body. But for Jesus, being confined in a skeleton and human skin *was* the unnatural state. The scars are, to him, an emblem of life on our planet, a permanent reminder of those days of confinement and suffering.

I take hope in Jesus' scars. From the perspective of heaven, they represent the most horrible event that has ever happened in the history of the universe. Even that event, though—the crucifixion—Easter turned into a memory. Because of Easter, I can hope that the tears we shed, the blows we receive, the emotional pain, the heartache over lost friends and loved ones, all these will become memories, like Jesus' scars. Scars never completely go away, but neither do they hurt any longer. We will have re-created bodies, a re-created heaven and earth. We will have a new start, an Easter start.

There are two ways to look at human history, I have concluded. One way is to focus on the wars and violence, the squalor, the pain and tragedy and death. From such a point of view, Easter seems a fairy-tale exception, a stunning contradiction in the name of God. That gives some solace, although I confess that when my friends died, grief was so overpowering that any hope in an after-life seemed somehow thin and insubstantial.

There is another way to look at the world. If I take Easter as the starting point, the one incontrovertible fact about how God treats those whom he loves, then human history becomes the contradiction and Easter a preview of ultimate reality. Hope then flows like lava beneath the crust of daily life.

This, perhaps, describes the change in the disciples' perspective as they sat in locked rooms discussing the incomprehensible events of Easter Sunday. In one sense nothing had changed: Rome still occupied Palestine, religious authorities still had a bounty on their heads, death and evil still reigned outside. Gradually, however, the shock of recognition gave way to a long slow undertow of joy. If God could do that ...

Part Three

What He Left Behind

12
Ascension:
A Blank Blue Sky

But God's own descent
Into flesh was meant
As a demonstration ...
Spirit enters flesh and for all it's worth
Charges into earth in birth after birth
Ever fresh and fresh.

Robert Frost

12

Ascension:
A Blank Blue Sky

Sometimes I think about how different the world would be had Jesus not resurrected from the dead. Although the disciples would not risk their lives trumpeting a new faith in the streets of Jerusalem, neither would they forget him. They had given three years to Jesus. He may not be the Messiah (not without Easter), but he had impressed them as the wisest teacher ever and had demonstrated powers that no one could explain.

After time, as emotional wounds began to heal, the disciples would seek some way to memorialize Jesus. Perhaps they would collect his sayings in a written form akin to one of our Gospels, though with the more sensational claims excised. Or, along with Jews from that period who were honoring other martyr-prophets, they might build a monument to Jesus' life. If so, we who live in modern times could still visit that monument and learn about the carpenter/philosopher from Nazareth. We could sift through his sayings, taking or leaving whatever we liked. Worldwide, Jesus would be esteemed in the same way Confucius or Socrates is esteemed.

In many respects I would find an unresurrected Jesus easier to accept. Easter makes him dangerous. Because of Easter I have to listen to his extravagant claims and can no longer pick and choose from his sayings. Moreover, Easter means he must be loose out there somewhere. Like the disciples, I never know where Jesus might turn up, how he might speak to me, what he might ask of me. As Frederick Buechner says, Easter means "we can never nail him down, not even if the nails we use are real and the thing we nail him to is a cross."

Easter puts Jesus' life in a whole new light. Apart from Easter I would think it a tragedy that Jesus died young after a few short years of ministry. What a waste for him to leave so soon, having affected so few people in such a small part of the world! Yet, viewing that same life through the lens of Easter, I see that was Jesus' plan all along. He stayed just long enough to gather around him followers who could carry the message to others. Killing Jesus, says Walter Wink, was like trying to destroy a dandelion seed-head by blowing on it.

When Jesus returned after death to vaporize all doubts among the remnant of believers, he tarried a mere forty days before vanishing for good. The time between Resurrection and Ascension was an interlude, nothing more.

If Easter Sunday was the most exciting day of the disciples' lives, for Jesus it was probably the day of Ascension. He the Creator, who had descended so far and given up so much, was now heading home. Like a soldier returning across the ocean from a long and bloody war. Like an astronaut shedding his spacesuit to gulp in the familiar atmosphere of earth. Home at last.

Jesus' prayer at the Last Supper with his disciples reveals something of this point of view. "I have brought you glory on earth by completing the work you gave me to do," Jesus prayed, "And now, Father, glorify me in your presence with the glory I had with you before the world began." Before the world began! Like an old man reminiscing—no, like an ageless God reminiscing—Jesus, who sat in a stuffy room in Jerusalem, was letting his mind wander back to a time before the Milky Way and Andromeda. On an earthly night dark with fear and menace, Jesus was making preparations to return home, to assume again the glory he had set aside.

On the day Jesus ascended, the disciples stood around dumbfounded, like children who have lost their parent. Two angels sent to calm them asked the obvious question, "Men of Galilee, why do you stand here looking into the sky?" The sky was blank, empty. Still they stood and gazed, not knowing how to go on or what to do next.

So many times in the course of writing this book I have felt like one of those disciples, peering intently at a blank blue sky. I look for some sign of Jesus, some visual clue. When I glance around me at the church he left behind, I want to avert my eyes. Like the disciples' eyes, mine ache for a pure glimpse of the One who ascended. Why, I ask again, did he have to leave?

But as I go back through the Gospels, trying to envision how Jesus himself viewed his time on earth, it seems obvious he planned this departure from the beginning. Nothing pleased Jesus more than the successes of his disciples; nothing disturbed him more than their failures. He had come to earth with the goal of leaving again, after transferring his mission to others. The angels' gentle rebuke might as well have been his own: "Why do you stand here looking into the sky?"

The first time Jesus sent the disciples out alone, he warned them about opposition that would likely take the form of floggings and public torture. "I am sending you out like sheep among wolves," he said. Reading these dire warnings, I cannot push from my mind a harrowing scene from Shusako Endo's novel *Silence*. A Portuguese missionary priest, bound, is forced to watch as samurai guards torture Japanese Christians, one by one, and throw them into the sea. The samurai swear they will keep on killing Christians until the priest renounces his faith. "He had come to this country to lay down his life for other men, but instead of that the Japanese were laying down their lives one by one for him."

What was it like for Jesus, who saw with piercing vision the terrible consequences of what he had set loose in the world, not only for himself but for the huddled few around him, his best friends in all the world? "Brother will betray brother to death, and a father his child ... All men will hate you because of me. ..."

I struggle to reconcile that point of view—a parent consigning her children to the gangs, a general ordering his troops into the line of fire—with what took place at the Last Supper. There, as Jesus disclosed plans for his departure in terms no one could mistake, he said,

"But I tell you the truth: It is for your good that I am going away." All along he had planned to depart in order to carry on his work in other bodies. Their bodies. Our bodies. The new body of Christ.

At the time the disciples had no idea what Jesus meant. *How can it be good that he is going away?* They ate the "body, broken for you" without comprehending the drastic change, that the mission God had assigned to the Son, the Son was now entrusting to them. "As you sent me into the world, I have sent them into the world," Jesus prayed.

Jesus left few traces of himself on earth. He wrote no books or even pamphlets. A wanderer, he left no home or even belongings that could be enshrined in a museum. He did not marry, settle down, and begin a dynasty. We would, in fact, know nothing about him except for the traces he left in human beings. That was his design. The law and the prophets had focused like a beam of light on the One who was to come, and now that light, as if hitting a prism, would fracture and shoot out in a human spectrum of waves and colors.

Six weeks later, the disciples would find out what Jesus had meant by the words *for your good*. As Augustine put it, "You ascended from before our eyes, and we turned back grieving, only to find you in our hearts."

Would it be too much to say that, ever since the Ascension, Jesus has sought other bodies in which to begin again the life he lived on earth? The church serves as an extension of the Incarnation, God's primary way of establishing presence in the world. We are "AfterChrists," in Gerard Manley Hopkins's coinage:

> ...*for Christ plays in ten thousand places,*
> *Lovely in eyes, and lovely in limbs not his*
> *To the Father through the features of men's faces.*

The church is where God lives. What Jesus brought to a few— healing, grace, the good-news message of God's love—the church can now bring to all. That was the challenge, or Great Commission, that Jesus gave just before vanishing from the numbed disciples' sight. "Unless a kernel of wheat falls to the ground and dies," he had explained earlier, "it remains only a single seed. But if it dies, it produces many seeds." Propagation by the dandelion method.

Such is the theory, at least. In truth, I must, though, place myself with the disciples who watch with jaws agape as Jesus lifts into the air like some wingless creature defying gravity. "Lord, are you at this time going to restore the kingdom to Israel?" they have just asked—and now this. He's gone! I sympathize with their bewilderment, because I too yearn for a power-Messiah to impose order on a world of evil and violence and poverty. Living two millennia after the disciples, I look back and marvel at how little difference the church has made in such a world. Why did Jesus leave us alone to fight the battles? How can it be good that he went away?

I have concluded, in fact, that the Ascension represents my greatest struggle of faith—not whether it happened, but why. It challenges me more than the problem of pain, more than the difficulty of harmonizing science and the Bible, more than belief in the Resurrection and other miracles. It seems odd to admit such a notion—I have never read a book or article conceived to answer doubts about the Ascension—yet for me what has happened since Jesus' departure strikes at the core of my faith. Would it not have been better if the Ascension had never happened? If Jesus had stayed on earth, he could answer our questions, solve our doubts, mediate our disputes of doctrine and policy.

I find it much easier to accept the fact of God incarnating in Jesus of Nazareth than in the people who attend my local church—and in me. Yet that is what we are asked to believe; that is how we are asked to live. The New Testament declares that the future of the cosmos is being determined by the church (see Romans 8:19–21; Ephesians 3:10). Jesus played his part and then left. Now it is up to us.

"It is a serious thing," wrote C. S. Lewis, "to live in a society of possible gods and goddesses, to remember that the dullest and most uninteresting person you talk to may one day be a creature which, if you saw it now, you would be strongly tempted to worship, or else a horror and a corruption such as you now meet, if at all, only in a nightmare. All day long we are, in some degree, helping each other to one or another of these destinations."

Ancient religions, such as the Roman paganism of Jesus' day, believed that the actions of gods in the heavens above affected the earth below. If Zeus got angry, thunderbolts shot out. Like kids dropping rocks off highway bridges onto the cars below, the gods rained cataclysm onto the earth. "As above, so below," went the ancient formula. Jesus, though, inverted that formula: "As below, so above." "He who listens to you listens to me," Jesus told his followers; "he who rejects you rejects me." A believer prays, and heaven responds; a sinner repents, and the angels rejoice; a mission succeeds, and Satan falls like lightning; a believer rebels, and the Holy Spirit is grieved. What we humans do here decisively affects the cosmos.

I believe these things, and yet somehow I keep "forgetting" them. I forget that my prayers matter to God. I forget that I am helping my neighbors to their eternal destinations. I forget that the choices I make today bring delight—or grief—to the Lord of the Universe. I live in a world of trees and telephones and fax machines, and the reality of this material universe tends to overwhelm my faith in a spiritual universe suffusing it all. I look into the blank blue sky and see nothing.

By ascending, Jesus took the risk of being forgotten.

Not long ago, as I was reading through Matthew, I noticed with a start that Jesus himself foresaw the very predicament of being forgotten. Four parables toward the end of Matthew, among the last that Jesus gave, have a common theme lurking in the background. An owner leaves his house vacant, an absentee landlord puts his servant in charge, a bridegroom arrives so late the guests grow drowsy and fall asleep, a master distributes talents among his servants and takes off— all these circle around the theme of the departed God.

In effect, Jesus' stories anticipated the central question of the modern era: "Where is God now?" The modern answer, from the likes of Nietzsche, Freud, Marx, Camus, and Beckett, is that the landlord has abandoned us, leaving us free to set our own rules. *Deus absconditus.* In places like Auschwitz and Rwanda, we have seen living versions of those parables, graphic examples of how some will act when they stop believing in a sovereign landlord. If there is no God, as Dostoevsky said, then anything is permissible.

Reading on, I came to one more parable, the Sheep and the Goats, probably the last one Jesus taught.

> When the Son of Man comes in his glory, and all the angels with him, he will sit on his throne in heavenly glory. All the nations will be gathered before him, and he will separate the people one from another as a shepherd separates the sheep from the goats. He will put the sheep on his right and the goats on his left.
>
> Then the King will say to those on his right, "Come, you who are blessed by my Father; take your inheritance, the kingdom prepared for you since the creation of the world. For I was hungry and you gave me something to eat, I was thirsty and you gave me something to drink, I was a stranger and you invited me in, I needed clothes and you clothed me, I was sick and you looked after me, I was in prison and you came to visit me."
>
> Then the righteous will answer him, "Lord, when did we see you hungry and feed you, or thirsty and give you something to drink? When did we see you a stranger and invite you in, or needing clothes and clothe you? When did we see you sick or in prison and go to visit you?"
>
> The King will reply, "I tell you the truth, whatever you did for one of the least of these brothers of mine, you did for me."
>
> Then he will say to those on his left, "Depart from me, you who are cursed, into the eternal fire prepared for the devil and his angels. For I was hungry and you gave me nothing to eat, I was thirsty and you gave me nothing to drink, I was a stranger and you did not invite me in, I needed clothes and you did not clothe me, I was sick and in prison and you did not look after me."
>
> They also will answer, "Lord, when did we see you hungry or thirsty or a stranger or needing clothes or sick or in prison, and did not help you?"
>
> He will reply, "I tell you the truth, whatever you did not do for one of the least of these, you did not do for me."
>
> Then they will go away to eternal punishment, but the righteous to eternal life.

I knew this last parable well. It is as potent and disturbing as anything Jesus ever said. But I had never before noticed its logical connection with the four parables that precede it.

In two ways the parable of the Sheep and the Goats directly addresses the question raised by the others: the issue of the absentee landlord, the missing God. First, it gives a glimpse of the landlord's return on judgment day, when there will be hell to pay—literally. The departed One will return, this time in power and in glory, to settle accounts for all that has happened on earth. "Men of Galilee," said the angels, "why do you stand here looking into the sky? This same Jesus, who has been taken from you into heaven, will come back in the same way you have seen him go into heaven."

Second, the parable refers to the meantime, the centuries-long interval we live in now, the time when God seems absent. The answer to that most modern question is at once profound and shocking. God has not absconded at all. Rather, he has taken on a disguise, a most unlikely disguise of the stranger, the poor, the hungry, the prisoner, the sick, the ragged ones of earth: "I tell you the truth, whatever you did for one of the least of these brothers of mine, you did it for me." If we cannot detect God's presence in the world, it may be that we have been looking in the wrong places.

Commenting on this passage, the great American theologian Jonathan Edwards said that God has designated the poor as his "receivers." Since we cannot express our love by doing anything to profit God directly, God wants us to do something profitable for the poor, who have been delegated the task of receiving Christian love.

One night I was absently flipping the channels of television when I came across what seemed to be a children's movie, starring the young Hayley Mills. I settled back and watched the plot unfold. She and two friends, while playing in a country barn, stumbled across a vagrant (Alan Bates) sleeping in the straw. "Who are you?" Mills demanded. The vagrant jerked awake and, seeing the children, muttered, "Jesus Christ!"

What he meant as an expletive, the children took as the truth. They actually believed the man to be Jesus Christ. For the rest of the movie (*Whistle Down the Wind*), they treated the vagrant with awe, respect, and love. They brought him food and blankets, sat and talked with him, and told him about their lives. In time their tenderness transformed the vagrant, an escaped convict who had never before known such mercy.

Mills's mother, who wrote the story, intended it as an allegory of what might happen if all of us took literally Jesus' words about the poor and the needy. By serving them, we serve Jesus. "We are a contemplative order," Mother Teresa told a rich American visitor who could not comprehend her fierce commitment to the dregs of Calcutta. "First we meditate on Jesus, and then we go out and look for him in disguise."

As I reflected on the last parable in Matthew 25, I became aware that many of my own questions of God are actually boomerang questions that come right back to me. Why does God allow babies to be born in Brooklyn ghettoes and by a river of death in Rwanda? Why does God allow prisons and homeless shelters and hospitals and refugee camps? Why did Jesus not clean up the world's messes in the years he lived here?

According to this parable, Jesus knew that the world he left behind would include the poor, the hungry, the prisoners, the sick. The decrepit state of the world did not surprise him. He made plans to cope with it: a long-range plan and a short-range plan. The long-range plan involves his return, in power and great glory, to straighten out planet earth. The short-range plan means turning it over to the ones who will ultimately usher in the liberation of the cosmos. He ascended so that we would take his place.

"Where is God when it hurts?" I have often asked. The answer is another question, "Where is the church when it hurts?"

That last question, of course, is the problem of history in a nutshell, and also the reason why I say the Ascension represents my greatest struggle of faith. When Jesus departed, he left the keys of the kingdom in our fumbling hands.

All through my own quest for Jesus has run a counterpoint theme: my need to strip away layers of dust and grime applied *by the church itself*. In my case the image of Jesus was obscured by the racism, intolerance, and petty legalism of fundamentalist churches in the South. A Russian or a European Catholic confronts a very different restoration process. "For not only dust, but also too much gold can cover up the true figure," wrote the German Hans Küng about his own search. Many, far too many, abandon the quest entirely; repelled by the church, they never make it to Jesus.

"What a pity that so hard on the heels of Christ come the Christians," observes Annie Dillard. Her statement reminds me of a T-shirt that can be spotted at contemporary political rallies: "Jesus save us ... from your followers." And of a line from the New Zealand film *Heavenly Creatures* in which two girls describe their imaginary kingdom: "It's like heaven only better—there aren't any Christians!"

The problem showed itself early on. Commenting on the church in Corinth, Frederick Buechner writes, "They were in fact Christ's body, as Paul wrote to them here in one of his most enduring metaphors—Christ's eyes, ears, hands—but the way they were carrying on, that could only leave Christ bloodshot, ass-eared, all thumbs, to carry on God's work in a fallen world." In the fourth century an exasperated St. Augustine wrote about the fractious church, "The clouds roll with thunder that the House of the Lord shall be built throughout the earth; and these frogs sit in their marsh and croak—'We are the only Christians!'"

I could fill several pages with such colorful quotations, all of which underscore the risk involved in entrusting God's own reputation to the likes of us. Unlike Jesus, we do not perfectly express the Word. We speak in garbled syntax, stuttering, mixing languages together, putting accent marks in wrong places. When the world looks for Christ it sees, like the cave-dwellers in Plato's allegory, only shadows created by the light, not the light itself.

Why don't we look more like the church Jesus described? Why does the body of Christ so faintly resemble him? If Jesus could foresee such disasters as the Crusades, the Inquisition, the Christian slave trade, apartheid, why did he ascend in the first place?

I cannot provide a confident answer to such questions, for I am part of the problem. Examined closely, my query takes on a distressingly personal cast: Why do *I* so poorly resemble him? I merely offer three observations that help me come to terms with what has transpired since Jesus' ascension.

First, the church has brought light as well as darkness. In the name of Jesus, St. Francis kissed the beggar and took off his robes,

Mother Teresa founded the Home for the Dying, Wilberforce freed the slaves, General Booth established an urban Army of Salvation, and Dorothy Day fed the hungry. Such work continues: as a journalist I have met educators, urban ministers, doctors and nurses, linguists, relief workers, and ecologists serving all over the world for little pay and less fame, all in the name of Jesus. In other ways, Michelangelo, Bach, Rembrandt, the masons of cathedrals, and many like them offered up the best of their creation "for the glory of God alone." God's hands on earth have reached wider since the Ascension.

I see no point in tallying up a balance sheet to weigh the church's failures against its successes. The final word will come from God's own judgment. The first few chapters of Revelation show how realistically God views the church, and yet elsewhere the New Testament makes clear that God takes pleasure in us: we are "peculiar treasures," a "pleasing aroma," "gifts that he delights in." I cannot fathom such statements; I merely accept them on faith. God alone knows what pleases God.

Second, Jesus takes full responsibility for the constituent parts of his body. "You did not choose me, but I chose you," he told his disciples, and these were the very scalawags who so exasperated him and would soon desert him at his hour of greatest need. I think of Peter, whose bluster, love, hot-headedness, misdirected passion, and faithless betrayal preview in embryo form nineteen centuries of church history. On "rocks" like him, Jesus built his church, and he promised that the gates of hell would not prevail against it.*

I take hope as I observe Jesus together with his disciples. Never did they disappoint him more than on the night of his betrayal. Yet it was then, says John, that Jesus "showed them the full extent of his love," and then that he conferred on them a kingdom.

Finally, the problem of the church is no different than the problem of one solitary Christian. How can an unholy assortment of men and women be the body of Christ? I answer with a different question:

---

*Charles Williams comments that Jesus "does not seem, to judge by his comments on the religious leaders of his day, ever to have hoped much from officers of a church. The most he would do was to promise that the gates of hell should not *prevail* against it. It is about all that, looking on the history of the Church, one can feel they have not done."

How can one sinful man, myself, be accepted as a child of God? One miracle makes possible the other.

I remind myself that the apostle Paul's soaring words about the bride of Christ and the temple of God were addressed to groups of hideously flawed individuals in places like Corinth. "We have this treasure in jars of clay to show that this all-surpassing power is from God and not from us," wrote Paul in one of the most accurate statements ever penned.

The novelist Flannery O'Connor, who could never be accused of glossing over human depravity, once answered a letter from a reader complaining about the state of the church. "All your dissatisfaction with the Church seems to me to come from an incomplete understanding of sin," O'Connor began:

> . . . what you seem actually to demand is that the Church put the kingdom of heaven on earth right here now, that the Holy Ghost be translated at once into all flesh. The Holy Spirit rarely shows Himself on the surface of anything. You are asking that man return at once to the state God created him in, you are leaving out the terrible radical human pride that causes death. Christ was crucified on earth and the Church is crucified in time . . . The Church is founded on Peter who denied Christ three times and who couldn't walk on the water by himself. You are expecting his successors to walk on the water. All human nature vigorously resists grace because grace changes us and the change is painful. Priests resist it as well as others. To have the Church be what you want it to be would require the continuous miraculous meddling of God in human affairs . . .

In two memorable phrases, O'Connor has captured the choices God faced, looking out on human history: to engage in "the continuous miraculous meddling in human affairs" or to allow himself to be "crucified in time" as his Son was on earth. With a few exceptions, God, whose nature is self-living love, has chosen the second option. Christ bears the wounds of the church, his body, just as he bore the wounds of crucifixion. I sometimes wonder which have hurt worse.

13
Kingdom:
Wheat Among the Weeds

The human comedy doesn't attract me enough. I am not entirely of this world. . . . I am from elsewhere. And it is worth finding this elsewhere beyond the walls. But where is it?

Eugene Ionesco

13
Kingdom: Wheat Among the Weeds

Each fall the childhood church I attended sponsored a prophecy conference. Silver-haired men of national repute would stretch their prophecy charts—stitched bedsheets covered with Day-Glo renditions of beasts and armies—across the platform and expound on "the last days" we were living in.

I listened in fear and fascination as they drew a straight line south from Moscow to Jerusalem and sketched in the movements of million-strong armies who would soon converge on Israel. I learned that the ten members of Europe's Common Market had recently fulfilled Daniel's prophecy about the beast with ten horns. Soon all of us would wear a number stamped on our foreheads, the mark of the beast, and be registered in a computer somewhere in Belgium. Nuclear war would break out and the planet would teeter on the brink of annihilation, until at the last second Jesus himself would return to lead the armies of righteousness.

That scenario seems far less likely now that Russia has declined and the Common Market (now European Union) has expanded beyond ten members. What sticks with me, though, is not so much the particulars of prophecy as their emotional effect on me. I grew up at once terrified and desperately hopeful. In high school I took courses in Chinese and my brother studied Russian so that one of us could communicate with invading armies from either direction. My uncle went further, packing up his family and moving to Australia. Yet in the midst of this terror we also had hope: though I felt certain the world would soon end, nevertheless I banked all my childhood faith on the belief that somehow Jesus would conquer.

Later, as I read church history, I learned that often before—during the first decades of Christianity, the end of the tenth century, the late 1300s, the Napoleonic era, World War I, the Axis of Hitler and Mussolini—visions of the end times had bubbled to the surface. As recently as the 1991 Gulf War, Saddam Hussein was being branded the Antichrist, the new trigger-man for the apocalypse. Each time, Christians went through a passionate cycle of fear, hope, and sheepish disillusionment. The end times had not arrived after all.

I also learned that the Jewish race has repeatedly undergone the exact same cycle, never more poignantly than in the first century A.D. At that time many Jews expected the Messiah to arise and liberate them from the terrors of Rome, a hope that the man from Nazareth at first ignited, and then dashed. To understand Jesus and the mission he left behind after his ascension, I need to return once more to his own era, to place myself again in his time, to listen to him speak on the topic he favored more than any other: the kingdom of God. What he said about God's kingdom in the first century has great relevance to me today in the twentieth.

In Jesus' day, Jews were poring over the same passages from Daniel and Ezekiel that would later figure so prominently in the prophecy conferences of my childhood.* We disagreed on some details—Northern Europe was then a forest full of barbarians not a Common Market, and Russia was unknown—yet our visions of the Messiah matched: we expected a conquering hero. Anyone

---

*The scribes who pored so assiduously over Old Testament prophecies did not recognize Jesus as the fulfillment of those prophecies. Should not their failure to interpret signs of the first coming sound a note of caution to those today who so confidently proclaim signs of the Second Coming?

who declared "The kingdom of God has come upon you!" would surely awaken in his listeners' minds the image of a political leader who would arise, take charge, and defeat the most powerful empire ever known.

In such an environment, Jesus well understood the explosive power of the word *Messiah*. In William Barclay's judgment, "If Jesus had publicly claimed to be Messiah, nothing could have stopped a useless flood tide of slaughter." Although Jesus did not use the title himself, he accepted it when others called him Messiah, and the Gospels show a gradual dawning on his disciples that their teacher was none other than the long-awaited King.

Jesus encouraged such beliefs by using the word that quickened the pulse of his people. "The *kingdom* of heaven is near," he proclaimed in his very first message. Each time he spoke it, that word stirred memories to life: bright banners, glittering armies, the gold and ivory of Solomon's day, the nation of Israel restored. What was about to happen, Jesus said, would far surpass anything from the past: "For I tell you that many prophets and kings wanted to see what you see but did not see it, and to hear what you hear but did not hear it." On another occasion he announced provocatively, "Now one greater than Solomon is here."

Zealots stood at the edge of Jesus' audience, armed and well-organized guerrillas spoiling for a fight against Rome, but to their consternation the signal for revolt never came. In time, Jesus' pattern of behavior disappointed all who sought a leader in the traditional mold. He tended to flee from, rather than cater to, large groups. He insulted the memory of Israel's glory days, comparing King Solomon to a common day lily. The one time a crowd tried to crown him king by force, he mysteriously withdrew. And when Peter finally did wield a sword on his behalf, Jesus healed the victim's wounds.

To the crowds' dismay, it became clear that Jesus was talking about a strangely different kind of kingdom. The Jews wanted what people have always wanted from a visible kingdom: a chicken in every pot, full employment, a strong army to deter invaders. Jesus announced a kingdom that meant denying yourself, taking up a cross, renouncing wealth, even loving your enemies. As he elaborated, the crowd's expectations crumbled.

By the time Jesus was nailed to wooden crossbeams, everyone had lost hope and fallen away. Scholars report that first-century Jews had no concept of a suffering Messiah. As for the Twelve, no matter how often or how plainly Jesus warned them of his impending death, it never sank in. No one could imagine a Messiah dying.

The word *kingdom* meant one thing to Jesus and quite another to the crowd. Jesus was rejected, in large part, because he did not measure up to a national image of what a Messiah was supposed to look like.

A question has long puzzled me. In view of their expectations, why did Jesus keep arousing his followers' hopes with the word *kingdom*? (It appears fifty-three times in Matthew's gospel alone.) He insisted on associating himself with a term that everyone seemed to misunderstand. What did Jesus mean by the *kingdom of God*?

It is a great irony that the one who so failed the expectations of his people became known to all history as a king—so much so that a form of the word became his "last name." Christ, or *Christos* in Greek, translates the Hebrew word *Messiah*, which means anointed and refers to the ancient manner of coronating kings. Now, all of us who call ourselves *Christ*-ians carry an echo of the word that so baffled the people of Jesus' day. I wonder, Do we understand the kingdom of God any better?

Jesus never offered a clear definition of the kingdom; instead he imparted his vision of it indirectly through a series of stories. His choice of images is telling: everyday sketches of farming, fishing, women baking bread, merchants buying pearls.

The kingdom of heaven is like a farmer going out to sow his seed. As every farmer knows, not all the seed you plant ends up yielding crops. Some falls among rocks, some gets eaten by birds and field mice, some gets crowded out by weeds. All this seems natural to a farmer, but heretical to a traditional kingdom-builder. Are not kings judged by their power, their ability to impose their will on a populace, their strength in repelling enemies? Jesus was indicating that the kingdom of God comes with a resistible power. It is humble and unobtrusive and coexistent with evil—a message that surely did not please patriotic Jews intent on revolt.

Consider the mustard seed, a seed so tiny it can fall to the ground and lie unnoticed by human beings and birds alike. Given time, though, the seed may sprout into a bush that overtakes every other plant in the garden, a bush so large and verdant that birds come and nest in its branches. God's kingdom works like that. It begins so small that people scorn it and give it no chance for success. Against all odds, God's kingdom will grow and spread throughout the world, bringing shade to the sick, the poor, the imprisoned, the unloved.

The kingdom of heaven is like a businessman who specializes in rare gems. One day he finds a pearl gorgeous enough to make princesses drool with envy. Recognizing its value, he liquidates his entire business in order to buy it. Although the purchase costs everything he owns, not for a moment does he regret it. He makes the trade with joy, as the crowning achievement of his life: the treasure will outlive him, enduring long after the family name has disappeared. God's kingdom works like that. The sacrifice—deny yourself, take up your cross—turns out to be a shrewd investment, its outcome not remorse but joy beyond all telling.

These are the stories Jesus told. As I review the parables of the kingdom, though, I realize how far my own understanding has drifted from such homespun images. I tend to envision the same kind of kingdom the Jews did: a visible, powerful kingdom. I think of Constantine leading his troops, crosses emblazoned on their armor, with the slogan "By this sign conquer." I think of the armies marching across the bedsheets at the prophecy conferences. Obviously, I need to listen again to Jesus' description of the kingdom of God.

Those of us in the twentieth century, an era that has few literal "kings," conceive of kingdoms in terms of power and polarization. We are the children of revolution. Two centuries ago in the U.S. and France the oppressed rose up and overturned the reigning powers.

Later, in places like Russia and China, Marxists led revolts with an ideology that became a kind of religion: they began, in fact, to view all history as an outgrowth of class struggle, or dialectical materialism. "Workers, unite! Throw off your chains!" cried Marx, and so they did for much of our bloody century.

For a period of time I tried to read the Gospels through the eyes of liberation theology. Ultimately I had to conclude that, whatever else it is, the kingdom of God is decidedly not a call to violent revolution. First-century Jews were doubtless looking for such an upheaval. Battle lines were clear: oppressed Jews versus the bad-guy Romans—pagans who collected taxes, trafficked in slaves, regulated religion, and quashed dissent. Under these conditions the Zealots issued a call much like Marx's: "Jews, unite! Throw off your chains!" But Jesus' message of the kingdom had little in common with the politics of polarization.

As I read the Gospels, Jesus seems to speak a two-pronged message. To the oppressors, he had words of warning and judgment. He treated the powers of government with an attitude of mild contempt, dismissing Herod as "that fox" (a Jewish expression for a worthless or insignificant person) and agreeing to pay a temple tax "so that we may not offend them." He placed little store in politics; it was government, after all, that tried to exterminate him.

To the oppressed, his primary audience, Jesus offered a message of comfort and consolation. He called the poor and the persecuted "blessed." Never did he incite the oppressed to rise up and throw off their chains. In words that must have galled the Zealots, he commanded, "Love your enemies." He invoked a different kind of power: love, not coercion.

People who looked to Jesus as their political savior were constantly befuddled by his choice of companions. He became known as a friend of tax collectors, a group clearly identified with the foreign exploiters, not the exploited. Though he denounced the religious system of his day, he treated a leader like Nicodemus with respect, and though he spoke against the dangers of money and of violence, he showed love and compassion toward a rich young ruler and a Roman centurion.

In short, Jesus honored the dignity of people, whether he agreed with them or not. He would not found his kingdom on the basis of race or class or other such divisions. Anyone, even a half-breed with five husbands or a thief dying on a cross, was welcome to join his kingdom. The person was more important than any category or label.

I feel convicted by this quality of Jesus every time I get involved in a cause I strongly believe in. How easy it is to join the politics of polarization, to find myself shouting across the picket lines at the "enemy" on the other side. How hard it is to remember that the kingdom of God calls me to love the woman who has just emerged from the abortion clinic (and, yes, even her doctor), the promiscuous person who is dying of AIDS, the wealthy landowner who is exploiting God's creation. If I cannot show love to such people, then I must question whether I have truly understood Jesus' gospel.

A political movement by nature draws lines, makes distinctions, pronounces judgment; in contrast, Jesus' love cuts across lines, transcends distinctions, and dispenses grace. Regardless of the merits of a given issue—whether a pro-life lobby out of the Right or a peace-and-justice lobby out of the Left—political movements risk pulling onto themselves the mantle of power that smothers love. From Jesus I learn that, whatever activism I get involved in, it must not drive out love and humility, or otherwise I betray the kingdom of heaven.

If I am tempted to see the kingdom of God as one more power structure, I need only turn to the account of the trial in Jerusalem, a scene that brings together the two kingdoms in striking apposition. On that climactic day the rulers of the "kingdom of this world" confronted Jesus and his kingdom face-to-face.

Two kings, Herod and Jesus, personified very different kinds of power. Herod had legions of Roman soldiers to enforce his will, and history records how Herod used his power: he stole his brother's wife, locked up all dissenters, beheaded John the Baptist as a party trick. Jesus too had power, but he used it compassionately, to feed the hungry and heal the sick. Herod had a gold crown, palaces, guards, and all the visible tokens of royalty. For Jesus, the closest thing to a formal coronation, or Messiah's "anointing," occurred in an embarrassing scene when a disreputable woman poured perfume over his head. He got the title "King of the Jews" as a criminal sentence. His "crown," made of thorns, was merely one more source of pain. And though he could have called on a legion of angels for protection, he declined.

Consistently, Jesus refused to use coercive power. He knowingly let one of his disciples betray him and then surrendered himself without protest to his captors. It never ceases to amaze me that Christian hope rests on a man whose message was rejected and whose love was spurned, who was condemned as a criminal and given a sentence of capital punishment.

Despite Jesus' plain example, many of his followers have been unable to resist choosing the way of Herod over that of Jesus. The Crusaders who pillaged the Near East, the conquistadors who converted the New World at the point of a sword, the Christian explorers in Africa who cooperated with the slave trade—we are still feeling aftershocks from their mistakes. History shows that when the church uses the tools of the world's kingdom, it becomes as ineffectual, or as tyrannical, as any other power structure. And whenever the church has intermingled with the state (the Holy Roman Empire, Cromwell's England, Calvin's Geneva), the appeal of the faith suffers as well. Ironically, our respect in the world declines in proportion to how vigorously we attempt to force others to adopt our point of view.

Sheep among wolves, a tiny seed in the garden, yeast in bread dough, salt in meat: Jesus' own metaphors of the kingdom describe a kind of "secret force" that works from within. He said nothing of a triumphant church sharing power with the authorities. The kingdom of God appears to work best as a minority movement, in opposition to the kingdom of this world. When it grows beyond that, the kingdom subtly changes in nature.

For this reason, I must say in an aside, I worry about the recent surge of power among U.S. Christians, who seem to be focusing more and more on political means. Once Christians were ignored or scorned; now they are courted by every savvy politician. Evangelicals especially are identified with a certain political stance, so much so that the news media use the terms "evangelical" and "religious right" interchangeably. When I ask a stranger, "What is an evangelical Christian?" I get an answer something like this: "Someone who supports family values and opposes homosexual rights and abortion."

This trend troubles me because the gospel of Jesus was not primarily a political platform. The issues that confront Christians in a secular society must be faced and addressed and legislated, and a democracy gives Christians every right to express themselves. But we dare not invest so much in the kingdom of this world that we neglect our main task of introducing people to a different kind of kingdom, one based solely on God's grace and forgiveness. Passing laws to enforce morality serves a necessary function, to dam up evil, but it never solves human problems. If a century from now all that historians can say about evangelicals of the 1990s is that they stood for family values, then we will have failed the mission Jesus gave us to accomplish: to communicate God's reconciling love to *sinners*.

Jesus did not say, "All men will know you are my disciples . . . if you just pass laws, suppress immorality, and restore decency to family and government," but rather " . . . if you love one another." He made that statement the night before his death, a night when human power, represented by the might of Rome and the full force of Jewish religious authorities, collided head-on with God's power. All his life, Jesus had been involved in a form of "culture wars" against a rigid religious establishment and a pagan empire, yet he responded by giving his life for those who opposed him. On the cross, he forgave them. He had come, above all, to demonstrate love: "For God so loved the world that he gave his one and only Son . . ."

When the Roman governor Pilate asked Jesus point-blank whether he was king of the Jews, he replied, "My kingdom is not of this world. If it were, my servants would fight to prevent my arrest by the Jews. But now my kingdom is from another place." Allegiance to a kingdom "not of this world" has emboldened Christian martyrs who, ever since the death of their founder, have met resistance from kingdoms that are of this world. Unarmed believers used that text against their Roman persecutors in the Colosseum, Tolstoy used it to undermine the authority of the tsars, and civil rights marchers used it to challenge apartheid laws in the southern United States and in South Africa. It speaks of a reign that transcends the boundaries—and sometimes the laws—of nation and empire.

On another occasion, Jesus was asked by the Pharisees when the kingdom of God would come. He replied, "The kingdom of God does not come with your careful observation, nor will people say, 'Here it is,' or 'There it is,' because the kingdom of God is within you."

Clearly, the kingdom of God operates by a set of rules different from any earthly kingdom's. God's kingdom has no geographical borders, no capital city, no parliament building, no royal trappings that you can see. Its followers live right among their enemies, not separated from them by a border fence or a wall. It lives, and grows, on the inside of human beings.

Those of us who follow Jesus thus possess a kind of dual citizenship. We live in an external kingdom of family and cities and nationhood, while at the same time belonging to the kingdom of God. In his command, "Give to Caesar what is Caesar's, and to God what is God's," Jesus underscored the fundamental tension that can result. For the early Christians, loyalty to God's kingdom sometimes meant a fatal clash with Caesar's visible kingdom. Historian Will Durant, in *The Story of Civilization*, concludes:

> There is no greater drama in human record than the sight of a few Christians, scorned and oppressed by a succession of emperors, bearing all trials with a fierce tenacity, multiplying quietly, building order while their enemies generated chaos, fighting the sword with the word, brutality with hope, and at last defeating the strongest state that history has known. Caesar and Christ had met in the arena, and Christ had won.

We have seen vivid demonstrations of the clash of kingdoms in our own time. In communist countries—Albania, the U.S.S.R., China—the government forced the Christian church to go underground so that it became, quite literally, invisible. In waves of persecution during the 1960s and 1970s, for instance, Chinese believers were fined, imprisoned, and tortured, and local regulations prohibited most religious activities. Yet despite this government oppression, a spiritual revival broke out that could well be the largest in the history of the church. As many as fifty million believers gave their allegiance to an invisible kingdom even as the visible kingdom made them suffer for it.

In fact, problems seem to arise when the church becomes too external, and gets too cozy with government. As one U.S. legislative aide said after a tour of China, "I believe there is a word of caution for us in the apolitical nature of China's underground church. They fervently pray for their leaders but maintain a careful independence. We are privileged to live in a participatory democracy, but having worked in American politics for almost a decade, I have seen more than a few believers trade in their Christian birthright for a mess of earthly pottage. We must continually ask ourselves: Is our first aim to change our government or to see lives in and out of government changed for Christ?"

To rephrase her question, Is our first aim to change the external, political kingdom or to further God's transcendent kingdom? In a nation like the U.S., the two easily get confused.

I grew up in a church that proudly displayed the "Christian flag" next to the Stars and Stripes, and we would pledge allegiance to both. People would apply to the United States passages from the Old Testament that were obviously intended for a time when God worked through a visible kingdom on earth, the nation of Israel. For example, I often heard this verse quoted as a formula for national revival: "If my people, who are called by my name, will humble themselves and pray and seek my face and turn from their wicked ways, then will I hear from heaven and will forgive their sin and will heal their land." The principle may apply in a general way, of course, but the specific national promise was given as part of God's covenant relationship with the ancient Hebrews; its occasion was the dedication of Solomon's temple, God's dwelling place on earth. Have we any reason to assume God has a similar covenant arrangement with the U.S.?

Indeed, have we any indication that God now judges the U.S. or any other country *as a national entity*? Jesus told his parables of the kingdom in part to correct such nationalistic notions. God is working not primarily through nations, but through a kingdom that transcends nations.

As I now reflect on Jesus' stories of the kingdom, I sense that much uneasiness among Christians today stems from a confusion of the two kingdoms, visible and invisible. Each time an election rolls around, Christians debate whether this or that candidate is "God's man" for the White House. Projecting myself back into Jesus' time, I have difficulty imagining him pondering whether Tiberius, Octavius, or Julius Caesar was "God's man" for the empire. The politics of Rome were virtually irrelevant to the kingdom of God.

Nowadays, as the U.S. grows increasingly secularized, it appears that church and state are heading in different directions. The more I understand Jesus' message of the kingdom of God, the less alarm I feel over that trend. Our real challenge, the focus of our energy, should not be to Christianize the United States (always a losing battle) but rather to strive to be God's kingdom in an increasingly hostile world. As Karl Barth said, "[The Church] exists . . . to set up in the world a new sign which is radically dissimilar to [the world's] own manner and which contradicts it in a way which is full of promise."

Ironically, if the United States is truly sliding down a slippery moral slope, that may better allow the church—as it did in Rome and also in China—to set up "a new sign . . . which is full of promise." I would prefer, I must admit, to live in a country where the majority of people follow the Ten Commandments, act with civility toward each other, and bow their heads once a day for a bland, nonpartisan prayer. I feel a certain nostalgia for the social climate of the 1950s in which I grew up. But if that environment does not return, I will not lose any sleep. As America slides, I will work and pray for the kingdom of God to advance. If the gates of hell cannot prevail against the church, the contemporary political scene hardly offers much threat.

In Stuttgart, Germany, in 1933 Martin Buber held a discussion with a New Testament scholar on why he, a Jew who admired Jesus, nevertheless could not accept him. To Christians, he began, Jews must seem stubborn as they steadfastly wait for a Messiah to come. Why not acknowledge Jesus as Messiah? "The church rests on its faith that the Christ has come, and that this is the redemption which God has bestowed on mankind. We, Israel, are not able to believe this.... We know more deeply, more truly, that world history has not been turned upside down to its very foundations—that the world is not redeemed. We *sense* its unredeemedness." Buber's classic statement took on added poignancy in the next few years, for 1933 was the year Adolf Hitler came to power in Germany, putting to rest any doubts about the unredeemed character of the world. How could a true Messiah allow such a world to continue?

The only possible explanation lies in Jesus' teaching that the kingdom of God comes in stages. It is "Now" and also "Not yet," present and also future. Sometimes Jesus stressed the present aspect, as when he said the kingdom is "at hand" or "within you." At other times he suggested the kingdom lay in the future as when he taught his disciples to pray, "Your kingdom come, your will be done, on earth as it is in heaven." Martin Buber is correct to observe that God's will is apparently not being done on earth as it is in heaven. In some important ways, the kingdom has not fully come.

Probably Jesus himself would have agreed with Buber's assessment of the state of the world. "In this world, you will have trouble," he told his disciples. He also warned of impending disasters: "You will hear of wars and rumors of wars, but see to it that you are not alarmed. Such things must happen, but the end is still to come." The presence of evil guarantees that history will be full of strife and that the world will look unredeemed. For a period of time, the kingdom of God must exist alongside an active rebellion against God. God's kingdom advances slowly, humbly, like a secret invasion force operating within the kingdoms ruled by Satan.

As C. S. Lewis expressed it,

> Why is God landing in this enemy-occupied world in disguise and starting a sort of secret society to undermine the devil? Why is He not landing in force, invading it? Is it that He is not strong enough? Well, Christians think He is going to land in force; we do not know when. But we can guess why He is delaying: He wants to give us the chance of joining His side freely.... God will invade. But I wonder whether people who ask God to

interfere openly and directly in our world quite realise what it will be like when He does. When that happens, it is the end of the world. When the author walks on to the stage the play is over.

Jesus' closest disciples had difficulty grasping this double view of the kingdom. After his death and resurrection, when they understood at last that the Messiah had come not as a conquering king but as one clothed in humility and weakness, even then one thought obsessed them: "Lord, are you at this time going to restore the kingdom to Israel?" No doubt they were thinking of a visible kingdom to replace the rule of Rome. Jesus brushed aside the question and commanded them to carry word of him to the ends of the earth. That is when, to their amazement, he ascended out of sight and when, a few moments later, the angels explained, "This same Jesus, who has been taken from you into heaven, *will come back* in the same way you have seen him go into heaven." The kind of kingdom they yearned for would indeed come, but not yet.

I must confess that for many years I avoided thinking about the Second Coming of Jesus—partly, I'm sure, as a reaction to the prophecy mania of my childhood church. The doctrine seemed an embarrassment, the kind of talk that attracted people who believed in flying saucers. I still have little certainty about details of the Second Coming, but I now see it as the necessary culmination of the kingdom of God. To the degree that the church loses faith in Christ's return and contents itself to be a comfortable part of this world and not the advance guard of a kingdom from another world, to that degree we risk losing faith in a sovereign God.

God has put his reputation on the line. The New Testament points to a time when "every knee should bow . . . and every tongue confess that Jesus Christ is Lord." Obviously, that has not yet happened. Several decades after Easter, the apostle Paul spoke of the whole creation groaning in labor pains for a redemption not yet realized. Jesus' first coming did not solve the problems of planet earth, rather it presented a vision of God's kingdom to help break the earthly spell of delusion.

Only at Christ's second coming will the kingdom of God appear in all its fullness. In the meantime we work toward a better future, always glancing back to the Gospels for a template of what that future will be like. Jürgen Moltmann has observed that the phrase "Day of the Lord" in the Old Testament inspired fear; but in the New Testament it inspires confidence, because those authors had come to know the Lord whose Day it was. They now knew what to expect.

When Jesus lived on earth he made the blind to see and the lame to walk; he will return to rule over a kingdom that has no disease or disability. On earth he died and was resurrected; at his return, death will be no more. On earth he cast out demons; at his return, he will destroy the Evil One. On earth he came as a baby born in a manger; he will return as the blazing figure described in the book of Revelation. The kingdom he set in motion on earth was not the end, only the beginning of the end.

Indeed, the kingdom of God will grow on earth as the church creates an alternative society demonstrating what the world is *not*, but one day will be: Barth's prescription of "a new sign which is radically dissimilar to [the world's] own manner and which contradicts it in a way which is full of promise." A society that welcomes people of all races and social classes, that is characterized by love and not polarization, that cares most for its weakest members, that stands for justice and righteousness in a world enamored with selfishness and decadence, a society in which members compete for the privilege of serving one another—this is what Jesus meant by the kingdom of God.

The Four Horsemen of the Apocalypse give a preview of how the world will end: in war, famine, sickness, and death. But Jesus gave a personal preview of how the world will be restored, by reversing the deeds of the Four Horsemen: he made peace, fed the hungry, healed the sick, and brought the dead to life. He made the message of God's kingdom powerful by living it, by bringing it to reality among the people around him. The prophets' fairy-tale predictions of a world free of pain and tears and death referred to no mythical world, but rather to *this* world.

We in the church, Jesus' successors, are left with the task of displaying the signs of the kingdom of God, and the watching world will judge the merits of the kingdom by us. We live in a transition time— a transition from death to life, from human injustice to divine justice, from the old to the new—tragically incomplete yet marked here and there, now and then, with clues of what God will someday achieve in perfection. The reign of God is breaking into the world, and we can be its heralds.

14
The Difference He Makes

The other gods were strong; but Thou wast weak;
They rode, but Thou didst stumble to a throne;
But to our wounds only God's wounds can speak,
And not a god has wounds but Thou alone.

Edward Shillito

14

The Difference He Makes

Scott Peck writes that he first approached the Gospels skeptically, suspecting he would find public-relations accounts written by authors who had tied together loose ends and embellished their biographies of Jesus. The Gospels themselves quickly disabused him of that notion.

> I was absolutely thunderstruck by the extraordinary *reality* of the man I found in the Gospels. I discovered a man who was almost continually frustrated. His frustration leaps out of virtually every page: "What do I have to say to you? How many times do I have to say it? What do I have to do to get through to you?" I also discovered a man who was frequently sad and sometimes depressed, frequently anxious and scared.... A man who was terribly, terribly lonely, yet often desperately needed to be alone. I discovered a man so incredibly real that no one could have made Him up.
>
> It occurred to me then that if the Gospel writers had been into PR and embellishment, as I had assumed, they would have created the kind of Jesus three quarters of Christians still seem to be trying to create ... portrayed with a sweet, unending smile on His face, patting little children on the head, just strolling the earth with this unflappable, unshakable equanimity.... But the Jesus of the Gospels—who some suggest is the best-kept secret of Christianity—did not have much "peace of mind," as we ordinarily think of peace of mind in the world's terms, and insofar as we can be His followers, perhaps we won't either.

How can we know the "real Jesus" of whom Scott Peck got a glimpse? I have made a conscious attempt to view Jesus "from below," to grasp as best I can what it must have been like to observe in person the extraordinary events unfolding in Galilee and Judea. Like Scott Peck, I too feel thunderstruck by what I have found.

Icons of the Orthodox Church, stained-glass windows in European cathedrals, and Sunday school art in low-church America all depict on flat planes a placid, "tame" Jesus, yet the Jesus I met in the Gospels was anything but tame. His searing honesty made him seem downright tactless in some settings. Few people felt comfortable around him; those who did were the type no one else felt comfortable around. He was notoriously difficult to predict, pin down, or even understand.

I conclude my survey of Jesus with as many questions as answers. I certainly have not succeeded in taming him, for myself, let alone for anyone else. I now have a built-in suspicion against all attempts to categorize Jesus, to box him in. Jesus is radically unlike anyone else who has ever lived. The difference, in Charles Williams' phrase, is the difference between "one who is an example of living and one who is the life itself."

To sum up what I have learned about Jesus, I offer a series of impressions. They do not form a whole picture by any means, but these are the facets of Jesus' life that challenge me and, I suspect, will never cease to challenge me.

A Sinless Friend of Sinners. When Jesus came to earth, demons recognized him, the sick flocked to him, and sinners doused his feet and head with perfume. Meanwhile he offended pious Jews with their strict preconceptions of what God should be like. Their rejection makes me wonder, Could religious types be doing just the reverse now? Could we be perpetuating an image of Jesus that fits our pious expectations but does not match the person portrayed so vividly in the Gospels?

Jesus was the friend of sinners. He commended a groveling tax collector over a God-fearing Pharisee. The first person to whom he openly revealed himself as Messiah was a Samaritan woman who had a history of five failed marriages and was currently living with yet another man. With his dying breath he pardoned a thief who would have zero opportunity for spiritual growth.

Yet Jesus himself was not a sinner. "Unless your righteousness surpasses that of the Pharisees and the teachers of the law, you will certainly not enter the kingdom of heaven," he taught. The Pharisees themselves searched in vain for proof that he had broken the law of Moses. He had defied certain of their traditions, yes, but at his formal trial the only "crime" that stuck was the one he finally acknowledged, his claim to be Messiah.

I view with amazement Jesus' uncompromising blend of graciousness toward sinners and hostility toward sin, because in much of church history I see virtually the opposite. We give lip service to "hate the sin while loving the sinner," but how well do we practice this principle?

The Christian church has always found ways to soften Jesus' strong words on morality. For three centuries Christians tended to take literally his command to "Resist not evil," but eventually the church developed a doctrine of "just war" and even "holy war." At various times small groups of Christians have followed Jesus' words about disposing of wealth, but most of these have lived on the fringe of a wealthy church establishment. Nowadays many of the same Christians who hotly condemn homosexuality, which Jesus did not mention, disregard his straightforward commands against divorce. We keep redefining sin and changing the emphasis.

At the same time, the institutional church expends much energy positioning itself against the sinful world outside. (A term like "Moral Majority" only sounds appealing to someone already included in it.) I recently attended a play based on stories from a support group comprising people with AIDS. The theater director said he decided to stage the play after hearing a local minister state that he celebrated each time he read an obituary of a young single man, believing each death to be yet another sign of God's disapproval. Increasingly, I fear, the church is viewed as an enemy of sinners.

All too often, sinners feel unloved by a church that, in turn, keeps altering its definition of sin—exactly the opposite of Jesus' pattern. Something has gone awry.

In one of his earlier books, *Shame*, Salman Rushdie said that the true battle of history is fought not between rich and poor, socialist and capitalist, or black and white, but between what he termed the epicure and the puritan. The pendulum of society swings back and forth between those who say, "Anything goes," and those who say, "Oh, no you don't!": the Restoration versus Cromwell, the ACLU versus the religious right, modern secularists versus Islamic fundamentalists. As if to prove his point, soon afterward Iran set a million-dollar bounty on Rushdie's head; he had crossed a line.

History gives ample precedent for legalism and also for decadence. But how does one hold to high standards of moral purity while at the same time showing grace to those who fail those standards? How to embrace the sinner without encouraging sin? Christian history offers few facsimiles of the pattern Jesus laid down.

While I was researching the life of Jesus, I also read several lengthy studies of the first three centuries of the faith. The early church began well, placing a high premium on moral purity. Baptismal candidates had to undergo long periods of instruction, and church discipline was rigorously enforced. Sporadic persecution by Roman emperors helped to purge the church of "lukewarm" Christians. Yet even pagan observers were attracted to the way Christians reached out to others by caring for the oppressed and devoting themselves to the sick and the poor.

A major change took place with the emperor Constantine, who first legalized Christianity and made it a state-subsidized religion. At the time his reign appeared to be the faith's greatest triumph, for the emperor was now using state funds to build churches and sponsor theological conferences rather than to persecute Christians. Alas, the triumph did not come without cost: the two kingdoms got confused. The state began appointing bishops and other church offices, and soon a hierarchy grew up that neatly replicated the hierarchy of the empire itself. As for their part, Christian bishops began imposing morality on society at large, not just the church.

Ever since Constantine, the church has faced the temptation of becoming the "morals police" of society. The Catholic Church in the Middle Ages, Calvin's Geneva, Cromwell's England, Winthrop's New

England, the Russian Orthodox Church—each of these has attempted to legislate a form of Christian morality, and each has in its own way found it hard to communicate grace.

I realize, as I look at the life of Jesus, how far we have come from the divine balance he set out for us. Listening to the sermons and reading the writings of the contemporary church in the U.S., I sometimes detect more of Constantine than of Jesus. The man from Nazareth was a sinless friend of sinners, a pattern that should convict us on both counts.

The God-Man. It would be easier, I sometimes think, if God had given us a set of ideas to mull over and kick around and decide whether to accept or reject. He did not. He gave us himself in the form of a person.

"Jesus saves," announce the bumper stickers—imagine how ridiculous it would sound if you substituted Socrates or Napoleon or Marx. The Buddha gave his disciples permission to forget him as long as they honored his teaching and followed his path. Plato said something similar of Socrates. Jesus, though, pointed to himself and said "*I am the way.*"

Looking at Jesus' life primarily "from below," I have not stressed such concepts as preexistence and divine essence and dual nature, which take up so much space in theology books. It required five centuries for the church to work out the details of Jesus' divinity/humanity, and I have deliberately stayed close to the viewpoint presented by Matthew, Mark, Luke, and John, not the interpretive screen provided by the rest of the New Testament and formalized by the councils of Nicea and Chalcedon.

Even so, the Gospels themselves present the mystery of Jesus' dual identity. How did this Galilean Jew with a family and hometown come to be worshiped as "Very God of Very God"? Simple: Read the Gospels, especially John. Jesus accepted Peter's prostrate worship. To a lame man and an adulterous woman and many others he said commandingly, "I forgive your sins." To Jerusalem he remarked, "I am sending you prophets and wise men and teachers," as if he was not a rabbi standing before them but the sovereign God of history. When challenged, Jesus answered bluntly, "I and the Father are one." "Before Abraham was born, *I am*," he said on another occasion, uttering the sacred Hebrew word for God in case they missed the point. Devout Jews did not miss the point; several times they picked up stones to punish him for blasphemy.

Jesus' audacious claims about himself pose what may be the central problem of all history, the dividing point between Christianity and other religions. Although Muslims and, increasingly, Jews respect Jesus as a great teacher and prophet, no Muslim can imagine Mohammed claiming to be Allah any more than a Jew can imagine Moses claiming to be Yahweh. Likewise, Hindus believe in many incarnations but not one Incarnation, while Buddhists have no categories in which to conceive of a sovereign God becoming a human being.

Could Jesus' disciples have back-filled his teaching to include such brazen claims as part of their conspiracy to launch a new religion? Unlikely. The disciples, as we have seen, were inept conspirators, and in fact the Gospels portray them as resistant to the very idea of Jesus' divinity. Every disciple, after all, belonged to the most fiercely monotheistic race on earth. As late as Jesus' last night with them, after they had heard all the claims and seen all the miracles, one of them asked the Teacher, "Show us the Father." Still they could not grasp it. Jesus was never clearer in his response: "Anyone who has seen me has seen the Father."

It is an incontestable fact of history that Jesus' followers, the same ones who were scratching their heads over his words at the Last Supper, a few weeks later were proclaiming him as the "Holy and Righteous One," the "Lord," the "author of life." By the time the Gospels were written they regarded him as the Word who was God, through whom all things were made. In a later letter John took pains to point out "That which was from the beginning, which we have heard, which we have seen with our eyes, which we have looked at and our hands have touched—this we proclaim concerning the Word of life." The book of Revelation describes Jesus as a blazing figure whose face "was like the sun shining in all its brilliance," but always the author connected this Cosmic Christ to the actual Galilean man the disciples had heard and seen and touched.

Why would Jesus' disciples invent these notions? Followers of Mohammed or Buddha, willing to lay down their lives for their master, did not make such a jump in logic. Why would Jesus' disciples, so slow to accept it themselves, require of us a belief so difficult to swallow? Why make it harder rather than easier to accept Jesus?

The alternative to a conspiracy theory, regarding Jesus himself as the source of the audacious claims, only magnifies the problem. As I read through the Gospels, I sometimes try to view them as an outsider might, in the same way I read the Qur'an or the *Upanishads*. When I take up that perspective I find myself repeatedly startled, even offended, by the arrogance of one who says, "I am the way, the truth and the life. No one comes to the Father except through me." I can read only a few pages before stumbling across one of these statements that seem outlandishly to undercut all his wise teaching and good deeds. If Jesus is not God, then he is badly deluded.

C. S. Lewis made this point forcefully. "The discrepancy between the depth and sanity and (let me add) *shrewdness* of His moral teaching and the rampant megalomania which must lie behind His theological teaching unless He is indeed God, has never been satisfactorily got over," he wrote in *Miracles*. Lewis phrased the argument more colorfully in a famous passage in *Mere Christianity*: "A man who was merely a man and said the sort of things Jesus said would not be a great moral teacher. He would either be a lunatic—on the level with the man who says he is a poached egg—or else he would be the Devil of Hell. You must make your choice. Either this man was, and is, the Son of God; or else a madman or something worse."

I remember reading that quote from *Mere Christianity* in college and thinking it a gross exaggeration. I knew many people who respected Jesus as a great moral teacher but judged him neither the Son of God nor a lunatic. That was, in fact, my own view at the time. As I have studied the Gospels, though, I have come to agree with Lewis. Jesus never temporized or waffled about his identity. He was either the Son of God sent to save the world or an impostor deserving of crucifixion. The people of his day understood the binary choice precisely.

I now see that Jesus' entire life stands or falls on his claim to be God. I cannot trust his promised forgiveness unless he has the authority to back up such an offer. I cannot trust his words about the other side ("I go to prepare a place for you . . .") unless I believe what he said about having come from the Father and returning to the Father. Most important, unless he was in some way God, I must view the cross as an act of divine cruelty rather than sacrificial love.

Sidney Carter wrote this disturbing poem:

> *But God is up in heaven*
> *And he doesn't do a thing,*
> *With a million angels watching,*
> *And they never move a wing. . . .*
> *It's God they ought to crucify*
> *Instead of you and me,*
> *I said to this Carpenter*
> *A-hanging on the tree.*

Theologically, the only answer to Carter's accusation is the mysterious doctrine that, in Paul's words, "God was in Christ reconciling the world to himself." In an incomprehensible way, God personally experienced the cross. Otherwise, Calvary would go down in history as a form of cosmic child abuse, rather than a day we call Good Friday.*

Portrait of God. George Buttrick, former chaplain at Harvard, recalls that students would come into his office, plop down on a chair and declare, "I don't believe in God." Buttrick would give this disarming reply: "Sit down and tell me what kind of God you don't believe in. I probably don't believe in that God either." And then he would talk about Jesus, the corrective to all our assumptions about God.

---

*In Frederick Buechner's words, "What is new about the New Covenant, therefore, is not the idea that God loves the world enough to bleed for it but the claim that here he is actually putting his money where his mouth is. Like a father saying about his sick child, 'I'd do anything to make you well,' God finally calls his own bluff and does it. Jesus Christ is what God does, and the cross where he did it is the central symbol of New Covenant faith."

Books of theology tend to define God by what he is not: God is *im*mortal, *in*visible, *in*finite. But what is God like, positively? For the Christian, Jesus answers such all-important questions. The apostle Paul boldly called Jesus "the image of the invisible God." Jesus was God's exact replica: "For God was pleased to have all his fullness dwell in him."

God is, in a word, Christlike. Jesus presents a God with skin on whom we can take or leave, love or ignore. In this visible, scaled-down model we can discern God's features more clearly.

I must admit that Jesus has revised in flesh many of my harsh and unpalatable notions about God. *Why am I a Christian?* I sometimes ask myself, and to be perfectly honest the reasons reduce to two: (1) the lack of good alternatives, and (2) Jesus. Brilliant, untamed, tender, creative, slippery, irreducible, paradoxically humble—Jesus stands up to scrutiny. He is who I want my God to be.

Martin Luther encouraged his students to flee the hidden God and run to Christ, and I now know why. If I use a magnifying glass to examine a fine painting, the object in the center of the glass stays crisp and clear, while around the edges the view grows increasingly distorted. For me, Jesus has become the focal point. When I speculate about such imponderables as the problem of pain or providence versus free will, everything becomes fuzzy. But if I look at Jesus himself, at how he treated actual people in pain, at his calls to free and diligent action, clarity is restored. I can worry myself into a state of spiritual ennui over questions like "What good does it do to pray if God already knows everything?" Jesus silences such questions: he prayed, so should we.

During my work on *The Student Bible* I spent several years immersed in the Old Testament. With a steady diet of "the Old Covenant," I absorbed something like the attitude of an Orthodox Jew. The Old Testament underscores the vast gulf between God and humanity. God is supreme, omnipotent, transcendent, and any limited contact with him puts human beings at risk. The worship instructions in a book like Leviticus remind me of a manual on handling radioactive material. Bring only spotless lambs to the tabernacle. Do not touch the Ark. Always let smoke cover it; if you look at the ark, you'll die. Never enter the Most Holy Place, except for the high priest on the one permitted day of the year. On that day, Yom Kippur, fasten a rope around his ankle, and a bell, so that if he makes a mistake and dies inside, his corpse can be dragged out.

Jesus' disciples grew up in such an environment, never pronouncing God's name, complying with the intricate code of cleanliness, heeding the requirements of Mosaic law. They took for granted, as did most other religions of the time, that worship must include sacrifice: something had to die. Their God had forbidden human sacrifice, and so on a festival day Jerusalem was filled with the bleats and cries of a quarter million animals destined for the temple altar. The noise and smell of sacrifice were sharp sensory reminders of the great gulf between God and themselves.

I worked in the Old Testament for so long that, when one day I skipped over to the book of Acts, the contrast jolted me. Now God's followers, good Jews most of them, were meeting in private homes, singing hymns, and addressing God with the informal *Abba*. Where was the fear, and the solemn protocol required of anyone who dared approach *mysterium tremendum*? No one brought animals to sacrifice; death did not enter into worship except for the solemn moment when they broke bread and drank wine together, reflecting on the once-for-all sacrifice Jesus had made.

In these ways, Jesus introduced profound changes in how we view God. Mainly, he brought God near. To Jews who knew a distant, ineffable God, Jesus brought the message that God cares for the grass of the field, feeds the sparrows, numbers the hairs on a person's head. To Jews who dared not pronounce the Name, Jesus brought the shocking intimacy of the Aramaic word *Abba*. It was a familiar term of family affection, onomatopoeic like "Dada," the first word many children spoke. Before Jesus, no one would have thought of applying such a word to Yahweh, the Sovereign Lord of the universe. After him, it became a standard term of address even in Greek-speaking congregations; imitating Jesus, they borrowed the foreign word to express their own intimacy with the Father.

An event happened as Jesus hung on the cross that seemed to seal the new intimacy for the young church. Mark records that just as Jesus breathed his last, "The curtain of the temple was torn in two from top to bottom." This massive curtain had served to wall off the Most Holy

Place, where God's presence dwelled. As the author of Hebrews would later note, the tearing of this curtain showed beyond doubt exactly what was accomplished by Jesus' death. No more sacrifices would ever be required. No high priest need tremble to enter the sacred room.

Those of us in modern times have lived under the new intimacy for so long that we take it for granted. We sing choruses to God and converse in casual prayers. To us, the notion of sacrifice seems primitive. Too easily we forget what it cost Jesus to win for us all—ordinary people, not just priests—immediate access to God's presence. We know God as *Abba*, the loving Father, only because of Jesus.

The Lover. Left on my own, I would come up with a very different notion of God. My God would be static, unchanging; I would not conceive of God "coming" and "going." My God would control all things with power, stamping out opposition swiftly and decisively. As a Muslim boy told psychiatrist Robert Coles, "Allah would tell the world, everyone, 'God is great, very great' . . . He would make everyone believe in Him, and if someone refused, he'd die—that's what would happen if Allah came here."

Because of Jesus, however, I must adjust my instinctive notions about God. (Perhaps that lay at the heart of his mission?) Jesus reveals a God who comes in search of us, a God who makes room for our freedom even when it costs the Son's life, a God who is vulnerable. Above all, Jesus reveals a God who is love.

On our own, would any of us come up with the notion of a God who loves and yearns to be loved? Those raised in a Christian tradition may miss the shock of Jesus' message, but in truth love has never been a normal way of describing what happens between human beings and their God. Not once does the Qur'an apply the word love to God. Aristotle stated bluntly, "It would be eccentric for anyone to claim that he loved Zeus"—or that Zeus loved a human being, for that matter. In dazzling contrast, the Christian Bible affirms, "God *is* love," and cites love as the main reason Jesus came to earth: "This is how God showed his love among us: He sent his one and only Son into the world that we might live through him."

As Søren Kierkegaard wrote, "The bird on the branch, the lily in the meadow, the stag in the forest, the fish in the sea, and countless joyful people sing: God is love! But under all these sopranos, as if it were a sustained bass part, sounds the *de profundis* of the sacrificed: God is love."

Jesus' own stories about God's love express a quality almost of desperation. In Luke 15 he tells of a woman who searches all night until she finds a valuable coin and of a shepherd who hunts in the darkness until he finds the one sheep who has wandered astray. Each parable concludes with a scene of rejoicing, a celestial party that erupts over the news of another sinner welcomed home. Finally, building to an emotional climax, Jesus tells the story of the lost son, a prodigal who spurns the love of his father and squanders his inheritance in a far country.

The priest Henri Nouwen sat in the Hermitage Museum in St. Petersburg, Russia, for many hours meditating on Rembrandt's great painting *Return of the Prodigal Son*. While staring at the painting, Nouwen gained a new insight into the parable: the mystery that Jesus himself became something of a prodigal son for our sakes. "He left the house of his heavenly Father, came to a foreign country, gave away all that he had, and returned through a cross to his Father's home. All of this he did, not as a rebellious son, but as the obedient son, sent out to bring home all the lost children of God ... Jesus is the prodigal son of the prodigal Father who gave away everything the Father had entrusted to him so that I could become like him and return with him to his Father's home."

In a nutshell, the Bible from Genesis 3 to Revelation 22 tells the story of a God reckless with desire to get his family back. God struck the decisive blow of reconciliation when he sent the Son on the long journey to planet earth. The Bible's last scene, like the parable of the lost son, ends in jubilation, the family united once again.

Elsewhere, the Gospels comment on the extent to which God went to accomplish that rescue plan of love.

> This is love: not that we loved God, but that he loved us and sent his Son as an atoning sacrifice for our sins.
> Greater love has no one than this, that he lay down his life for his friends.

For God so loved the world that he gave his one and only Son ...

I remember a long night sitting in uncomfortable Naugahyde chairs in O'Hare Airport, waiting impatiently for a flight that was delayed for five hours. I happened to be next to a wise woman who was traveling to the same conference. The long delay and the late hour combined to create a melancholy mood, and in five hours we had time to share all the dysfunctions of childhood, our disappointments with the church, our questions of faith. I was writing the book *Disappointment with God* at the time, and I felt burdened by other people's pains and sorrows, doubts and unanswered prayers.

My companion listened to me in silence for a very long time, and then out of nowhere she asked a question that has always stayed with me. "Philip, do you ever just let God love you?" she said. "It's pretty important, I think."

I realized with a start that she had brought to light a gaping hole in my spiritual life. For all my absorption in the Christian faith, I had missed the most important message of all. The story of Jesus is the story of a celebration, a story of love. It involves pain and disappointment, yes, for God as well as for us. But Jesus embodies the promise of a God who will go to any length to win us back. Not the least of Jesus' accomplishments is that he made us somehow lovable to God.

The novelist and literary critic Reynolds Price put it this way: "He says in the clearest voice we have the sentence that mankind craves from stories—*The Maker of all things loves and wants me* ... In no other book our culture owns can we see a clearer graph of that need, that tall enormous radiant arc—fragile creatures made by God's hand, hurled into space, then caught at last by a man in some ways like ourselves."

Portrait of Humanity. When a light is brought into a room, what was a window becomes also a mirror reflecting back the contents of that room. In Jesus not only do we have a window to God, we also have a mirror of ourselves, a reflection of what God had in mind when he created this "poor, bare, forked animal." Human beings were, after all, created in the image of God; Jesus reveals what that image should look like.

"The Incarnation shows man the greatness of his misery by the greatness of the remedy which he required," said Pascal. In a most unsettling way Jesus exposed our failures as human beings. We tend to excuse our many faults by saying, "That's just human." A man gets drunk, a woman has an affair, a child tortures an animal, a nation goes to war: that's just human. Jesus put a stop to such talk. By enacting what we ought to be like, he showed who we were meant to be and how far we miss the mark.

"Behold the man!" Pilate cried. Behold the best example yet of humanity. Yet look at what it got him. Jesus unmasked for all time the jealousy, the lust for power, the violence that infects this planet like a virus. In a weird sort of way, that was the intent of the Incarnation. Jesus knew what he was getting into by coming to this planet; his death had been decreed from the beginning. He came to make an exchange of the most preposterous kind, as described in the Epistles:

> ... though he was rich, yet for your sakes he became poor,
> so that you through his poverty might become rich.
>
> Who, being in very nature God ... made himself nothing, taking the very nature of a servant, being made in human likeness.
>
> God made him who had no sin to be sin for us, so that in him we might become the righteousness of God.
>
> And he died for all, that those who live should no longer live for themselves but for him who died for them and was raised again.

Our riches for poverty, deity for servanthood, perfection for sin, his death for our life—the exchange seems entirely one-sided. But elsewhere in the Epistles can be found intriguing hints that the Incarnation had meaning for God as well as for human beings. Indeed, the suffering endured on earth served as a kind of "learning experience" for God. Such words sound faintly heretical, but I am merely following Hebrews: "Although he was a son, he learned obedience from what he suffered." Elsewhere, that book tells us that the author of our salvation was "made perfect" through suffering. Commentaries often avoid these phrases, for they are difficult to reconcile with traditional notions of an unchanging

God. To me, they demonstrate certain "changes" that had to take place within the Godhead before we could be reconciled.

During that wrinkle in time known as the Incarnation, God experienced what it is like to be a human being. In thirty-three years on earth God's Son learned about poverty and about family squabbles and social rejection and verbal abuse and betrayal. He learned, too, about pain. What it feels like to have an accuser leave the red imprint of his fingers on your face. What it feels like to have a whip studded with metal lashed across your back. What it feels like to have a crude iron spike pounded through muscle, tendon, and bone. On earth, God's Son "learned" all that.

God's character did not permit the option of simply declaring about this defective planet, "It doesn't matter." God's Son had to encounter evil personally in a way that perfect deity had never before encountered evil. He had to forgive sin by taking on our sin. He had to defeat death by dying. He had to learn sympathy for human beings by becoming one. The author of Hebrews reports that Jesus became a "sympathetic" advocate for us. There is only one way to learn sympathy, as signified by the Greek roots of the word, *syn pathos*, "to feel or suffer with." Because of the Incarnation, Hebrews implies, God hears our prayers in a new way, having lived here and having prayed as a weak and vulnerable human being.*

In one of his last statements before dying, Jesus prayed, "Father, forgive them"—all of them, the Roman soldiers, the religious leaders, his disciples who had fled in darkness, you, me, who have denied him in so many ways—"forgive them, for they do not know what they are doing." Only by becoming a human being could the Son of God truly say with understanding, "They do not know what they are doing." He had lived among us. Now, he understood.

* * *

---

*As a doctor who works in hospice told me, "When my patients pray, they are talking to someone who has actually died—something that's not true of any other adviser, counselor, or death expert."

The Wounded Healer. Goethe asked, "There the cross stands, thickly wreathed in roses. Who put the roses on the cross?"

In my travels to foreign countries, I have noticed the striking differences of the symbols used by the great religions. In India, where the four largest religions coexist, I took a brisk walk through the large city of Bombay in the course of which I came upon worship centers of all four.

Hindu temples were everywhere, even portable temples on mobile carts such as sidewalk vendors use, and each had an elaboration of carved, brightly painted images depicting some of the thousands of gods and goddesses in the Hindu pantheon. In stark contrast, a large Muslim mosque in the center of the city contained no images; a soaring spire or minaret pointed skyward, toward the one God, Allah, who could never be reduced to a graven image. Looking at Hindu and Muslim buildings, virtually side by side, I could better understand why each religion finds the other so incomprehensible.

I also visited a Buddhist center that afternoon. Compared to the crowded, noisy streets outside, it offered an atmosphere of serenity. Monks in saffron robes knelt in prayer in the dark, quiet room suffused with the smell of incense. A gilded statue of the Buddha dominated the room, his sly smile expressing the Buddhist belief that the key to contentment lies in developing inner strength that allows one to surmount any suffering in life.

And then I came across a Christian church, a Protestant church of a kind that discouraged images. It most closely resembled the Muslim mosque, with one exception: atop the spire above the church stood a large, ornate cross.

In a foreign country, uprooted from my own culture, I saw the cross with new eyes, and suddenly it struck me as bizarre. What possessed Christians to seize upon this execution device as a symbol for faith? Why not do everything within our power to squelch the memory of the scandalous injustice? We could stress the Resurrection, mentioning the cross only as an unfortunate footnote of history. Why make it the centerpiece of the faith? "Why, that picture might make some people lose their faith!" cried one of Dostoevsky's characters after viewing Holbein's painting of the crucified Christ.

There is, of course, the plain fact that Jesus commanded us to remember his death when we gather together in worship. He did not need to say, "This do in remembrance of me," about Palm Sunday or Easter, but clearly he did not want us to forget what happened on Calvary. Christians have not forgotten. In John Updike's words, the cross "profoundly offended the Greeks with their playful, beautiful, invulnerable pantheon and the Jews with their traditional expectations of a regal Messiah. Yet it answered, as it were, to the facts, to something deep within men. God crucified formed a bridge between our human perception of a cruelly imperfect and indifferent world and our human need for God, our human sense that God is present."

I realized, as I stood on a Bombay street corner with pedestrians, bicyclists, and farm animals swarming around me, why the cross had come to mean so much to Christians, why it had come to mean so much to me. The cross enacts for us deep truths that would make no sense apart from it. The cross gives hope when there is no hope.

The apostle Paul heard from God, "My [God's] power is made perfect in weakness," and then concluded about himself, "When I am weak, then I am strong." "That is why," he added, "I delight in weakness, in insults, in hardships, in persecutions, in difficulties." He was pointing to a mystery which goes several steps beyond the Buddhist way of coming to terms with suffering and hardship. Paul spoke not of resignation but of transformation. The very things that make us feel inadequate, the very things that plunder hope, these are what God uses to accomplish his work. For proof, look at the cross.

I wish someone with the talents of Milton or Dante would render the scene that must have transpired in hell on the day that Jesus died. No doubt an infernal celebration broke out. The snake of Genesis had struck at the heel of God; the dragon of Revelation had devoured the child at last. God's Son, sent to earth on a rescue mission, had ended up dangling from a cross like some ragged scarecrow. Oh, what a diabolical victory!

Oh, what a short-lived victory. In the most ironic twist of all history, what Satan meant for evil, God meant for good. Jesus' death on the cross bridged the gap between a perfect God and a fatally flawed humanity. On the day we call Good Friday, God defeated sin, routed death, triumphed over Satan, and got his family back. In that act of transformation, God took the worst deed of history and turned it into the greatest victory. No wonder the symbol never went away; no wonder Jesus commanded that we never forget.

Because of the cross, I have hope. It is through the Servant's wounds that we are healed, said Isaiah—not his miracles. If God can wrest such triumph out of the jaws of apparent defeat, can draw strength from a moment of ultimate weakness, what might God do with the apparent failures and hardships of my own life?

Nothing—not even the murder of God's own Son—can end the relationship between God and human beings. In the alchemy of redemption, that most villainous crime becomes our healing strength.

The fatally wounded healer came back on Easter, the day that gives a sneak preview of how all history will look from the vantage point of eternity, when every scar, every hurt, every disappointment will be seen in a different light. Our faith begins where it might have seemed to end. Between the cross and the empty tomb hovers the promise of history: hope for the world, and hope for each one of us who lives in it.

The German theologian Jürgen Moltmann expresses in a single sentence the great span from Good Friday to Easter. It is, in fact, a summary of human history, past, present, and future: "God weeps with us so that we may someday laugh with him."

The author and preacher Tony Campolo delivers a stirring sermon adapted from an elderly black pastor at his church in Philadelphia. "It's Friday, but Sunday's Comin'" is the title of the sermon, and once you know the title you know the whole sermon. In a cadence that increases in tempo and in volume, Campolo contrasts how the world looked on Friday—when the forces of evil won over the forces of good, when every friend and disciple fled in fear, when the Son of God died on a cross—with how it looked on Easter Sunday. The disciples who lived through both days, Friday and Sunday, never doubted God again. They had learned that when God seems most absent he may be closest of all, when God looks most powerless he may be most powerful, when God looks most dead he may be coming back to life. They had learned never to count God out.

Campolo skipped one day in his sermon, though. The other two days have earned names on the church calendar: Good Friday and Easter Sunday. Yet in a real sense we live on Saturday, the day with no name. What the disciples experienced in small scale—three days, in grief over one man who had died on a cross—we now live through on cosmic scale. Human history grinds on, between the time of promise and fulfillment. Can we trust that God can make something holy and beautiful and good out of a world that includes Bosnia and Rwanda, and inner-city ghettoes and jammed prisons in the richest nation on earth? It's Saturday on planet earth; will Sunday ever come?

That dark, Golgothan Friday can only be called Good because of what happened on Easter Sunday, a day which gives a tantalizing clue to the riddle of the universe. Easter opened up a crack in a universe winding down toward entropy and decay, sealing the promise that someday God will enlarge the miracle of Easter to cosmic scale.

It is a good thing to remember that in the cosmic drama, we live out our days on Saturday, the in-between day with no name. I know a woman whose grandmother lies buried under 150-year-old live oak trees in the cemetery of an Episcopal church in rural Louisiana. In accordance with the grandmother's instructions, only one word is carved on the tombstone: "Waiting."

Sources

Chapter 1

13: *Dickens*: Charles Dickens, *The Life of Our Lord*. London: Associated Newspapers Ltd., 1934.

15: *Pasolini*: Richard H. Campbell and Michael R. Pitts, *The Bible on Film*. Metuchen, N.J.: The Scarecrow Press, 1981, p. 54.

16: *Milliken*: Bill Milliken, *So Long, Sweet Jesus*. New York: Prometheus Press, n.d.

17: *H. G. Wells*: Quoted from *The Greatest Men in History* in Mark Link, S.J., *He Is the Still Point of the Turning World*. Chicago: Argus Communications, 1971, p. 111.

17: *"I tell you, whoever"*: Luke 12:8.

17: *"Do you have eyes"*: Job 10:4.

18: *Blake*: William Blake, "The Everlasting Gospel," *The Portable Blake*. New York: The Viking Press, 1968, p. 612.

18: *Barth*: Karl Barth, *The Word of God and the Word of Man*. New York: Harper & Row, Publishers, 1957, p. 62.

19: *Lakota*: Cullen Murphy, "Who Do Men Say That I Am?" *The Atlantic Monthly*, December 1986, p. 58.

19: *Norm Evans*: Quoted in "Making It Big," *The Reformed Journal*, December 1986, p. 4.

19: *Fritz Peterson*: Quoted in *The Chicago Tribune*, May 24, 1981.

20: *"scholar at the University of Chicago"*: David Tracy, quoted in Murphy, "Who Do Men Say That I Am?" op cit., p. 38.

20: *Phillips*: J. B. Phillips, *Ring of Truth*. Wheaton, Ill.: Harold Shaw Publishers, 1977, p. 79.

20: *"With a loud cry"*: Mark 15:37.

21: *"Blessed is he"*: Matthew 11:6, RSV.

21: *McGrath*: Alister McGrath, *Understanding Jesus*. Grand Rapids: Zondervan Publishing House, 1987, p. 52.

22: *Kasper*: Walter Kasper, *Jesus the Christ*. New York: Paulist Press, 1977, p. 46.

23: *"Get behind me"*: Matthew 16:23.

23: *Wink*: Walter Wink, *Engaging the Powers*. Minneapolis: Fortress Press, 1992, p. 129.

23: *Sayers*: Dorothy Sayers, *Christian Letters to a Post-Christian World*. Grand Rapids: William B. Eerdmans Publishing Company, 1969, p. 15.

24: *Tuchman*: Barbara Tuchman, *Practicing History*. New York: Alfred A. Knopf, 1981, p. 22.

24: *Pascal*: Blaise Pascal, *Pensées*. New York: E. P. Dutton, Inc., 1958, p. 228.

24: *Luther*: Quoted in Jürgen Moltmann, *The Way of Jesus Christ*. San Francisco: Harper-SanFrancisco, 1990, p. 84.

Chapter 2

30: *"salvation from"*: Luke 1:71.

30: *"sword will pierce"*: Luke 2:35.

31: *Lewis*: C. S. Lewis, "The Grand Miracle," in *God in the Dock: Essays on Theology and Ethics*. Grand Rapids: William B. Eerdmans Publishing Company, 1972, p. 84.

32: *Muggeridge*: Malcolm Muggeridge, *Jesus: the Man Who Lives*. New York: Harper & Row, 1975, p. 19.

32: "*I am the Lord's*": Luke 1:38.

33: *Ricci*: Jonathan D. Spence, *The Memory Palace of Matteo Ricci*. New York: Penguin Books, 1984, p. 245.

33: "*This child is destined*": Luke 2:34.

33: *Augustus*: John Dominic Crossan, *The Historical Jesus: The Life of a Mediterranean Jewish Peasant*. San Francisco: HarperCollins Publishers, 1991, p. 31.

34, see also p. 57: *Herod the Great*: Joseph Klausner, *Jesus of Nazareth: His Life, Times, and Teaching*. London: George Allen & Unwin, Ltd, 1925, p. 146.

34: *Auden*: *The Collected Poetry of W. H. Auden*. New York: Random House, 1945, p. 455.

36: *Donne*: John Donne, "Nativity," *The Complete English Poems*. New York: Penguin Books, 1971, p. 307.

36: "*made himself nothing*": Philippians 2:7.

36: "*silver as common*": 1 Kings 10:27.

36: *Figgis*: Neville Figgis, *The Gospel and Human Needs*. London: Longmans, Green, 1909, p. 11.

37: "*O here and now*": W. H. Auden, *The Collected Poetry*, op cit., pp. 443–44.

39: "*brought down rulers*": Luke 1:52.

39: *Tokes*: Laszlo Tokes, *The Fall of Tyrants*. Wheaton, Ill.: Crossway Books, 1990, p. 186.

41: *Lubavitcher*: David Remnick, "Waiting for the Apocalypse in Crown Heights," *The New Yorker*, December 21, 1992, p. 52ff.

42: "*Isn't his mother's name*": Matthew 13:54–55.

42: "*Nazareth!*": John 1:46.

42: "*demon-possessed*": John 10:20.

42: *Chesterton*: G. K. Chesterton, *Orthodoxy*, Garden City, N.Y.: Doubleday/Image Books, 1959, p. 137.

43: *Phillips*: J. B. Phillips, *New Testament Christianity*. London: Hodder & Stoughton, 1958, pp. 27–33.

44: *Apollo astronauts*: Quoted in William M. Justice, *Our Visited Planet*. New York: Vantage Press, 1973, p. 167.

45: "*He is the image*": Colossians 1:15, 17.

Chapter 3

50: *Buber*: Quoted in Geza Vermes, *Jesus the Jew: A Historian's Reading of the Gospels*. London: Collins, 1973, p. 9.

51: *Moltmann*: Jürgen Moltmann, *The Way of Jesus Christ*, op cit., p. 168.

52: "*My God, my God*": Matthew 27:46.

52: "*I am not*": John 3:28.

52: "*Are you the one*": Matthew 11:3.

53: "*rend the heavens*": Isaiah 64:1.

53: "*he hath practised sorcery*": Joseph Klausner, *Jesus of Nazareth*, op cit., p. 27.

54: "*God did not beget*": Jürgen Moltmann, *The Crucified God*. New York: Harper & Row, 1974, p. 235.

55: *Dodd*: C. H. Dodd, *The Founder of Christianity*. London: The Macmillan Company, 1970, p. 103.

55: *Pelikan*: Jaroslav Pelikan, *Jesus Through the Centuries*. New Haven, Conn.: Yale University Press, 1985, p. 20

56: *Bonhoeffer*: Dietrich Bonhoeffer, *Christ the Center*. San Francisco: Harper & Row, Publishers, 1978, p. 61.

56: *Virgil*: Quoted in Jaroslav Pelikan, *Jesus Through the Centuries*, op cit., p. 35.

57: *Barclay*: Quoted in Malcolm Muggeridge, *Jesus: the Man Who Lives*, op cit., p. 74.

57: *Antiochus*: Donald B. Kraybill, *The Upside-Down Kingdom*. Scottsdale, Pa.: The Herald Press, 1990, p. 38.

57: "*Would the Romans*": Joseph Klausner, *Jesus of Nazareth*, op cit., p. 144.

58: *Muggeridge*: Malcolm Muggeridge, *Jesus: the Man Who Lives*, op cit., p. 13.

60: "*How can the Christ*": John 7:41.

60: "*Nazareth!*": John 1:46.

60: "*Galilee, Galilee, you hate*": Vermes, *Jesus the Jew*, op cit., p. 53.

60: "*Are you from Galilee*": John 7:52.

60: "*You ought to leave*": John 7:3.

61: "*His high priests*": Joseph Klausner, *Jesus of Nazareth*, op cit., p. 151.

62: *Josephus*: A. N. Wilson, *Jesus*. New York: W. W. Norton & Company, 1992, p. xii.

62: "*It is better*": John 11:50.

64: "*If anyone comes*": Luke 14:26.

64: "*I am able*": Matthew 26:61.

Chapter 4

70: "*Jesus, full of the Holy Spirit*": Luke 4:1–2.

71: *Hopkins*: *The Sermons and Devotional Writings of Gerard Manley Hopkins*. London: Oxford University Press, 1959, pp. 180–83.

71: *Luther*: Quoted in F. Forrester Church, *Entertaining Angels*. San Francisco: Harper & Row, Publishers, 1987, p. 54.

72: *Muggeridge*: Malcolm Muggeridge, *Jesus: the Man Who Lives*, op cit., p. 52ff.

73: "*Out of my sight*": Matthew 16:23.

73: "*Never, Lord*": Matthew 16:22.

73: "*Aren't you*": Luke 23:39.

73: "*Let him come down*": Matthew 27:42–43.

74: *Milton*: "Paradise Regained," *The Complete Poems of John Milton*. New York: Washington Square Press, Inc., 1964, p. 393.

74: *Karamazov*: Fyodor Dostoevsky, *The Brothers Karamazov*. Garden City, N.Y.: Nelson Doubleday, Inc., n.d., pp. 229–39.

76n.: *Sayers*: Dorothy Sayers, *The Man Born to Be King*. Grand Rapids: William B. Eerdmans Publishing Company, n.d., p. 35.

76: *Kierkegaard*: Quoted in D. R. Davies, *On to Orthodoxy*. London: Hodder and Stoughton, 1939, p. 162.

77: *MacDonald*: George MacDonald, *Life Essential, The Hope of the Gospel*. Wheaton, Ill.: Harold Shaw Publishers, 1974, pp. 24–25.

77: "*O Jerusalem*": Matthew 23:37.

78: "*I, when I am*": John 12:32–33.

80: "*Jesus looked at him*": Mark 10:21.

80: "*Because of the increase*": Matthew 24:12.

80: "*held it more humane*": Milton, "Paradise Regained," op cit., 368.

80: "*I have prayed*": Luke 22:32.

80: "*You do not*": John 6:67.

80: "*Take up your cross*": Matthew 16:24.

81: *Thielicke*: Helmut Thielicke, *Our Heavenly Father*. Grand Rapids: Baker Book House, 1974, p. 123.

81: "*We do not have*": Hebrews 4:15; 2:18.

Chapter 5

86: *Lentulus*: Sherwood Wirt, *Jesus, Man of Joy*. Nashville: Thomas Nelson, 1991, p. 28.

86: "*a gluttonous man*": Luke 7:34, KJV.

87: "*How can the guests*": Mark 2:19.

87: "*Just as there were many*": Isaiah 52:14; 53:2–3.

87: *John the Baptist admitted*: John 1:33.

88: "*My soul is*": Matthew 26:38.

88: "*Your faith*": Matthew 9:22.

88: "*a true Israelite*": John 1:47.

89: *Mary Gordon*: Alfred Corn, ed., *Incarnation: Contemporary Writers on the New Testament*. New York: Viking Penguin, 1990, p. 21.

90: *Lewis*: C. S. Lewis, *The Four Loves*. London: Geoffrey Bles, 1960, p. 67.

90: "*Son, why*": Luke 2:48–49.

90: "*Quiet!*": Mark 4:39.

91: *Maritain*: Quoted in John S. Dunne, *The Church of the Poor Devil*. New York: Macmillan Publishing Co., Inc., 1982, p.111.

91: "*If it is possible*": Matthew 26:39.

91: *Crossan*: John Dominic Crossan, *The Historical Jesus*, op cit., p. xi.

91: "*Isn't he*": Matthew 13:54–55, paraphrased.

92: "*wicked and adulterous*": Matthew 12:39.

92: "*Believe me*": John 14:11.

93: *Buechner*: Frederick Buechner, *Peculiar Treasures*. San Francisco: Harper & Row, Publishers, 1979, p. 70.

93: "*Foxes*": Matthew 8:20.

94: *Berryman*: John Berryman, "Eleven Addresses to the Lord," in *Love & Fame*. New York: Farrar, Straus and Giroux, 1970, p. 92.

94: *Pelikan*: Jaroslav Pelikan, *Jesus Through the Centuries*, op cit., p. 13.

95: "*full of grace*": John 1:14.

95: "*not impose*": Joseph Klausner, *From Jesus to Paul*, quoted in Everett F. Harrison, *A Short Life of Christ*. Grand Rapids: Wm. B. Eerdmans Publishing Company, 1968, p. 98.

96: "*Be perfect*": Matthew 5:48.

96: *Trueblood*: Elton Trueblood, *The Yoke of Christ and Other Sermons*. Waco, Tex.: Word Books, 1958, p. 113.

96: "*Count the cost*": Luke 14:28, RSV.

96: *Neusner*: Jacob Neusner, *A Rabbi Talks with Jesus*. New York: Doubleday, 1993, pp. 24, 29, 31, 53.

96: "*he taught*": Matthew 7:29.

96: "*You have heard*": Matthew 5:21, et al.

97: "*This fellow*": Matthew 9:3.

97: "*No one ever*": John 7:46.

97: "*Be quiet*": Mark 1:25.

97: "*You deaf*": Mark 9:25.

97: "*We had hoped*": Luke 24:21.

97: "*the whole world*": John 12:19.

98: "*Whoever finds*": Matthew 10:39.

98: *"You don't know"*: Matthew 20:22.

99: *"Are you so dull"*: Mark 7:18.

99: *"How long"*: Matthew 17:17.

99: *"that they might"*: Mark 3:14.

100: *"At that time"*: Luke 10:21.

Chapter 6

105: *"Blessed are . . ."*: All Beatitudes taken from Matthew 5.

109: *"The spirit of self-sacrifice"*: Quoted in Alister Hardy, *The Biology of God*. New York: Taplinger Publishing Company, 1975, p. 146.

111: *Lewis*: C. S. Lewis, *The Weight of Glory*. Grand Rapids: William B. Eerdmans Publishing Company, 1965, pp. 1–2.

113: *Phillips*: J. B. Phillips, *Good News*. London: Geoffrey Bles, 1964, pp. 33–4.

113n.: *Kasper*: Walter Kasper, *Jesus the Christ*, op cit., p. 84.

115: *Hellwig*: Monika Hellwig, "Good News to the Poor: Do They Understand It Better?" in *Tracing the Spirit*, James E. Hug, ed. Mahwah, N.J.: Paulist Press, 1983, p. 145.

118: *Mauriac*: François Mauriac, *What I Believe*. New York: Farrar, Straus and Company, 1963, pp. 47–56.

120: *"Adam is a 25-year-old"*: Henri Nouwen, "Adam's Peace," in *World Vision Magazine*, August-September 1988, pp. 4–7.

122: *"Christianity has always insisted"*: Martin Luther King Jr. Quoted in David J. Garrow, *Bearing the Cross*. New York: William Morrow and Company, Inc., 1986, p. 532.

122: *"to awaken a sense"*: Ibid, p. 81.

125: *"Whoever wants"*: Matthew 16:25, et al.

125: *"life to the full"*: John 10:10.

125: *"in his joy"*: Matthew 13:44.

Chapter 7

129: *"Be perfect"*: Matthew 5:48.

129: *"I tell you, not seven"*: Matthew 18:22.

129: *"In everything"*: Matthew 7:12.

130: *Owens*: Virginia Stem Owens, "God and Man at Texas A&M," in *The Reformed Journal*, November 1987, pp. 3–4.

131: *"Do not think"*: Matthew 5:17, 20.

132: *"You shall not misuse"*: Exodus 20:7.

132: *bleeding Pharisees*: Mary Stewart Van Leeuwen, "Why Christians Should Take the Men's Movement Seriously," in *Radix*, Vol. 21, no. 3, p. 6.

133: *"I tell you . . ."*: All such statements taken from Sermon on the Mount, Matthew 5–7.

133: *Updike*: John Updike, "Even the Bible Is Soft on Sex," in *The New York Times Book Review*, June 20, 1993, p. 3.

134: *"Give to Caesar"*: Matthew 22:21.

136n.: *Muggeridge*: Malcolm Muggeridge, "Books," in *Esquire*, April 1972, p. 39.

137: *Tolstoy*: See William L. Shirer, *Love and Hatred: The Stormy Marriage of Lev and Sonya Tolstoy*. New York: Simon & Schuster, 1994.

138: *"There is so little genuine warmth"*: From Sonya Tolstoy's diary, January 26, 1895.

139: *"What about you"*: Quoted in A. N. Wilson, *The Lion and the Honeycomb: The Religious Writings of Tolstoy*. San Francisco: Harper & Row, Publishers, pp. 147–8.

140: *Wilson*: Ibid, p. 17.

140: *Dostoevsky*: See Joseph Frank: *Dostoevsky, The Years of Ordeal, 1850–1859*. Princeton, N.J.: Princeton University Press, 1983.

141: "*We love because*": 1 John 4:19.

142: "*Where sin increased*": Romans 5:20.

142: "*There is now no*": Romans 8:1.

143: "*Be perfect*": Matthew 5:48.

143: "*Love the Lord*": Matthew 22:37.

143: "*Father, forgive*": Luke 23:34.

Chapter 8

150: "*Do you see*": Luke 7:44–47.

151: "*the poor, the crippled*": Luke 14:21.

151: "*For the Son*": Luke 19:10.

151: "*It is not*": Matthew 9:12.

152: "*If any one of you*": John 8:7–11.

152: *Lewis*: C. S. Lewis, *The Problem of Pain*. New York: The Macmillan Company, 1962, p. 98.

152: *Kaminer*: Wendy Kaminer, from *By the Book: America's Self-Help Habit*, quoted in "Saving Therapy: Exploring the Religious Self-Help Literature," *Theology Today*, October 1991, p. 301.

153: "*No madman*": Hans Küng, *On Being a Christian*. Garden City, N.Y.: Doubleday & Company, Inc., 1976, p. 235.

153: "*Blessed art thou*": Marcus J. Borg, *Jesus, A New Vision*. San Francisco: Harper & Row, 1987, 133–34.

154: *Wink*: Wink, *Engaging the Powers*, op cit., p. 129.

154: "*There is neither*": Galatians 3:28.

154n.: *Sayers*: Dorothy L. Sayers, *Are Women Human*. Downers Grove, Ill.: InterVarsity Press, 1971, p. 47.

154: *Wink*: Wink, *Engaging the Powers*, op cit., p. 130.

155: "*God, have mercy*": Luke 18:13–14.

155: *Wilson*: A. N. Wilson, *Jesus*, op cit., p. 30.

156: "*Son, remember*": Luke 16:25.

156n.: *Constantine, early Christians*: See Robin Lane Fox, *Pagans and Christians*. New York: Alfred A. Knopf, 1989.

157: *Third World base communities*: See Robert McAfee Brown, *Unexpected News: Reading the Bible with Third World Eyes*. Philadelphia: The Westminster Press, 1984.

157: "*he has anointed*": Isaiah 61:1.

158: *Endo*: See Shusaku Endo, *A Life of Jesus*. New York: Paulist Press, 1973.

160: "*O Jerusalem*": Matthew 23:37.

160: "*offered up loud*": Hebrews 5:7.

161: "*My God*": Matthew 27:46.

Chapter 9

167: *Miracle of water into wine*: John 2:1–11

168: *Lewis*: C. S. Lewis, "Miracles," in *God in the Dock*, op cit., p. 29.

169: "*There is no death*": Footnote to John 9:2 in *The NIV Study Bible*. Grand Rapids: Zondervan Publishing House, 1985, p. 1614.

170: *Miracle of healed blindness*: John 9: 1–41.

171: *Koop*: From personal interview.

172: *Miracle of healed leprosy*: Matthew 8:1–4; Mark 1:40–44; Luke 5:12–14.

173n.: "*Holy Disease*": Patrick Feeny, *The Fight Against Leprosy*. New York: American Leprosy Mission, 1964, pp. 25, 32.

173: *Teresa*: From television interview.

173: *Miracle of healed paralysis*: Matthew 9:1–8; Mark 2:1–12; Luke 5:17–26.

174n.: "*Any disabled person*": Donald Senior, C. P., "With New Eyes," in *Stauros Notebook*, vol. 9, no. 2, p. 1.

176: *Miracle of feeding five thousand*: Matthew 14:13–21; Mark 6:30–44; Luke 9:10–17; John 6:5–71.

177: *Capon*: Robert Farrar Capon, *Parables of the Kingdom*. Grand Rapids: Zondervan Publishing House, 1985, p. 27.

177: "*A wicked and adulterous*": Matthew 12:39.

178: "*he would not entrust*": John 2:24.

178: *Miracle of raising Lazarus*: John 11:1–54.

181: "*If they do not listen*": Luke 16:31.

181: "*not one [sparrow]*": Matthew 10:29.

181: *Askew*: Eddie Askew, *Disguises of Love*. London: The Leprosy Mission International, 1983, p. 50.

181: "*I do believe*": Mark 9:24.

182: *John the Baptist*: Matthew 11:1–7.

183: *Moltmann*: Jürgen Moltmann, *The Way of Jesus Christ*, op cit., p. 99.

Chapter 10

189: "*Blessed is the king*": Luke 19:38.

189: "*I tell you*": Luke 19:40.

189: "*Look how*": John 12:19.

191: "*I confer on you*": Luke 22:29.

191: "*I have overcome*": John 16:33.

191: "*Jesus knew*": John 13:3–4.

191: *Peck*: M. Scott Peck, *The Different Drum*. New York: Touchstone/Simon & Schuster, 1988, p. 293.

192: "*the greatest*": Luke 22:26.

192: "*stared at one another*": John 13:22.

192: "*Surely not I?*": Mark 14:19.

193: "*I don't know*": Matthew 26:74.

193: "*Satan entered*": John 13:27.

194: "*Father, forgive*": Luke 23:34.

194: *Gethsemane*: Matthew 26:36–56; Mark 14:32–52; Luke 22:39–53.

195: *Yoder*: John Howard Yoder, *The Politics of Jesus*. Grand Rapids: William B. Eerdmans Publishing Company, 1972, pp. 55–56, 61.

196: "*Did not the Christ*": Luke 24:26.

197n.: *Klausner*: Joseph Klausner, *Jesus of Nazareth*, op cit., p. 348.

198: "*I charge you . . .*": Matthew 26:63–65.

198: "*Are you the king*": Luke 23:3.

199: *Barth*: Karl Barth, *The Word of God and the Word of Man*, op cit., p. 82.

200: *Cicero*: Quoted in Walter Kasper, *Jesus the Christ*, op cit., p. 113.

200: "*anyone who is hung*": Deuteronomy 21:23.

201: "*I thirst*": John 19:28, KJV.

201: "*Father, into*": Luke 23:45.

201: "*It is finished*": John 19:30.

201: *"My God, my God"*: Matthew 27:46; Mark 15:33.
201: *Lewis*: C. S. Lewis, *Letters to Malcolm: Chiefly on Prayer*. London: Geoffrey Bles, 1964, p. 65.
202: *"a curse for us"*: Galatians 3:13.
202: *"God made him"*: 2 Corinthians 5:21.
202: *Sayers*: Sayers, *The Man Born to Be King*, op cit., p. 5.
20n.: *Constantine*: Michael Grant, *Constantine the Great*. New York: Charles Scribner's Sons, 1994, pp. 149, 222.
203: *Lewis*: *Letters to Malcolm: Chiefly on Prayer*, op cit., p. 113.
203: *"Having disarmed"*: Colossians 2:15.
203: *"Surely this man"*: Mark 15:39.
203: *"remember me"*: Luke 23:42.
204: *Justin Martyr*: Hans Küng, *On Being a Christian*, op cit, p. 339.
204: *Peck*: M. Scott Peck, *People of the Lie*. New York: Simon and Schuster, 1983, p. 269.
205: *Sölle*: Dorothy Sölle, *Of War and Love*. Maryknoll, N.Y.: Orbis Books, 1984, p. 97.

Chapter 11
210: *May*: Rollo May, *My Quest for Beauty*. Dallas: Saybrook Publishing Company, 1985, p. 60.
211: *"And if Christ"*: 1 Corinthians 15:14.
212: *"nonsense"*: Luke 24:11.
212: *"some doubted"*: Matthew 28:17.
213: *"afraid yet"*: Matthew 28:8.
213: *"trembling and bewildered"*: Mark 16:8.
213: *Gospel of Peter*: Quoted in Frederick Buechner, *The Faces of Jesus*. San Francisco: Harper & Row Publishers, 1989, p. 218.
214: *"His disciples came"*: Matthew 28:13.
214: *"If they do not listen"*: Luke 16:31.
214: *"He is not here"*: Cited in Hans Küng, *On Being a Christian*, op cit, p. 365.
214: *Buechner*: Frederick Buechner, *Whistling in the Dark*. San Francisco: Harper & Row Publishers, 1988, p. 42.
214: *Emmaus story*: Luke 24:13–49
216: *"Because you have seen"*: John 20:29.
217: *Dodd*: C. H. Dodd, *The Founder of Christianity*, op cit., p. 163.
217: *Updike*: John Updike, "Seven Stanzas at Easter," in *Collected Poems 1953–1993*. New York: Alfred A. Knopf, 1993, p. 20. Used by permission.
218n. *Tolkien*: J. R. R. Tolkien, "On Fairy Tales," quoted in Robert McAfee Brown, *Persuade Us to Rejoice*. Louisville, Ky.: Westminster/John Knox Press, 1992, p. 145.
218: *Sayers*: Dorothy L. Sayers, *The Mind of the Maker*. London: Methuen & Co. Ltd., 1959, p. 67.

Chapter 12
226: *Buechner*: Frederick Buechner, *The Magnificent Defeat*. New York: The Seabury Press, 1979, p. 86.
226: *Wink*: Walter Wink, *Engaging the Powers*, op cit., p. 143.
226: *"I have brought you glory..."*: John 17:4–5.
227: *"Men of Galilee"*: Acts 1:11.
227: *"I am sending"*: Matthew 10:16.
227: *Endo*: Shusaku Endo, *Silence*. New York: Taplinger Publishing Company, 1979, p. 203.

227: *"Brother will betray"*: Matthew 10:21–22.

228: *"But I tell you"*: John 16:7.

228: *"As you sent"*: John 17:18.

228: *Hopkins*: "Inversnaid," in Gerard Manley Hopkins, *Poems and Prose*. Baltimore, Md.: Penguin Books, 1953, p. 51.

228: *"Unless a kernel"*: John 12:24.

229: *"Lord, are you at this time"*: Acts 1:6.

229: *Lewis*: C. S. Lewis, *The Weight of Glory*, op cit., p. 15.

230: *"He who listens"*: Luke 10:16.

231: *"When the Son"*: Matthew 25:31–46.

232: *"Men of Galilee"*: Acts 1:11.

232: *Edwards*: Gerald R. McDermott, "What Jonathan Edwards Can Teach Us About Politics," *Christianity Today*, July 18, 1994, p. 35.

234: *Küng*: Hans Küng, *On Being a Christian*, op cit., p. 132.

234: *Dillard*: Alfred Corn, *Incarnation,* op cit., p. 36.

234: *Buechner*: Ibid, p. 123.

234: *Augustine*: Quoted in Paul Johnson, *A History of Christianity*. New York: Atheneum, 1976, p. 115.

235: *"You did not choose"*: John 15:16.

235n.: *Williams*: Charles Williams, *He Came Down from Heaven*. London: William Heinemann Ltd., 1938, p. 108.

235: *"showed them the full"*: John 13:1.

236: *"We have this treasure"*: 2 Corinthians 4:7.

236: *O'Connor*: Flannery O'Connor, *The Habit of Being*. New York: Vintage Books, 1979, p. 307.

Chapter 13
241: *"The kingdom of God"*: Matthew 12:28.

241: *Barclay*: Quoted in Malcolm Muggeridge, *Jesus: the Man Who Lives*, op cit., p. 74.

241: *"The kingdom of heaven"*: Matthew 3:2.

241: *"For I tell you"*: Luke 10:24.

241: *"Now one greater"*: Matthew 12:42.

244: *"that fox"*: Luke 13:32.

244: *"so that we may not offend"*: Matthew 17:27.

244: *"Love your enemies"*: Matthew 5:44.

247: *"All men will know"*: John 13:35.

247: *"For God so loved"*: John 3:16.

247: *"My kingdom is not"*: John 18:36.

248: *"The kingdom of God does not come"*: Luke 17:20.

248: *"Give to Caesar"*: Matthew 22:21.

248: *Durant*: Will Durant, *The Story of Civilization Part III: Caesar and Christ*. New York: Simon & Schuster, 1944, p. 652.

249: *Legislative aide in China*: Karen M. Feaver, "Chinese Lessons," *Christianity Today*, May 16, 1994, p. 33.

249: *"If my people"*: 2 Chronicles 7:14.

250: *Barth*: Karl Barth, from *Church Dogmatics*, quoted in Stanley Hauerwas and William H. Willimon, *Resident Aliens*. Nashville: Abingdon Press, 1989, p. 83.

250: *Buber*: Quoted in Jürgen Moltmann, *The Way of Jesus Christ*, op cit., p. 28.

251: *"Your kingdom come"*: Matthew 6:10.

251: *"In this world"*: John 16:33.

251: *"You will hear of wars"*: Matthew 24:6.

251: *Lewis*: C. S. Lewis, *Mere Christianity*. New York: The Macmillan Company, 1960, p. 65.

252: *"Lord, are you at this time"*: Acts 1:6.

252: *"This same Jesus"*: Acts 1:11.

252: *"every knee should bow"*: Philippians 2:10–11.

Chapter 14

257: *Peck*: M. Scott Peck, *Further Along the Road Less Traveled*. New York: Simon & Schuster, 1993, p. 160.

259: *"Unless your righteousness"*: Matthew 5:20.

261: *"I am the way"*: John 14:6.

261: *"I am sending"*: Matthew 23:34.

262: *"I and the Father"*: John 10:30.

262: *"Before Abraham"*: John 8:58.

262: *"Show us"*: John 14:8.

262: *"Anyone who has seen"*: John 14:9.

262: *"That which was"*: 1 John 1:1.

262: *"was like the sun"*: Revelation 1:16.

263: *"I am the way"*: John 14:6.

263: *Lewis*: C. S. Lewis, *Miracles*. New York: The Macmillan Company, 1947, p. 113.

263: *Lewis*: *Mere Christianity*, op cit., p. 56.

264: *"I go to prepare"*: John 14:2, KJV.

264: *Carter*: Quoted in Gordon Bridger, *A Day That Changed the World*. Downers Grove, Ill.: InterVarsity Press, 1975, p. 56.

264n.: *Buechner*: Frederick Buechner, *Wishful Thinking*. San Francisco: Harper & Row Publishers, p. 17.

265: *"image of the invisible"*: Colossians 1:15.

265: *"For God was pleased"*: Colossians 1:19.

266: *"The curtain"*: Mark 15:38.

267: *Coles*: Robert Coles, *The Spiritual Life of Children*. Boston: Houghton Mifflin Company, 1990, p. 231.

267: *Aristotle*: Aristotle, *Magna Moralia*, Quoted in Diogenes Allen, *Love*. Cambridge, Mass.: Cowley Publications, 1987, p. 115.

267: *"God is love"*: 1 John 4:8.

267: *"This is how God"*: 1 John 4:9.

268: *Kierkegaard*: Quoted in Karl Barth, *The Word of God and the Word of Man*, p. 84.

268: *Nouwen*: Henri J. M. Nouwen, *The Return of the Prodigal Son*. New York: Image Books/Doubleday, 1994, p. 55.

268: *"This is love"*: 1 John 4:10.

268: *"Greater love"*: John 15:13.

269: *"For God so loved"*: John 3:16.

269: *Price*: Quoted in Alfred Corn, *Incarnation*, op cit., p. 72.

270: *Pascal*: Blaise Pascal, *Pensées*, op cit., p. 143.

270: *"Behold the man"*: John 19:5.

270: *"though he was rich"*: 2 Corinthians 8:9, KJV.

270: *"Who, being in very nature"*: Philippians 2:6–7.

270: *"God made him"*: 2 Corinthians 5:21.

270: *"And he died for all"*: 2 Corinthians 5:15.

270: *"Although he was a son"*: Hebrews 5:8.

271: "*Father, forgive them*": Luke 23:34.
272: *Goethe*: Quoted in Walter Kasper, *Jesus the Christ*, op cit., p. 182.
272: *Dostoevsky*: Quoted in Hans Küng, *On Being a Christian*, op cit., p. 142.
273: *Updike*: Alfred Corn, *Incarnation*, op cit., p. 10.
273: "*my power is made perfect*": 2 Corinthians 12:9–10.
274: *Moltmann*: Jürgen Moltmann, *The Way of Jesus Christ*, op cit., p. 322.

Others

In addition to the specific citations above, I must express gratitude to the following authors for helping me understand Jesus better:

Anderson, Sir Norman. *Jesus Christ: the Witness of History*. Downers Grove, Ill.: InterVarsity Press, 1985.
Baillie, John. *The Place of Jesus Christ in Modern Christianity*. Edinburgh: T&T Clark, 1929.
Bainton, Roland H. *Behold the Christ*. New York: Harper & Row, 1974.
Baker, John Austin. *The Foolishness of God*. Atlanta: John Knox Press, 1970.
Barclay, William. *Jesus As They Saw Him*. Grand Rapids: William B. Eerdmans Publishing Company, 1962.
Barton, Bruce. *The Man Nobody Knows*. New York: Macmillan Publishing Company, 1987.
Batey, Richard. *Jesus and the Poor*. San Francisco: Harper & Row, Publishers, 1972.
Berkhof, Hendrik. *Christ and the Powers*. Scottsdale, Pa.: Herald Press, 1977.
Bright, John. *The Kingdom of God*. Nashville: Abingdon, 1980.
Brown, Colin. *Miracles and the Critical Mind*. Grand Rapids: William B. Eerdmans Publishing Company, 1984.
Bruce, F. F. *Jesus and Christian Origins Outside the New Testament*. Grand Rapids: William B. Eerdmans Publishing Company, 1974.
Bruce, F. F. *What the Bible Teaches About What Jesus Did*. Wheaton, Ill.: Tyndale House Publishers, 1979.
Capon, Robert Farrar. *Hunting the Divine Fox*. New York: The Seabury Press, 1974.
Cullman, Oscar. *Jesus and the Revolutionaries*. New York: Harper & Row, Publishers, 1970.
Ellul, Jacques. *The Subversion of Christianity*. Grand Rapids: William B. Eerdmans Publishing Company, 1986.
Falk, Harvey. *Jesus the Pharisee: A New Look at the Jewishness of Jesus*. New York: Paulist Press, 1985.
Fretheim, Terence E. *The Suffering of God*. Philadelphia: Fortress Press, 1984.
Guardini, Romano. *The Lord*. Chicago: Regnery Gateway, Inc., 1954.
Guthrie, Donald. *A Shorter Life of Christ*. Grand Rapids: Zondervan Publishing, 1970.
Hellwig, Monika. *Jesus, The Compassion of God*. Wilmington, Del.: Michael Glazier, Inc., 1983.
Hengel, Martin. *The Charismatic Leader and His Followers*. New York: Crossroad, 1981.
Kierkegaard, Søren, *Training in Christianity*. Princeton, N.J.: Princeton University Press, 1947.
Ladd, George Eldon. *The Gospel of the Kingdom*. Grand Rapids: William B. Eerdmans Publishing Company, 1959.
Macquarrie, John. *The Humility of God*. Philadelphia: The Westminster Press, 1978.
Macquarrie, John. *Jesus Christ in Modern Thought*. Philadelphia: Trinity Press International, 1990.
Mason, Steve. *Josephus and the New Testament*. Peabody, Mass.: Hendrickson Publishers, 1992.

McGrath, Alister. *Understanding Jesus*. Grand Rapids: Zondervan Publishing House, 1988.

Meier, John P. *A Marginal Jew*. New York: Doubleday, 1991.

Moltmann, Jurgen. *The Trinity and the Kingdom*. San Francisco: Harper & Row Publishers, 1981.

Morison, Frank. *Who Moved the Stone?* London: Faber and Faber Limited, 1944.

Niebuhr, H. Richard. *Christ and Culture*. New York: Harper & Brothers Publishers, 1956.

Oppenheimer, Helen. *Incarnation and Immanence*. London: Hodder and Stoughton, 1973.

Pfeiffer, Charles. *Between the Testaments*. Grand Rapids: Baker Book House, 1959.

Stott, John. *Christian Counter-Culture: The Message of the Sermon on the Mount*. Downers Grove, Ill.: InterVarsity Press, 1978.

van Buren, Paul M. *A Theology of the Jewish-Christian Reality: Part III, Christ in Context*. San Francisco: Harper & Row, 1988.

Willis, Wendell, ed. *The Kingdom of God in 20th-Century Interpretation*. Peabody, Mass.: Hendrickson Publishers, 1987.

Wright, N. T. *Who Was Jesus?* Grand Rapids: William B. Eerdmans Publishing Company, 1992.

Ziolkowski, Theodore. *Fictional Transfigurations of Jesus*. Princeton, N.J.: Princeton University Press, 1972.

THE BIBLE JESUS READ

PHILIP YANCEY

Best-selling author Philip Yancey once read the Old Testament like taking medicine: as small a dose as possible, and bigger doses only when extremely necessary. Then he realized he'd missed the whole point. And he'd missed the plot. That's when he discovered an Old Testament he'd never known. Coming in September of 1999 discover what's so amazing about the Old Testament in the new book by Philip Yancey—*The Bible Jesus Read*.

In *The Bible Jesus Read*, Yancey describes how he personally came to love the Old Testament by getting an overview of the entire plotline and by seeing the canon of Old Testament books as a tunnel at the end of which appeared a solitary but imposing figure: Jesus Christ.

A preview of *The Bible Jesus Read* has been added as a bonus chapter to this special limited edition of *The Jesus I Never Knew*. Now that you've reacquainted yourself with the real Jesus, take a new look at the Bible he read. Then watch for Philip Yancey's new book.

Want to share this chapter with a friend? E-mail it to them.
It's available on-line at www.zondervan.com/biblejesusread.
We'd also love to hear your comments.

1

Is the Old Testament Worth the Effort?

Faith is not the clinging to a shrine but an endless pilgrimage of the heart. Audacious longing, burning songs, daring thoughts, an impulse overwhelming the heart, usurping the mind—these are all a drive toward [loving the One] who rings our heart like a bell.

Abraham Heschel

My brother, who attended a Bible College during a very smart-alecky phase in his life, enjoyed shocking groups of believers by sharing his "life verse." After listening to others quote pious phrases from Proverbs, Romans, or Ephesians, he would stand and with a perfectly straight face recite this verse very rapidly:

At Parbar westward, four at the causeway, and two at Parbar. (1 Chronicles 26:18 KJV)

Other students would screw up their faces and wonder what deep spiritual insight they were missing. Perhaps he was speaking another language?

If my brother felt in a particularly ornery mood, he would quote an alternative verse:

O daughter of Babylon … Happy shall he be, that taketh and dasheth thy little ones against the stones. (Psalm 137:9 KJV)

In his sassiness my brother had, quite ingeniously, identified the two main barriers to reading the Old Testament: It doesn't always make sense, and what sense it does make offends modern ears. For these and other reasons the Old Testament, three-fourths of the Bible, often goes unread.

As a result, knowledge of the Old Testament is fading fast among Christians and has virtually vanished in popular culture. In a comedy routine, Jay Leno tested his audience's knowledge of the Bible by asking them to name one of the Ten Commandments. A hand shot up: "God helps those who help themselves?" Everybody laughed, but no one else could do better. Polls show that eighty percent of Americans claim to believe in the Ten Commandments, but very few can name as many as four of them.

More surprisingly, a Wheaton College professor named Gary Burge has found that ignorance of the Old Testament—fourteen percent of Americans identify Joan of Arc as Noah's wife—extends to the church as well. For several years Burge has been testing incoming freshman at his school, a premier evangelical institution. His surveys show that students who have attended Sunday school all their lives, have watched innumerable episodes of VeggieTales, and listened to countless sermons, cannot identify basic facts about the Old Testament.

The experience of Barry Taylor, former rock musician and now pastor, suggests a reason why. "In the early 1970s my best friend became a Jesus freak. I thought he was crazy, so I started searching the Bible to find arguments to refute him. For the life of me, I could not figure out why God was concerned with the bent wing of a dove or why he would give an order to kill, say, 40,000 Amalekites. And who were the Amalekites anyway? Fortunately, I kept reading, plowing through all the hard books. When I got to the New Testament, I couldn't find a way around Jesus. So I became a Jesus freak too."

I am glad Barry Taylor made it to Jesus, but I recognize that he raises some good questions in the process. Why does the Bible spend so much time on temples, priests, and rules governing sacrifices that no longer even exist? Why does God care about defective sacrificial animals—limping lambs and bent-winged doves—or about a young goat cooked in its mother's milk, and yet apparently not about people like the Amalekites? How can we make sense of the strange Old Testament, and how does it apply to our lives today? In short, is the Old Testament worth the effort it takes to read and understand it?

I have heard from missionaries in places like Africa and Afghanistan that people there respond immediately to the Old Testament, for its stories of land disputes, water rights, tribal feuds, and arranged marriages relate directly to how they live now. But such customs are far removed from a Greek-thinking sophisticate like the Apostle Paul, and much further removed from the average suburbanite living, say, in Tampa, Florida. Those of us in developed countries who pick up the Old Testament and simply start reading may well feel boredom, confusion, or even outrage at the violence portrayed there. Jesus we identify with, the Apostle Paul we think we understand, but what of those barbaric people living in the Middle East several thousand years ago? What to make of them?

Most people get around this dilemma by avoiding the Old Testament entirely. Or, perhaps worse, they mine it for a nugget of truth that can be extracted and held up to the light, like a diamond plucked from a vein of coal. That technique can backfire, however—remember my brother's life verses.

Why Bother?

This book recounts how I came to stop avoiding and start reading—ultimately loving—the Old Testament. I confess that I began with ignoble motives: I read it because I was paid to, as part of my editorial assignment to produce *The Student Bible*. Long after *The*

Student Bible had been published and stocked on bookstore shelves, however, I kept returning to the Old Testament on my own.

My reading experience with the Old Testament parallels one I had with William Shakespeare's plays. In a moment of idealism, I made a New Year's resolution to read all thirty-eight of Shakespeare's plays in one year. Due to travel, a cross-country move, and other interruptions, I had to extend that deadline. Yet, to my surprise, fulfilling the task seemed far more like entertainment than like work. At first I would have to look up archaic words, concentrate on keeping the characters straight, and adjust to the sheer awkwardness of reading plays. I found, though, that as I kept at it and got accustomed to the rhythm and language, these distractions faded and I felt myself being swept up in the play. Without fail I looked forward to the designated Shakespeare evenings.

I expected to learn about Shakespeare's world and the people who inhabited it. I found, though, that Shakespeare mainly taught me about my world. He endures as a playwright because of his genius in probing the hidden recesses of humanity, a skill that gives him appeal in places as varied as the United States, China, and Peru several centuries after his death. We find ourselves in his plays.

I went through precisely that same process in encountering the Old Testament. From initial resistance, I moved to a reluctant sense that I ought to read the neglected three-quarters of the Bible. As I worked past some of the barriers (much like learning to read Shakespeare), I came to feel a need to read, because of what it was teaching me. Eventually I found myself wanting to read it. Those thirty-nine books satisfied in me some hunger that nothing else had—not even, I must say, the New Testament. They taught me about Life with God: not how it is supposed to work, but how it actually does work.

The rewards offered by the Old Testament do not come easily, I admit. Learning to feel at home in its pages take time and effort. All achievements—climbing mountains, mastering the guitar, competing in a triathlon—require a similar process of hard work; we persevere because we believe rewards will come.

A reader of the Old Testament confronts obstacles not present in other books. For example, I was put off at first by its disarray. The

Old Testament does not read like a cohesive novel; it consists of poetry, history, sermons, and short stories written by various authors and mixed up together. In its time, of course, no one conceived of the Old Testament as one book. Each book had its own scroll, and a long book like Jeremiah would occupy a scroll twenty or thirty feet long. A Jewish person entering a synagogue would see stacks of scrolls, not a single book, and aware of their differences would choose accordingly. (Indeed, on certain solemn holidays Jews were only permitted to read from Job, Jeremiah, and Lamentations in order to stay appropriately mournful; the other books might provide too much pleasure.)

Yet I find it remarkable that this diverse collection of manuscripts written over a period of a millennium by several dozen authors possesses as much unity as it does. To appreciate this feat, imagine a book begun five hundred years before Columbus and just now completed. The Bible's striking unity is one strong sign that God directed its composition. By using a variety of authors and cultural situations, God developed a complete record of what he wants us to know; amazingly, the parts fit together in such a way that a single story does emerge.

The more I persevered, the more passages I came to understand. And the more I understood, the more I found myself in those passages. Even in a culture as secular as the United States, best-sellers such as *Care of the Soul* by Thomas Moore and *Cloister Walk* by Kathleen Norris reveal a deep spiritual hunger. The Old Testament speaks to that hunger like no other book. It does not give us a lesson in theology, with abstract concepts neatly arranged in logical order. Quite the opposite: it gives an advanced course in Life with God, expressed in a style at once personal and passionate.

Neither Testament Is Enough

Christians of all stripes hold one thing in common: we believe the Old Testament is not enough. Jesus the Messiah came to introduce a "New Covenant," or New Testament, and following the Apostle Paul we look back on the Old Testament period as a time of preparation. Without question I agree. Yet I am increasingly convinced that neither is the New Testament enough. On its own, it proves insufficient for understanding God or our world.

When Thomas Cahill wrote the book *The Gifts of the Jews*, he chose the subtitle, "How a Tribe of Desert Nomads Changed the Way Everyone Thinks and Feels." He is surely right. Western civilization builds so directly on foundations laid in the Old Testament era that it would not otherwise make sense. As Cahill points out, the Jewish belief in monotheism gave us a Great Whole, a unified universe that can, as a product of one Creator, be studied and manipulated scientifically. Ironically, our technological modern world traces back to that tribe of desert nomads.

The Jews also gave us what Cahill calls "the Conscience of the West," the belief that God expresses himself not primarily through outward show, rather through the "still, small voice" of conscience. A God of love and compassion, he cares about all of his creatures, especially human beings created "in his own image," and he asks us to do the same. Every person on earth has inherent human dignity. Following that God, the Jews gave us a pattern for the great liberation movements of modern history, and for just laws to protect the weak and minorities and the oppressed.

According to Cahill, without the Jews,

> … we would never have known the abolitionist movement, the prison-reform movement, the antiwar movement, the labor movement, the civil rights movement, the movements of indigenous and dispossessed peoples for their human rights, the anti-apartheid movement in South Africa, the Solidarity movement in Poland, the free-speech and pro-democracy movements in such Far Eastern countries as South Korea, the Philippines, and even China.

So many of the concepts and words we use daily—new, individual, person, history, freedom, spirit, justice, time, faith, pilgrimage, revolution—derive from the Old Testament that we can hardly imagine the world and our place in it without relying on the Jewish heritage. A comic character in one of Molière's plays suddenly discovers, "I am speaking prose! I am speaking prose!" Our roots go so deep in Old Testament thinking that in many ways—human rights, government, the treatment of neighbors, our understanding of God—we are already speaking and thinking Old Testament.

Most assuredly we cannot understand the New Testament apart from the Old. The proof is simple: try reading Hebrews, Jude, or Revelation without any reference to Old Testament allusions or concepts. It cannot be done (which may explain why many modern Christians avoid those books too). The Gospels can be read as stand-alone stories, but a reader unacquainted with the Old Testament will miss many layers of richness in them. Paul constantly appealed to the Old Testament. Without exception, every New Testament author wrote about the new work of God on earth while looking through the prism of the earlier or "old" work.

A Chinese philosopher insisted on riding his mule backwards so that he would not be distracted by where he was going and could instead reflect on where he had been. The Bible works in somewhat the same way. The Epistles shed light backward on the events of the Gospels, so that we understand them in a new way. Epistles and Gospels both shed light backward on the Old Testament.

For centuries the phrase "as predicted by the prophets" was one of the most powerful influences on people coming to faith. Justin the Martyr credited his conversion to the impression made on him by the Old Testament's predictive accuracy. The brilliant French mathematician Blaise Pascal also cites fulfilled prophecies as one of the most important factors in his faith. Nowadays, few Christians read the prophets except in search of Ouija-board-like clues into the future. We have lost the Reformers' profound sense of unity between the two testaments.

Understanding our civilization and understanding the Bible may be important reasons for reading the Old Testament, but the title of this book hints at perhaps the most important reason: It is the Bible Jesus read. He traced in its passages every important fact about himself and his mission. He quoted from it to settle controversies with opponents such as the Pharisees, Sadducees, and Satan himself. The images—Lamb of God, shepherd, sign of Jonah, stone which the builders rejected—that Jesus used to define himself came straight from the pages of the Old Testament.

Once, a government tried to amputate the Old Testament from Christian Scriptures. The Nazis in Germany forbade study of this

"Jewish book," and Old Testament scholarship disappeared from German seminaries and journals. In 1940, at the height of Nazi power, Dietrich Bonhoeffer defiantly published a book on Psalms and got slapped with a fine. In letters of appeal he argued convincingly that he was explicating the prayer book of Jesus Christ himself. Jesus quoted often from the Old Testament, Bonhoeffer noted, and never from any other book. Besides, much of the Old Testament explicitly or implicitly points to Jesus.

When we read the Old Testament, we read the Bible Jesus read and used. These are the prayers Jesus prayed, the poems he memorized, the songs he sang, the bedtime stories he heard as a child, the prophecies he pondered. He revered every "jot and tittle" of the Hebrew Scriptures. The more we comprehend the Old Testament, the more we comprehend Jesus. Said Martin Luther, "the Old Testament is a testamental letter of Christ, which he caused to be opened after his death and read and proclaimed everywhere through the Gospel."

In a poignant passage from his Gospel, Luke tells of Jesus spontaneously appearing by the side of two disciples on the road to Emmaus. Even though rumors of the Resurrection were spreading like wildfire, clearly these two did not yet believe, as Jesus could tell by looking into their downcast eyes. In a kind of practical joke, Jesus got them to repeat all that had happened to this man Jesus—they had not yet recognized him—over the past few days. Then he gave them a rebuke:

> "How foolish you are, and how slow of heart to believe all that the prophets have spoken! Did not the Christ have to suffer these things and then enter his glory?" And beginning with Moses and all the Prophets, he explained to them what was said in all the Scriptures concerning himself. (24:25–27)

Today we need an "Emmaus road" experience in reverse. The disciples knew Moses and the Prophets but could not conceive how they might relate to Jesus the Christ. The modern church knows Jesus the Christ but is fast losing any grasp of Moses and the Prophets.

Elsewhere, Jesus told a story of two men who built houses that, from the outside, looked alike. The true difference between them came to light when a storm hit. One house did not fall, even though rain poured down, streams rose, and winds beat against it, because its foundation was built on rock. The second house, foolishly built on sand, fell with a great crash. In theology as well as in construction, foundations matter.

Quick, What Is God Like?

According to Elaine Storkey, that question, "Quick, what is God like?" was asked by a five-year-old girl who rushed up to her newborn brother in his hospital room. She shrewdly figured that, having just come from Heaven, he might have some inside information. Alas, he merely made a gurgling sound and rolled his eyes.

The Old Testament provides an answer to the little girl's question, a different answer than we might get from the New Testament alone. Although Jesus is the "image of the invisible God," he emptied himself of many of the prerogatives of God in order to become a man. The late professor Langdon Gilkey used to say that if evangelical Christianity has a heresy it is the neglect of God the Father, the Creator, Preserver, and Ruler of all human history and every human community, in favor of Jesus the Son, who relates to individual souls and their destinies.

If we had only the Gospels, we would envision a God who seems confined, all-too-human, and rather weak—after all, Jesus ended up hanging on a cross. The Jews objected so strongly to Jesus because, despite his audacious claims, he did not match their conception of what God is like; they rejected him for not measuring up. The book of Revelation gives a different glimpse of Jesus—blazing light, stunning in glory, unlimited in power—and the Old Testament likewise fills in a different portrayal of God. Like Jesus' original disciples, we need that background picture to appreciate how much love was involved in the Incarnation—how much God gave up on our behalf.

Apart from the Old Testament we will always have an impoverished view of God. God is not a philosophical construct but a Person who acts in history: the one who created Adam, who gave a promise to Noah, who called Abraham and introduced himself by name to Moses, who deigned to live in a wilderness tent in order to live close to his people. From Genesis 1 onward, God has wanted himself to be known, and the Old Testament is our most complete revelation of what God is like.

John Updike has said that "our brains are no longer conditioned for reverence and awe." The very words sound old-fashioned, and to the degree that they do, to that degree we have strayed from the picture of God revealed in the Old Testament. We cannot box him in, explain him away. God seems wild and mysterious, definitely not a God we can easily figure out. No one tells him what to do (the main point in God's blistering speech to Job).

I admit that the Old Testament introduces some problems I would rather avoid. Throughout this book I will struggle with the revelation of God I find there. "Consider therefore the kindness and sternness of God," wrote Paul to the Christians in Rome. I would rather consider only the kindness of God, but by doing so I would construct my own image of God instead of relying on God's self-revelation. I dare not speak for God without listening to God speak for himself.

It makes an enormous difference how we picture God. Is God an aloof Watchmaker who winds up the universe and steps back to watch it wind down on its own? Or is God a caring parent, who holds not just the universe but individual men and women in his hands? I cannot conceive of a more important project than restoring a proper notion of what God is like.

Unavoidably, we transfer to God feelings and reactions that come from our human parents. George Bernard Shaw had difficulty with God because his father had been a scoundrel, an absentee father who cared mostly about cricket and pubs. Likewise, C. S. Lewis struggled to overcome the imprint left by his own father, a harsh man who would revert to quoting Cicero to his children when scolding them. When his mother died, Lewis said, it was like Atlantis falling off and leaving him stranded on a tiny island. After studying at a public school led by a cruel headmaster who was later certified insane and committed to an institution, Lewis had to overcome the impact of these male figures to find a way to love God.

The Old Testament portrays God as a father, yes, but a different kind of father than that encountered by Shaw and Lewis. It portrays God as a lion but also a lamb, an eagle but also a mother hen, a king but also a servant, a judge but also a shepherd. Just when we think we have God pinned down, the Old Testament introduces a whole new picture of him: as a whistler, a barber, a vineyard keeper.

Like a drumbeat that never stops, in the pages of the Old Testament we hear the consistent message that this world revolves around God, not us. The Jews had incessant reminders built into their culture. They dedicated their firstborn livestock and children to God, wore portions of the law on their heads and wrists, posted visible reminders on their doorways, even wore distinctive hairstyles and sewed tassels on their garments. A devout Jew could barely make it through an hour, much less an entire day, without running smack into some reminder that he or she lived in God's world. Even the Hebrew calendar changed so that they marked years by the Passover and Day of Atonement, not merely by the harvest cycle and the moon. The world, they believed, is God's property. And human life is "sacred," which simply means that it belongs to God to do with what he wills.

This Old Testament notion sounds very un-American. Do not our founding documents guarantee us the right to life, liberty, and the pursuit of happiness? We rebel against anyone interfering with our personal rights, anyone who attempts to set boundaries that might encroach on our personal space. In our secularized, industrialized environment, we can go through an entire week, not just a day, without bumping into a reminder that this is God's world.

I remember hearing a chapel message at Wheaton College during the 1970s, when the Death of God movement had reached its peak. Professor Robert Webber chose to speak on the third commandment, "Thou shalt not take the name of the Lord thy God in vain." We usually interpret that commandment in a narrow sense of prohibiting swearing, said Webber, who then proceeded to expand its meaning to, "Never live as though God does not exist." Or, stated positively, "Always live in awareness of God's existence." The more I study the commandment in its Old Testament environment, the more I agree with Webber. Any key to living in such awareness must be found in the great Jewish legacy of the Old Testament.

I am not proposing that we return to forelocks, phylacteries, and a diet that excludes pork and lobster. Nevertheless, I do believe we have much to learn from a people whose daily lives centered on God. When we look back on the covenant between God and the ancient Hebrews, what stands out to us is its strictness, the seeming arbitrariness of some of its laws. I see no such reaction among the Hebrews themselves. Few of them pleaded with God to loosen the dietary restrictions or eliminate some of their religious obligations. They seem, rather, relieved that their God, unlike the pagan gods around them, had agreed to define a relationship with them.

As the Puritan scholar Perry Miller has said, when you have a covenant with God, you no longer have an ineffable, remote, unapproachable Deity; you have a God you can count on. They and God had entered into a kind of story together, and everything about their lives sent back echoes of that story. The story was a love story, from the very beginning. God chose the Hebrews not because they were larger and stronger than other tribes—quite the contrary. Nor did he choose them for their moral superiority. He chose them because he loved them.

Like any starstruck lover, God yearned for a response. All the commands given the Hebrews flowed out of the very first commandment, "Love the Lord your God with all your heart and with all your soul and with all your strength." The Hebrews failed to keep that command, of course, but the reason Christians now call three-fourths of the Bible the "Old" Testament is that not even that terrible failure could cancel out God's love. God found a new way—a new covenant, or testament, of his love.

Søren Kierkegaard offers two suggestions for the reader who tackles difficult portions of the Bible. First, read it like a love letter, he says. As you struggle with language, culture, and other barriers, look on them as the necessary work to get to the main, crucial message from Someone who loves you. Second, act on what you do understand. Kierkegaard dismisses the objection, "There are so many obscure passages in the Holy Scriptures, whole books which are almost riddles," with the reply that he would only consider that objection from someone who had fully complied with all the passages that are easy to understand!

Is God Really Good?

For thousands of years the Jews have prayed this prayer: "Give thanks to the Lord Almighty, for the Lord is good; his love endures forever." It makes a good prayer to reflect on, because we doubt precisely those two things today. Is the Lord good? Does his love endure forever? A glance at history, or any day's headlines, and any reasonable person begins to wonder about those bold assertions. For this reason, too, the Old Testament merits our attention, for the Jews loudly doubted the very prayer they prayed. As befitting an intimate relationship, they took those doubts to the other party, to God himself, and got a direct response.

We learn from the Old Testament how God works, which is not at all as we might expect. God moves slowly, unpredictably, paradoxically. The first eleven chapters of Genesis describe a series of human failures that call the entire creation project into question. As a remedy to those failures, God declares a plan in Genesis 12: to deal with the general problem of humanity by establishing one particular family, a tribe known as the Hebrews (later called the Jews). Through them, the womb for the Incarnation, God will bring about restoration of the entire earth, back to its original design.

That plan declared, God proceeds in a most mysterious manner. To found his tribe, God chooses a pagan from the region that is now Iraq and puts him through a series of tests, many of which he fails. In Egypt, for example, Abraham demonstrates a morality inferior to that of the Sun worshipers.

After promising to bring about a people numerous as the stars in the sky and the sand on the seashore, God then proceeds to conduct a clinic in infertility. Abraham and Sarah wait into their nineties to see their first child; their daughter-in-law Rebekah proves barren for a time; her son Jacob must wait seven years for the wife of his dreams, only to discover her barren as well. Three straight generations of infertile women hardly seems an efficient way to populate a great nation.

After making similar promises to bring about possession of a great land (Abraham himself possessed only a grave site in Canaan), God arranges a detour for the Israelites into Egypt, where they molder for four centuries until Moses arrives to lead them to the Promised Land—a wretched journey that takes forty years instead of the expected two weeks. Clearly, God operates on a different timetable than that used by impatient human beings.

The surprises continue on into New Testament times, for none of the vaunted Jewish scholars recognizes Jesus of Nazareth as the Messiah trumpeted in the Psalms and Prophets. In fact, they continue today, as self-appointed prophets confidently identify a succession of tyrants and world figures as the Antichrist, only to see Hitler, Stalin, Kissinger, and Hussein fade from view.

Christians living today face many unfulfilled promises. World poverty and population continue to soar and, as a percentage of population, Christianity barely holds its own. The planet lurches toward self-destruction. We wait, and keep on waiting, for the glory days promised in the Prophets and in Revelation. From Abraham and Joseph and Moses and David we gain at least the knowledge that God moves in ways we would not predict or even desire. At times God's history seems to operate on an entirely different plane from ours.

The Old Testament gives clues into the kind of history God is writing. Exodus identifies by name the two Hebrew midwives who helped save Moses' life, but does not bother to record the name of the Pharaoh ruling Egypt (an omission that has baffled scholars ever since). First Kings grants a total of eight verses to King Omri, even though secular historians regard him as one of Israel's most powerful kings. In his own history, God does not seem impressed by size or power or wealth. Faith is what he wants, and the heroes who emerge are heroes of faith, not strength or wealth.

God's history thus focuses on those who hold faithful to him regardless of how things turn out. When Nebuchadnezzar, one of many tyrants who persecute the Jews, threatens three young men with torture by fire, they respond: "If we are thrown into the blazing furnace, the God we serve is able to save us from it, and he will rescue us from your hand, O king. But even if he does not, we want you to know,

O king, that we will not serve your gods or worship the image of gold you have set up." (Daniel 3:17–18)

Empires rise and fall, powerful leaders soar to power then topple from it. The same Nebuchadnezzar who tossed these three into a fiery furnace ends up brainless, grazing on grass in the field like a cow. The succession of empires that follow his—Persia, Greece, Rome—so mighty in their day, join the dustbin of history even as God's people the Jews survive murderous pogroms. Slowly, painstakingly, God writes his history on earth through the deeds of his faithful followers, one by one.

Out of their tortured history, the Jews demonstrate the most surprising lesson of all: You cannot go wrong personalizing God. God is not a blurry power living somewhere in the sky, not an abstraction like the Greeks proposed, not a sensual super-human like the Romans worshiped, and definitely not the absentee Watchmaker of the Deists. God is personal. He enters into people's lives, messes with families, shows up in unexpected places, chooses unlikely leaders, calls people to account. Most of all, God loves.

As the great Jewish theologian Abraham Heschel put it,

> To the prophet, God does not reveal Himself in an abstract absoluteness, but in a personal and intimate relation to the world. He does not simply command and expect obedience; He is also moved and affected by what happens in the world, and reacts accordingly. Events and human actions arouse in Him joy or sorrow, pleasure or wrath…. man's deeps may move Him, affect Him, grieve Him or, on the other hand, gladden and please Him.
>
> … the God of Israel is a God Who loves, a God Who is known to, and concerned with, man. He not only rules the world in the majesty of His might and wisdom, but reacts intimately to the events of history.

More than any other word pictures, God chooses "children" and "lovers" to describe our relationship with him as being intimate and personal. The Old Testament abounds with husband-bride imagery. God woos his people, and dotes on them like a lover doting on his beloved. When they ignore him, he feels hurt, spurned, like a jilted lover. Shifting metaphors, it also announces that we are

God's children. In other words, the closest we can come to understanding how God looks upon us is by thinking about the people who mean most to us: our own child, our lover.

Think of a doting parent with a video camera, coaxing his year-old daughter to let go of the living room coffee table and take three steps toward him. "Come on, sweetie, you can do it! Just let go. Daddy's here. Come on." Think of a love-struck teenager with her phone permanently attached to her ear, reviewing every second of her day with a boy who is himself infatuated enough to be interested. Think of those two scenes, and then imagine God on one end and you on the other. That is the message of the Old Testament.

The Company God Keeps

You learn a lot about a person by the friends he selects, and nothing about God proves more surprising than his choice of companions, the hand-picked objects of his intimacy. Abraham pimped for his wife, Jacob cheated his brother, Moses murdered, David murdered and committed adultery both—yet all of these ended up on God's list of favorites. Jacob got his new name Israel (God-struggler) after an all-night wrestling match with God, and ever since the name for God's people has harked back to that contest. God's people are, literally, the children of struggle.

God has it out with loud complainers like Job, Jeremiah, and Jonah. He engages Abraham and Moses in lengthy arguments—and sometimes lets them win! In his wrestling match with Jacob, God waits until daybreak to inflict the wound; till then, Jacob holds his own. Quite obviously, God prefers honest disagreement to dishonest submission. He takes human beings seriously, conducts dialogues with them, includes them in his plans, listens to them.

If the Old Testament's overwhelming lesson about God is that he is personal and intimate, its overwhelming lesson about human beings is that we matter. What we say, how we behave, even what we think and feel—these things have an enormous effect on God. They have, in fact, cosmic implications.

Those of us who live in an era that has viewed our planet from the perspective of spacecraft, as a tiny globe of blue and green suspended in the unimaginable vastness of the universe, have trouble believing that we matter. Ironically, it was our most advanced technological accomplishments, such as the Hubble telescope, that exposed our cosmological tininess. Ernst Becker says that we carry in our breast "the ache of cosmic specialness," wondering how we can be an object of primary value in the universe.

Basketball bad-boy Dennis Rodman expresses the modern point of view, "If there is a supreme being, he/she/it has a hell of a lot more to worry about than my stupid problems." Actually, much of the Old Testament is devoted to overcoming that very same objection among the ancient Hebrews.

> When I consider your heavens,
>   the work of your fingers,
>   the moon and the stars,
>   which you have set in place,
> what is man that you are mindful of him,
>   the son of man that you care for him? (Psalm 8:3–4)

Mesopotamian creation accounts portray human beings as almost incidental to creation, inferior beings made to serve at the whims of the gods to satisfy their personal needs. Genesis, in contrast, puts man and woman at the peak of all creation and invests in them the freedom and power to determine—and spoil—all the rest. According to Cicero, "The gods attend to great matters; they neglect small ones." The Old Testament disagrees, showing instead a God who "takes delight in his people." The same psalm that begins with wonder at God's concern for humans continues:

> You made him a little lower than the heavenly beings
>   and crowned him with glory and honor.
> You made him ruler over the works of your hands;
>   you put everything under his feet.... (8:5–6)

David and the other psalmists seem stunned by the notion that a God "high up" in the heavens could care about what happens on this puny planet, but again and again God irrefutably proves it to them. The message that our actions do matter practically defines the Old Testament. We profoundly affect God. A verse from Zephaniah in the old King James Version expresses it well: "The Lord thy God in the midst of thee is mighty; he will save, he will rejoice over thee with joy; he will rest in his love, he will joy over thee with singing."

Scientists today, even agnostics, grudgingly acknowledge an "anthropic principle," for the universe is so finely tuned that it seems designed to support the existence of human life. The Old Testament pictures far more than an anthropic principle at work. God reverses the flow of all religion which, until then, had pictured the gods as supernatural beings whose actions filter down to affect life on earth. A god cries, it rains on earth; a god gets mad, and lightning strikes. The Old Testament shows—and nowhere more clearly than in Job— just the reverse. A desperate woman prays, and God sends a prophet; a disheartened old man refuses to curse God, and the impact reverberates throughout the cosmos.

For this reason, it can truly be said that the Jews invented history. For them, history did not simply replay cycles of eternity; human actions on earth mattered, and those very responses created history. The Sovereign Lord of history allows people to exert an influence on him, just as he exerts influence on them.

Visit a museum that contains artifacts from Israel's neighbors, and you can see the shift. In Egypt or Syria you can view the gods Osiris or Lil or Astarte. A Jew can point to no such image, for graven images of God have always been forbidden. All he can do is repeat Jewish history, the story of a relationship: Our God spoke to Abraham, called Moses, summoned us out of Egypt. "God," says Jack Miles, "is like a novelist who … can only tell his own story through his characters."

In the end, I came to love the Old Testament because it gives me a history to enter into. As I got to know the characters who sought in their various ways to "get along with God," I found myself in them. In different seasons I identified with Job, with Jacob, with the Teacher of Ecclesiastes, with the psalmists in their fluctuating moods. Through their lives with God I discovered my own.

For some time now I have been asking friends, "What is a relationship with God really like? How does it work?" Imagine the varied answers I would get to that question from Abraham, Enoch, Jeremiah,

Isaiah, Moses, Jacob, David, Jonah, and Job. Each of these had radically different experiences of God, and I can enter into and learn from their encounters. Life with God is an individual matter, and general formulas do not easily apply.

Kathleen Norris tells of her experiences as a guest at a Benedictine monastery, where the monks chant the psalms daily, proceeding through all 150 psalms in a month. At first Norris felt confused and jarred by the dissonance of the psalms, some of which express pious comfort while others cry out against God's absence or unfairness. Over time, though, as she got to know the monks and other guests who chanted the psalms, she realized that someone in the cloister was identifying with the words of each psalm. Each one reflected some facet of life with God, and those with eyes to see and ears to hear perceived the needed message.

Contemporary Christianity, with its narrow focus on the Epistles, has, for me, neglected this truth. Growing up in evangelical churches, I got my pictures of the Christian life exclusively from Paul who, I would suggest, is hardly a "typical" Christian. Paul had a miraculous conversion experience, had a history of miracles and supernatural interventions, and—apart from Romans 7, bless that chapter—apparently had an easy time living out the lofty ideals of the Christian life—or at least an easier time than I have. Once Paul understood something intellectually, his emotions tended to line up in good order. Trying to imitate Paul (which he encouraged) is, in my experience, no simpler than trying to imitate Jesus.

In the Old Testament I discovered a rich tapestry of encounters with God that added an important background to Paul's example. In the Psalms, for example, I found disorientation, confusion, rage, despair, and anguish such that I had never heard discussed in my church. We were too quick to move on to a "higher" experience of spiritual victory. Astonishingly, I learned that these "problematic" psalms were the ones the New Testament—and especially Jesus—quoted most often!

I have long struggled with the impossible ideals of the Sermon on the Mount, and the self-assured, God-said-it-so-do-it tone of the Epistles. I found a remarkably different approach in books like

Proverbs and Ecclesiastes. They use a moderate "Golden Mean" approach: Make money but not too much; have fun without getting hedonistic. These are, in fact, the principles parents have always used in raising children; I cannot imagine raising a three-year-old on the principles of the Sermon on the Mount.

I do not mean to draw a sharp distinction between the New Testament and the Old. Quite the contrary. It would be a mistake to read the Old Testament merely to contrast it with the New, or to add to our understanding of the New. It has a reality in itself. The Old Testament is not, as one theologian suggested, "reading someone else's mail"; it is our mail as well. The people who appear in it were real people learning to get along with the same God that I worship. I need to learn from their experience even as I try to incorporate the marvelous new message brought by Jesus and developed by Paul and the others.

Spiritual Journal

As I was in the process of writing this very chapter, a sad event occurred: my father-in-law died. Hunter Norwood lived a rich, full life of eighty years. He sailed to South America as a missionary in 1942, built a house in the jungle by hand, founded a church and Bible Institute, and later returned to the United States to direct a mission organization. Along the way he and his wife raised six daughters, one of whom I married.

Hunter was a Bible teacher par excellence. Even after retirement he sought out ways to teach the Bible. He taught extension courses for Moody Bible Institute. He drove forty-five minutes each Sunday to teach the Bible to a Presbyterian church class. When his health began failing, he would sit in front of the class in a wheelchair, speaking into a microphone in a bare whisper. A few years ago I hired him to help with some revisions of *The Student Bible* because I knew no one I could better trust with biblical research.

Eventually, due to cancer and a nerve-degenerating disease, the time came when Hunter Norwood could no longer teach the Bible. He still studied it faithfully each day and prayed through a list of all the people he had ministered to over the years. He believed wholeheartedly in the Victorious Christian Life and named Romans as his favorite book, his guidebook on relating to God. As illness progressed, however, he began questioning the Victorious Christian Life. Little wonder, in view of his condition. He had a catheter installed. He lost control of his bowels. His gums shriveled so that he could hardly keep dentures in, and visitors kept asking him to repeat what he had said. His hands trembled, and he often dropped things. It is hard to maintain a spirit of joy and victory when your body rebels against you, when you must call for help to drink a glass or water or blow your nose.

During the last two years of his life, Hunter's world shrank to the size of a single bedroom, then to the size of a hospital bed that he rarely left. There, up until the day he could no longer hold a pen, he recorded his journal of wrestling with God. I am holding that journal, a spiral-bound notebook, in my hands as I write. Starting from the back, I find lists of the people he prayed for faithfully, seventeen pages of lists: his extended family (there is my own name, beside my wife's), the Indians in South America, the students in his many Bible classes, the missionaries he used to lead, his church, widows, his neighbors. Stains—coffee, food, tears—mark the pages.

If I flip the notebook and start from the other side, I find Hunter Norwood's journal of relating to God. It goes on for nineteen pages, and I can watch the progression of his disease in the handwriting that deteriorates on each page. Mostly, he quotes a Bible verse, or briefly comments on it. A few times he writes about his physical condition: sore back, legs not working, losing strength, dehydrated. The last entry, barely legible, is marked August 7, almost exactly one year before he died. Throughout that final year, he could not write.

What strikes me about the journal is this: of the hundreds of entries, I can find only nine referring to verses in the New Testament. I see entries like this:

Psalm 28. Father help! I feel low, sad, fearful.
2 Kings 11–14. So few seem faithful to God, but He has compassion and mercy!
Psalm 53:5. There they were overwhelmed with dread when there was nothing to dread.
Psalm 59:4. Arise to help me, look on my plight.

Job 42:2. I know You can do all things. No plan of Yours can be thwarted!

Psalms 71:14. But as for me, I will always have hope!

Psalm 20:1. May the Lord answer you when you are in distress, and may the Lord protect you!

2 Chronicles 28:20. Do not be afraid or discouraged for the Lord my God is with you.

Lamentations 3:26. It is good to wait quietly for the salvation of the Lord.

Psalm 139. Fearfully and wonderfully made.

Psalm 27. The Lord is the stronghold of my life, of whom shall I be afraid?

Job 23:10. When He has tested me I will come forth as gold.

Psalm 40:17. O my God do not delay!

Job 36:15. He speaks to them in their affliction.

Jeremiah 46:28. Do not fear, O Jacob, my servant, for I am with you, declares the Lord.

Psalm 116:15. Precious in the sight of the Lord is the death of His saints.

Psalm 121:2. My help comes from the Lord.

Psalm 10:14. But You, O God do see trouble and grief.

Those of us who knew Hunter Norwood well know that the last few years of his life were by far the hardest. Opponents of his faith had stoned him in Colombia. He fought alligators, boa constrictors, and piranhas in South America. He brought up six daughters in two different cultures. But none of these compared to the difficulties of lying in bed all day, his body defying his every command, waiting to die. Toward the end, it took all his effort to accomplish the simple acts of swallowing and breathing.

Hunter went through a crisis of faith in those last few years, which he talked about openly. Answers that used to satisfy him no longer did. He lost spiritual confidence, not in God but in himself. As he grew anxious, impatient, and fearful, he wept bitter tears over his own inability to maintain composure. In the face of death, he longed to "finish well," a phrase he kept using. Yet again and again he disappointed himself. He feared disappointing God.

The wavering yet rock-solid faith Hunter found in the Old Testament sustained him when nothing else could. Even at his most doubt-filled moments, he took comfort in the fact that some of God's favorites had battled the very same demons. He learned that the arms of the Lord are long, and wrap around those he loves, not just in prosperous and happy times but especially in times of travail. I am glad, in those dark days, that Hunter Norwood had the Old Testament to fall back on.

Other books by Philip Yancey

Disappointment with God
Where Is God When It Hurts?
Church: Why Bother?
Discovering God
Finding God in Unexpected Places
The Gift of Pain (with Dr. Paul Brand)
Fearfully and Wonderfully Made (with Dr. Paul Brand)
In His Image (with Dr. Paul Brand)
The Student Bible, NIV (with Tim Stafford)
The Jesus I Never Knew Study Guide (with Brenda Quinn)
What's So Amazing About Grace?
What's So Amazing About Grace? Study Guide (with Brenda Quinn)

The Jesus I Never Knew

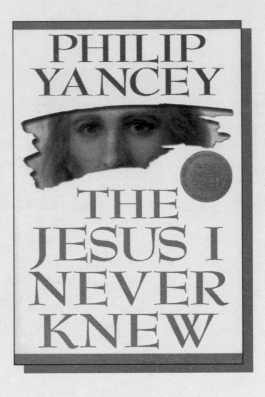

In this Book-of-the-Year Award-winning work, Philip Yancey peels away 2000 years of history to reveal the real Jesus—the Jesus beyond the stereotypes—revolutionizing your passion for Christ.

Original Edition Hardcover 0-310-38570-9
Audio Pages 0-310-20418-6

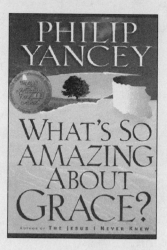

What's So Amazing About Grace?

"There is nothing we can do to make God love us more. There is nothing we can do to make God love us less."

We speak often of grace. But do we understand it? More important, do we truly believe in it . . . and do our lives proclaim it as powerfully as our words? Grace is the church's great distinctive. It's the one thing the world cannot duplicate, and the one thing it craves above all else—for only grace can bring hope and transformation to a jaded world.

In this book, Yancey explores grace at street level. If grace is God's love for the undeserving, he asks, then what does it look like in action? And if Christians are its sole dispensers, then how are we doing at lavishing grace on a world that knows far more of cruelty and unforgiveness than it does of mercy?

Grace does not excuse sin, says Yancey, but it treasures the sinner. True grace is shocking, scandalous. It shakes our conventions with its insistence on getting close to sinners and touching them with mercy and hope.

In his most personal and provocative book ever, which won a Book-of-the-Year Award, Yancey offers compelling, true portraits of grace's life-changing power. He searches for its presence in his own life and in the church. He asks, How can Christians contend graciously with moral issues that threaten all they hold dear? And he challenges us to become living answers to a world that desperately wants to know, *What's So Amazing About Grace?*

Pick up your copy of *What's So Amazing About Grace?* at Christian bookstores near you.

Hardcover 0-310-21327-4
Audio Pages 0-310-21578-1

Look for these award-winning books by Philip Yancey

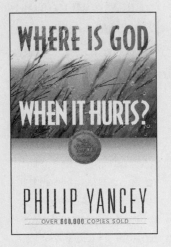

Where Is God When It Hurts?
A perennial best-seller, now in a revised and expanded edition, with a study guide. Yancey focuses on the role of pain in God's plan for life and how we can respond to it.

Disappointment with God
Philip Yancey answers the three questions no one asks aloud: Is God listening? Can he be trusted? And does he even exist? Yancey tackles the crisis of faith in this best-selling and award-winning book.

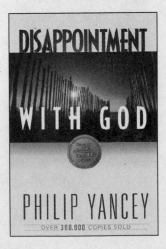

The Gift of Pain

The autobiography of Dr. Paul Brand follows his dramatic career in medicine across three continents.

Fearfully and Wonderfully Made

Philip Yancey teams with Dr. Paul Brand to offer insight into the marvelous details of the human body and draw analogies to the relationship expressed by New Testament writers in the metaphor of the body of Christ.

In His Image

The companion to *Fearfully and Wonderfully Made* unfolds spiritual truths through a physician's knowledge of the blood, the head, the spirit, and pain.

We want to hear from you. Please send your comments about this
book to us in care of the address below. Thank you.

ZondervanPublishingHouse
Grand Rapids, Michigan 49530
http://www.zondervan.com